HAPPY
WARRIORS

HAPPY WARRIORS

THE LIVES AND IDEAS OF THE POSITIVE-MIND MYSTICS

MITCH HOROWITZ

MEDIA

Published 2024 by Gildan Media LLC
aka G&D Media
www.GandDmedia.com

Front cover design by Tom McKeveny

Interior design by Meghan Day Healey of Story Horse, LLC.

Library of Congress Cataloging-in-Publication Data is available upon request

ISBN: 978-1-7225-0675-9

10 9 8 7 6 5 4 3 2 1

To the memory of
Jean-Gabriel Castel
(1928–2023)

"Tous les jours, à tous points de vue,
je vais de mieux en mieux."

Contents

Who is the happy Warrior? Who is he
That every man in arms should wish to be?

—CHARACTER OF THE HAPPY WARRIOR,
WILLIAM WORDSWORTH, 1806

Introduction

Warriors on Unhappiness

A shop rule among carpenters is: measure twice, cut once. In devising this book—a portrait of the most persuasive and fascinating, if inevitably flawed, figures in New Thought, an umbrella term for modernity's affirmative-mind theologies popularized in the mid-to-late 1890s—I have measured many times before cutting. Indeed, one of the key questions I faced was: who to include?

I privileged those figures and ideas I deemed most rewarding, lasting, and efficacious, without whom the philosophy of New Thought as we know it today would seem less familiar and practical. In making my selections, I can disavow neither personal taste nor error. There is, it must be acknowledged, a degree of affinity present. I warrant only earnestness of effort and consistency of criteria.

Happy Warriors explores not just New Thought's most intellectually and spiritually stimulating figures, or so I reckon, but those who remain *widely read* and *influential*. On that last count, I permit several exceptions, including the late-nineteenth-century journalist-seeker

Prentice Mulford with whom the book opens; Mulford deserves widespread rediscovery. I begin with the fitful seeker because he, perhaps more than any other figure in New Thought, elevated the genre to the conversational, widely accessible language on which it soared to influence.

Many of these chapter essays are new to book form, others have appeared elsewhere but are revised and expanded. The men and women who compose this biographical landscape are met more or less in chronological order of their careers, beginning in the late-nineteenth century and progressing to the late twentieth.

As a study of those who refined and communicated positive-mind metaphysics, *Happy Warriors* dwells chiefly on second-generation figures and less on the movement's early progenitors, such as mental healer Phineas Quimby, minister and author Warren Felt Evans, Christian Science founder Mary Baker Eddy (a complex figure distinctive from New Thought), and seminal teacher Emma Curtis Hopkins, who are explored in my earlier books *Occult America* (2009), *One Simple Idea* (2014), and *Modern Occultism* (2023). These pioneers are, of course, referenced in many individual chapters.

I mentioned my earlier book, *One Simple idea*, which is an overall history of the positive-thinking movement. Once upon a time, I had planned to call that volume *Happy Warriors*. Publishing professionals discouraged it and I complied. Yet I continued to hold a flame for the title, which is drawn from William Wordsworth's 1806 poem, "Character of the Happy Warrior." In reclaiming it here, I think I do justice to my subjects. The term *happy warriors* captures my affection for these men and women, amid their affinities, strivings, aims—and failures. To contextualize Wordsworth's use of the term, his full poem appears in the appendix.

Wordsworth praises the individual who, "Among the tasks of real life, hath wrought/Upon the plan that pleased his boyish thought." He means not childishness but youthful enthusiasm and moxie. This invites another question: Are the ideas championed by these radical optimists any good?

The division over whether a spiritual, ethical, or therapeutic philosophy is "good" or "bad" depends not on whether someone likes or approves of it but whether *it works*. In matters of personal philosophy, the sole meaningful measure of utility appears in the conduct and experience of the user.

As asked—sincerely—by twentieth-century mystic Vernon Howard, who appears in these pages: "Will you trust a religion or philosophy that does not produce a truly poised and decent human being?"

By these simple standards, the figures in *Happy Warriors* provide perhaps the most readily *applicable* and *testable* personal philosophy available to us. Their intellectual and spiritual gambit can be summarized: *you are as your mind is*, also the title of the chapter on writer-lecturer Neville Goddard (1905–1972).

For these reasons, this book is at once *historical* and *practical*—its ideas and methods are offered with sufficient detail to be tried if the reader desires. In terms of historicism, each chapter includes references either within the text, as footnotes, or in source essays at the end, and sometimes all three. These references are intended to be read and used for further study.

Like all intimate queries into spiritual, therapeutic, or ethical philosophies, experiments into New Thought must be ventured amid life's frictions and disappointments. Such frictions marked the existence of these purveyors as much as they do yours and my own. I call myself a "believing historian" and, as such, I have personally worked with the ideas in this book, alternately as publisher, writer, and seeker—sometimes wearing all hats simultaneously—for about twenty-five years. What have I to show for it?

My best assessment is that the mind-causation thesis *works* over the long term, although countervailing forces exist and make themselves felt. I wrote this in my 2022 *Daydream Believer*:

As I once walked through the darkened streets of a slightly humid Brooklyn spring evening and reflected on my life up to and encompassing of that moment, I realized with an overwhelming sense of actuality that *life assumes the contours of consistently held thought.* (In fact, what you just read was the first line written of this book [*Daydream Believer*].) The arrival of this perspective or realization—which I suspect you have also felt at one time or another—may be experienced as a surprise; it may reflect myriad joyous or painful possibilities; it may convey an understanding of how others have been affected (and raise questions, too, about the ultimate nature of all our experiences, a point I revisit); it may present you with momentary awareness of the impact of your alienated or unacknowledged selections; and it may leave unanswered critical questions—such as the seismically powerful force of physical limitations and the organic framework within which we function. But this realization will also leave you, or already has, with the indelible and somewhat jarringly ecstatic and frightening notion that there *is* functional truth in the proposition that thought plays a decisive role that is molding, instigative, and formative of your lived experience or conception of reality.

I refer to thought not strictly as a tool of decision, although that too is an aspect of life, but as a galvanic and selective *force*. To assume otherwise is to ascribe too much facility, I think, to the rational, prioritizing facets of intellect, which, experience also teaches, wield so little actual control over the order of life, including our emotions, intimacies, and physically felt urges—much less so control over those of others. And to default to the viewpoint that thought is a limited expression of the physical senses or neuro-system is no longer supportable in our post-materialist era . . .

To shape a life—and this can creep up on us unawares—is not so much a matter of rational plans, the perception of which we often impose as an illusory order on the past after the fact. Nor is your life wholly the domain of accident since we can divine early in the existence of any individual personality traits that doggedly even deterministically linger. But, rather, life is, in consort with other factors, including some that we cannot gain perspective on, an out-picturing of attitude, hunger, fear, striving, and long-sustained thought. Take this very moment to gaze back on your earliest fantasies, good or ill, or on wishes and fears, passionately harbored during periods of discontent and joy, and see if you do not detect a symmetry.

I return to some of these suppositions—and evidence for them—but I wish to make another observation here. As I've often noted, even if consciousness is the ultimate arbiter of reality—for which a compelling case can be made—there is no "mental super law" controlling all of our day-to-day affairs and outcomes. Natural laws, when they exist, are conditioned by surrounding circumstances. Complex forces, many more than we may ever know, interweave through our experience.

One of the prejudices resonant from New Thought's founding lies in its roots in a bustling and sometimes booming late-nineteenth and early twentieth-century America where money could seem to appear from out of the ether, especially as the stock market expanded, and, for many people, more so today, physical safety and satiety were and remain a relative given. Inexpensive consumer goods—sometimes produced through objectionable labor conditions—were and remain relatively plentiful. In earlier eras, issues of end-of-life care and widespread needs of a geriatric population were less known as, frankly, diseases and other burdens took people at an earlier age. Hence, previous generations of New Thoughters did not contend with the same emotional and social issues now intrinsic to aging and illness. Finally, American shores have, as of this writing, been relatively untouched by war and overwhelming natural disaster. To suggest that these factors foster tunnel vision—including within New Thought—is a relative given.

That said, I believe that New Thought's early generations, beginning in the mid-to-late nineteenth century and extending into the twentieth, demonstrated extraordinary instincts for the perceptual basis of reality, a contention later supported in fields including quantum mechanics, neuroplasticity, psychical research, and mind-body medicine.

At the same time, the New Thought field, so promising in its start and so attracting of world-class intellects, some of whom, such as philosopher William James (1842–1910) and physician-scientist Richard C. Cabot (1868–1939), appear in this book, ultimately did a better job of *popularizing* than of *refining* itself.

Hence, amid the many bestselling communicators of New Thought (not all of whom used the term) many pressing and even urgent questions, including those suggested earlier, are either addressed without depth or ignored. Notably, New Thought never devised a persuasive theology of suffering.

I try to amend this in my work and in this volume raise questions of tragedy, opposition, and purpose at various points, including the epilogue, which highlights the outlook of a different kind of happy warrior: traditionalist social critic Christopher Lasch (1932–1994). The twentieth-century philosopher foresaw much of the division in our present culture and offered probably the most trenchant and informed critique of popular mysticism. His voice, too, must be heard—with it, I provide my rejoinder.

In surveying these voices, I aim not only to document the lives of influential modern seekers—all possessed of their own greatness and limits—but to highlight the best ideas that have been spoken, written, and lived within New Thought tradition. In so doing, I wish to provide a yardstick for where the philosophy has been and where it must go.

Seekers, and virtually all of us, require a practical philosophy of living—Ralph Waldo Emerson called for a "Philosophy for the People." Such an outlook must harness the individual's greatest possibilities yet not abandon him or her in method or meaning when incomprehensible tragedy strikes.

I hope, finally, that the careers of these intrepid seekers point to the splendorous possibilities of New Thought—and the lacunas that our generation and the next are called to fill.

Chapter I

Thoughts Are Things:
The Struggle of Prentice Mulford

The modern writer who most decisively advocated the health-and-wealth-building powers of the mind is an American journalist, essayist, and mystic troubadour whose legacy, while etched across motivational literature, has faded like pencil on a water-logged page: Prentice Mulford (1834–1891).

In a sense, Mulford's work forged the missing link in the transition of America's positive-mind philosophies or New Thought from a predominantly health-based outlook, often called "mind cure," into an all-purpose metaphysical system for happiness and success.

Indeed, Mulford's tracts of the late 1880s and early 1890s mark the critical moment when the movement's abstruse, nineteenth-century tone fell away; from Mulford's writing emerged a remarkably modern and appealing vernacular, which won a vastly expanded, enduring audience for mind-power metaphysics—if not for the author himself.

In some regards, Mulford was the most influential of all early self-improvement writers. His personal journey itself proved an exercise in repeat transformations—and, toward its end, the pioneering writer-seeker struggled to live by the principles whose modern form he devised.

Mulford was born to a wealthy Long Island family in 1834. His father's early death cut short his fortunes. At age fifteen, Mulford was forced to leave school to support his mother and three sisters by running the family's sole remaining property: a four-story hotel in Sag Harbor, Long Island. In about four years the hotel failed. Day labor was too dull and dead-end a prospect for the restless and curious young man. He instead went to sea, joining the last leg of Sag Harbor's whaling industry.*

By the late 1850s, with whaling in decline, Mulford found himself stranded in San Francisco. With the Gold Rush booming, he took up life as a prospector, working in mining camps among other migratory or displaced men. It was a punishing daily routine spent bending over, digging and panning. American readers were hungry for news about prospecting, which was heavily romanticized at the time.** Although Mulford hadn't yet set his mind on becoming a writer, in late 1861 he began producing wry newspaper portraits of mining life, under the penname "Dogberry." Unlike other writers, who made the Gold Rush seem like a great adventure, Mulford vividly depicted its losses, hit-and-miss luck, and physical hardship. In Dogberry, miners found a voice of their own.

In 1866, with his mining ventures stagnating and his freelance articles paying meagerly, Mulford finally got a break. He was offered

---

* On the life of Prentice Mulford, I benefited from the essay "About Prentice Mulford," which appeared in volume VI of his *book Your Forces, and How to Use Them* (White Cross Library, 1892). It combined Mulford's autobiographical reflections with the biographical notes of others. Of further help was "Passing of Prentice Mulford" by Charles Warren Stoddard, *National Magazine*, September 1906, from which Mulford's journal passages are quoted.

** I am grateful for Enoch Anderson's foreword to a reissue of Mulford's 1889 *Life by Land and Sea* (Santa Ana River Press, 2004), a memoir of his whaling and mining years; Anderson provides an excellent overview of Mulford's San Francisco days and early life.

an editing position at *The Golden Era*, a San Francisco literary journal whose contributors included Mark Twain and Ambrose Bierce. A friend recalled Mulford showing up in the city looking like "a weatherbeaten young man, as shy as a country boy, and with many traits that must have resembled Thoreau in his youth."* Mulford recalled arriving with "an old gun, a saddle, a pair of blankets, an enfeebled suit of clothes and a trunk with abundant room for many things not in it."**

Mulford's writing at *The Golden Era* contributed to a post–Gold Rush literary boom in San Francisco. Historian Franklin Walker considered Mulford one of a handful of writers whose muckraking, realistic portraiture helped birth that renaissance.***

Yet the former gold-digger soon fell back on old business instincts—which, in actuality, were never very sharply honed. In 1872, Mulford raised $500 from local businessmen to send himself on a writing and lecture tour of England promoting business opportunities in California, still a relatively little-known place. Some biographers viewed the English tour as typical of Mulford's guile; but it was, in fact, a period as financially difficult as his gold-prospecting days. The writer-lecturer was forced to scrape by on ten shillings a week, the equivalent of less than $2. After two years, he returned home newly married with just $9 to his name. The transatlantic foray proved more hardship than triumph.

Back in the U.S., Mulford found work as a newspaper reporter in New York City. But in time he "grew thoroughly tired and sick of

---

* See Charles Warren Stoddard's article "Prentice Mulford, the New Gospeler," *National Magazine,* April 1905, which is quoted regarding Mulford's Thoreau-like traits.

** For Mulford's own recollection of the period, I quote from his autobiographical essay in *Your Forces.*

*** See *Prentice Mulford's California Sketches* edited and introduced by Franklin Walker (Book Club of California, 1935).

chronicling in short meter day after day the eternal round of murders, scandals, burglaries, fires, accidents and other events which people deem it indispensable to know and swallow after breakfast."*

Bored and depressed—familiar themes in his life—and suffering a split in his new marriage, Mulford quit newspaper work in 1883 and spent $50 building a cabin in the swampy woods of northern New Jersey, about seventeen miles from New York City. He entered the woods to live like Thoreau, but his forest idyll became yet another struggle.

Lonely, rainy days were difficult to bear. At such times, he recalled in *The Swamp Angel*, "I raked up certain old griefs out of the ashes of the past, borrowed some new troubles out of the future and put them all under the powerful microscope of a morbid imagination, which magnifies the awful about a thousand times, and diminishes the cheerful."

Mulford experimented with using directed thoughts to control his moods. "But I couldn't," he continued. "I failed." The mind and emotions, he discovered without precisely saying so, run on different tracks.

Yet the forest-dweller clung to his belief that the psyche—which might be considered a compact of thought and emotion—could bring light to life's darkened corners. "I do retain a faith in its curative properties for the blues, if long enough persisted in," he journaled about his mental exertions.

For all his personal difficulty, and perhaps due to it, Mulford's struggle with depression delivered him to a new type of work. In 1884 he left his cabin to resume writing—but in a newfound way that allowed him

---

* On Mulford's experiences, I quote from his memoir *The Swamp Angel* (F. J. Needham, 1888), which Mulford wrote as his equivalent of *Walden*.

THOUGHTS ARE THINGS 23

to pursue topics of his choosing, without facing newspaper deadlines or the dreary repetitions of a police blotter.

That year, Mulford conceived of his own line of advice-oriented, essay pamphlets. Although his mental therapeutics failed in the woods, Mulford believed that the mind, while perhaps too weak on its own, could summon *spiritual laws* to its aid—and these laws could be codified for use among a broad, general readership.

Mulford experienced his first inkling of mind metaphysics back in San Francisco, where he had covered seances and the local Spiritualist scene for *The Golden Era*. Mulford initially participated as a bemused skeptic and later a believer, though always with a touch of sardonic remove. Writing in *The Golden Era* in tones that could have come from H.L. Mencken had the jaundiced skeptic awakened one morning, to his horror, to find himself a believer in talking to the dead, Mulford clarified:

I am not particular that my readers should imagine that I am a sort of spiritual Barnum keeping a keen look-out for curiosities of this sort. Nearly all I have seen of this science has come into my path. I have been forced to see it. I have no inclination for [seance] circles. As a general rule I detest them. I rank them with wakes and revival prayer meetings. I am perfectly willing to grant that what we term wonderful things can be done through invisible agencies . . . I am already being sought after as a sort of inspector general and ghost detective for haunted houses. I waive the honor. Catch your own ghosts and convince yourselves that it is a reality or a humbug. True, the subject is very interesting to me. But it has slums and I desire not to wade through them.*

---

* Mulford's quotes on Spiritualism are from "The Invisible in Our Midst," a series of sketches for *The Golden Era*, written from December 1869 to March 1870; they are reprinted in the rare *Prentice Mulford's California Sketches* edited and introduced by Walker (1935). On Mulford's interest in Spiritualism I greatly benefited from Walker's *San Francisco's Literary Frontier* (Alfred A. Knopf, 1939). Also helpful is a section on Mulford in *The American Idea of Success* by Richard M. Huber (Pushcart Press, 1971, 1987).

Nonetheless, Mulford's forays into Spiritualism persuaded him of "invisible agencies" and higher laws. His hunch that these hidden forces could aid the individual in daily life appeared to crystallize when he visited Boston in 1884. There he fell under the influence of the mind-cure culture, or as it was sometimes called, the "Boston Craze." The city was developing a reputation, parallel to Chicago's, as the northeastern capital of New Thought. Mulford acknowledged this influence caustically: "It was for some mysterious reason necessary to go to Boston to start any new idea or movement."* He sounded like an idealist version of Mencken himself.

In May 1886, Mulford raised enough money to finance his first run of advice pamphlets, which he published under the name "The White Cross Library." He produced them steadily, seventy-four in all, until his death in 1891. First sold by mail subscription, Mulford's pamphlets were later repackaged into a six-volume collection, *Your Forces, and How to Use Them*, issued by a New York publisher beginning in 1890 and completed posthumously. This body of work arguably became Mulford's steadiest, most influential literary achievement—and certainly his most commercially successful.

Mulford was never wholly explicit about his sources, but he evidently drew upon the work of eighteenth-century Swedish scientist-mystic Emanuel Swedenborg (1688–1772) and nineteenth-century American minister and mind-power theorist Warren Felt Evans (1817–1889).

The writer repeatedly used the phrase *thoughts are things*, which sometimes appeared as a running footer in his books. It became one of the mottos of the mind-power movement and a keynote of self-motivation. The expression was first tucked into Warren Felt Evans'

---

* *Your Forces, and How to Use Them*, volume VI, "About Prentice Mulford" (1892).

1876 book, *Soul and Body*. Evans used the term in a Swedenborgian manner to describe the spiritual world in which our inner-selves dwell. "In that world," he wrote, "thoughts are things, and ideas are the most real entities of the universe." What transpires in the ethereal realm, Evans believed, is mirrored in our own.

Mulford had a knack for detaching such ideas and phrases from their esoteric moorings. In his hands, "thoughts are things" became a cause-and-effect formula for profitable thinking.

Mulford's writing in *Your Forces, and How to Use Them* could be seen as the most successful popularization of Swedenborg. Echoing the Swedish mystic, Mulford described the worlds of spirit and of thought as a symbiosis or yin-yang with mutually felt effects. While only once naming Swedenborg, Mulford argued that every individual routinely experiences the same astral journeys reported by the seer, writing in his inaugural 1888 essay "You Travel When You Sleep," which opened *Your Forces*:

> You travel when your body is in the state called sleep. The real "you" is not your body; it is an unseen organization, your spirit. It has senses like those of the body, but far superior. It can see forms and hear voices miles away from the body. Your spirit is not in your body. It never was wholly in it; it acts on it and uses it as an instrument. It is a power which can make itself felt miles from your body.

In a tantalizing passage for New Thought acolytes, Mulford explained his perspective on the mind's greater power: "Thought is a substance as much as air or any other unseen element of which chemistry makes us aware. It is of many and varying degrees in strength. Strong thought or mind is the same as strong will." And elsewhere: "In the chemistry of the future, thought will be recognized as substance as much as the acids, oxides, and all other chemicals of to-day." This seemed to complete the promise that "thoughts are things."

To sympathetic readers, Mulford's explanation of the powers of thought sounded at once mystical and scientific. In particular, his approach combined New Thought with reports of experiments emerging from the British Society for Psychical Research, founded in 1882 to test claims of after-death communication and non-local mental phenomena, such as extrasensory perception (ESP) and psychokinesis. In essence, Mulford's ideas conjoined the nascent field of parapsychology to a contemporary-sounding iteration of Swedenborgian theology. Whereas the published case studies of the British psychical researchers were clinical and demanding, and Swedenborg's translations often proved dense and verbose, Mulford's writing was delightfully accessible, exuding pithiness, practicality, and applicability.

Unlike many contemporaneous New Thoughters, such as influential teacher Emma Curtis Hopkins (1839–1925) and poet-essayist Ella Wheeler Wilcox (1850–1919), for whom prosperity was just one factor among many in the march of the happy warrior, Mulford tackled the wealth question head-on.

Among the first chapters in *Your Forces, and How to Use Them* appeared an essay called "The Law of Success." The title probably came from Ralph Waldo Emerson's like-named lecture, which the philosopher adapted into his 1870 essay, "Success." Emerson's work celebrated the power of enthusiasm but with tough-minded world weariness that denied man the ability to seize upon his every wish. Mulford was nowhere as discriminating but neither was he without persuasiveness and formidability. Indeed, Mulford's 1886 "Law of Success" pretty thoroughly laid down the template for spiritual self-help. He wrote in terms that the genre has never really deviated from—or surpassed:

Your prevailing mood, or frame of mind, has more to do than anything else with your success or failure in any undertaking . . . The mind is a magnet. It has the power, first of attracting thought, and next of sending that thought out again . . . What kind of thought you most charge that magnet (your mind) with, or set it open to receive, it will attract most of that kind to you. If, then, you think, or keep most in mind, the mere thought of determination, hope, cheerfulness, strength, force, power, justice, gentleness, order, and precision, you will attract and receive more and more of such thought elements. These are among the elements of success.

In his 1888 essay "The Necessity of Riches," Mulford grew even blunter on material matters, sounding like a modern prosperity guru: "It is right and necessary that you should have the very best of all this world's goods—of clothing, food, house, surroundings, amusements, and all of which you are appreciative; and you should aspire to these things." He disputed the old-fashioned ethic of self-sacrifice: "Does 'Early to bed and early to rise make men wealthy?' Who get up the earliest, work the most hours, and go to bed earliest? Thousands on thousands of the poor . . ."

To this predicament, Mulford proffered a spiritual solution: "All material wealth is gained through following a certain spiritual law." What is this law? Only the simple dictum of Christ: "Seek ye first the kingdom of God, and all these things shall be added unto you." Once more, Mulford was bringing in his version of Swedenborg. The "kingdom of God," he argued, is a "kingdom of spiritual law" in which your thoughts are creative forces. And "if you put those thoughts or forces in one direction, they will bring you health and the good of this world to use and enjoy . . . Your every thought is a force, as real as a current of electricity is a force."

Mulford set the parameters of New Thought philosophy as it played out in much of the twentieth and twenty-first centuries. In his writing, physical healing, while not absent, was downplayed while prosperity, success, and power were pushed to the front.

Mulford's gift for wrestling spiritual philosophies into facile practicalities may have irked some but his skills did not escape literary notice. He was among a handful of New Thought authors whom philosopher William James mentioned by name. James, in a letter of March 29, 1888, to his wife, Alice—with whom the philosopher explored mind-power methods—wrote: "I will send you a mind-cure theosophist book by one Mulford . . . Pray read it if you can and tell me what is in it when we meet."* The term "theosophist," as James used it, was sometimes shorthand for all esoteric inquiries rather than a direct reference to the Theosophical Society, the occult organization cofounded by Madame H.P. Blavatsky in 1875.

In any case, Alice's report must have been reasonably positive, as Mulford remained on James's mind more than a decade later when he appeared in the philosopher's 1899 essay on mind-power therapeutics, "The Gospel of Relaxation." James noted Mulford, past-and-future student Horatio Dresser (1866–1954), and best-selling eminence Ralph Waldo Trine (1866–1958), met in the next chapter, as New Thought figures who moved him to conclude that "it really looks as if a good start might be made in the direction of changing our American mental habit into something more indifferent and strong." By *indifferent,* James meant intellectual steadiness and utilitarianism in the face of circumstance: a kind of Yankee stoicism.

---

* James's letter appears in *William James: His Life and Thought* by Gerald E. Myers (Yale University Press, 1987).

At a time when Mulford was finally enjoying sizable readership, his life slipped away. The seeker died not only relatively young, just marking his fifty-seventh birthday, but also mysteriously.

In late May 1891, Mulford set out from Sheepshead Bay, Brooklyn, on his small sailboat, *White Cross*. He told friends that he planned to make a leisurely trek to his childhood home of Sag Harbor, Long Island. It was a seaborne version of his hermitage in the New Jersey woods. His boat was well stocked with food, an oil stove, pens, ink, writing paper, art supplies, blankets, and a banjo. Ever the inventive explorer, Mulford had fitted the boat with an awning that could enclose, tent-style, the vessel's sixteen-foot frame, providing shelter from the weather and snug sleeping quarters.

But when onlookers from the shore of Sheepshead Bay noticed that the covered boat had been unattended for a few days, they went to explore. On May 30, they found Mulford's body aboard. He had been dead three days. There was no sign of illness, injury, or foul play.

"How or why Mulford should have died on an open boat within easy reach of assistance and where the sound of his voice could have been heard ashore is the only mysterious feature that remains of this remarkable case," the *New York Times* reported on June 1.*

Suicide could not be ruled out. Mulford had once again been writing of his old depression, and struggling to apply his mind-power ideas to himself in search of a way forward. On May 11, he wrote in terms of Cartesian dualism in his journal: "The depression you feel is the old self of six years ago . . . You will soon throw it off and enjoy more than ever before. Exercise very gently and when your old condition comes out, complain in words, for you then materialize it—which helps to get rid of it much faster."

---

* "It Was Prentice Mulford: Sheepshead Bay's Mystery Was Solved Yesterday," June 1, 1891.

And on May 25, two days before his death: "Now you see your mind seizes immediately on trifles and makes mountains of them. I brought you under these conditions that I might more clearly show you this. It is the fear of these things, so bred in the mind, that does the injury; and your mind, in these periods of isolation, will be more readily cleared of these tendencies than in any other way."

In his struggle, Mulford seemed to think not only of his dual selves—material and spiritual—but, finally, of the many admiring readers who took succor from his work, and of what he owed them: "You are now fighting for thousands, as well as for yourself and me . . . Remember the chief end and object of the boat is to help you get into an element of thought. It is not going so far with the boat—it is going into that new element . . . Your material part does not like to get out of the world—your spiritual part does. (The body and the soul did not fit each other.) Recognize the first feeling of gloom that comes as an evil thought. Push it off directly and it is not so apt to find lodgment."

Toward the end, the physical and spiritual worlds seemed to converge for Mulford. Friends had already expressed concerns over his renewed interest in Spiritualism, automatic writing, and rein-carnation. Indeed, two old colleagues swore on the day of his death that they encountered Mulford's apparition vainly trying to speak to them.

Contrary to what some may have thought, Mulford's reignited interest in Spiritualism was less morbidity than a reflection of the spiritual-physical struggle evident in his diaries. In his personal tradition of self-sufficiency—from his whaling days through gold prospecting, from newspaper reporting to his sojourn in the woods—Mulford strove to employ the agencies of the unseen, specifically the metaphysical laws he perceived in a spiritualized thought-world, to push back the darkness and rescue his worldly self. It may not have been enough.

Other writers quickly picked over Mulford's legacy. In the years following his death, his essays were, if not pilfered, liberally borrowed from.

In 1910, inspirational writer Christian D. Larson, who is met in chapter IX, appropriated Mulford's iconic title, *Your Forces, and How to Use Them*, for a book of his own. In 1928, a young Napoleon Hill, who appears in chapter XI, called his first series of books *The Law of Success*, echoing Mulford. Mulford's insistence that "the mind is a magnet" found new expression again in 1928 in a series of pamphlets called *The Life Magnet* by motivational writer Robert Collier. Mulford's ever-ready slogan "thoughts are things" became a mantra of inspirational literature, appearing in countless books and articles and finally in Norman Vincent Peale's 1952 *The Power of Positive Thinking*, which is considered in chapter XVI.

Although his words spread like seedlings on the wind, Mulford himself was forgotten. Today, one of the few memorials is his tombstone in his hometown of Sag Harbor—erected thirty years after Mulford's body sat in an unmarked grave.

It bears the epitaph: "Thoughts Are Things."*

This might conclude my study of Mulford—but for a small act of kismet that not infrequently occurs during my exploration of New Thought's complex and sometimes confounding shapers.

As I was wrapping this chapter, a longtime reader, John Finley, messaged me a well-timed and previously unknown (to me, at least)

---

* Details on Mulford's tombstone appear at findagrave.com: www.findagrave.com/memorial/39949340/prentice-mulford

historical tribute to the author. It came from the pen of none other than William Walker Atkinson (1862–1932), the energetic New Thought writer and publisher who in 1908 produced the occult classic *The Kybalion* under the byline "Three Initiates," along with much else under his own name and varied pseudonyms, including Yogi Ramacharaka. We meet him more fully in chapter VI.

A preternaturally prolific publisher and author, Atkinson was positioned to know of what he wrote about his near-contemporary in "Prentice Mulford: An Appreciation," appearing in the March 1910 issue of the journal *New Thought*. I find Atkinson's remarks all-the-more poignant in that they appeared not twenty years after the death of "this almost forgotten writer," enunciating a melancholy truth that endures today.

As any writer knows, quotes ought to be brief and precise. In this case, however, justice to my subject trumps brevity:

> I have often wondered at the fact that the New Thought writers and lecturers of to-day show so little appreciation of the work of Prentice Mulford, one of the pioneers of the movement, who did so much to create popular interest in the subject in the early days. While he was far from being one of the original founders of the new school of thought, yet he was probably the first to place the teachings before the general public in such form as to be grasped and applied by the multitude who had no previous knowledge of the subject, and who were repelled rather than attracted by the metaphysical aspect of the teachings. Prentice Mulford did more toward making the general public "sit up and take notice" of New Thought than did any other one of its earlier writers. He brought the teachings down or up, to the plane of practical application by the average man or woman. He, like Franklin, sent up his kite to the clouds and brought down to earth the electrical power so that it would "spark" in actual earthly manifestation.

When one realizes the quality and quantity of the pioneer work performed by this almost forgotten writer—when one realizes that a large part of the "stock in trade" of the practical New Thought worker of to-day was originally furnished by this modest genius—one is surprised, and often shocked, to realize that so little recognition is accorded to his work, and so little credit awarded to the worker. Others have freely availed themselves of his splendid store of "raw material"—have partaken freely of his feast of good things—have reaped the reward which should have been his—and have forgotten to give him credit. In fact, many of the very persons of to-day who are most indebted to him for ideas received through the medium of third persons, have never read his works nor acquainted themselves with the history of his labors.

For this forgetfulness, Atkinson blamed three chief factors: 1) "this writer lived a little ahead of his time, and before his real audience was ready for him;" 2) Mulford had little knack or taste for publicity—"he worked for work's sake;" and 3) future publishers failed to market his work attractively and affordably.

Atkinson's article included a tribute from Indiana circuit court judge Joseph D. Ferrall (1838–1904), which may be a universal elegy for any truly independent thinker. Mulford, the jurist reckoned,

> refused to take his ideas of life and death second-hand, but delved himself in the mine of speculative inquiry, respected no creed or dogma because of its age, rejected no doctrine because it was a target of ridicule. He had a philosophy and religion of his own which came to be recognized and shared by many at the time of his sudden removal.

Chapter II

In Tune with the Infinite: Ralph Waldo Trine

n one of my favorite scenes from *The Wizard of Oz*, Dorothy is running away from home and happens upon the wagon of Professor Marvel who sympathetically invites her inside his fortunetelling parlor. Seating Dorothy before a crystal ball, Professor Marvel tells the wide-eyed girl:

> This is the same genuine, magic, authentic crystal used by the Priests of Isis and Osiris in the days of the Pharaohs of Egypt—in which Cleopatra first saw the approach of Julius Caesar and Marc Anthony, and—and so on—and so on. Now, you—you'd better close your eyes, my child, for a moment—in order to be better in tune with the infinite.

In tune with the infinite. It was the title of an enormously popular and now largely unread 1897 inspirational book by pioneering New Thought writer Ralph Waldo Trine (1866–1958). More than a generation after its publication, Trine's *In Tune With the Infinite*—the author's catchphrase for numinous realities—left its mark on one of America's best-loved movies. Neither the scene nor phrase appear in Theosophist L. Frank Baum's original novel from 1900.

The movie's 1939 reference testifies to the posterity of Trine's cultural reach and recognition in the first half of the twentieth century. He was the Jordan Peterson of popular spirituality but without the political baggage (and Trine was, for a time, an avowed socialist—true of a young Peterson, too). In many respects, *In Tune With the Infinite* was the nation's first mass bestseller of therapeutic spirituality, laying the template for future works such as *Alcoholics Anonymous* in 1939 and Norman Vincent Peale's *The Power of Positive Thinking* in 1952, both of which use Trine's phraseology, if not always with attribution.

Although the *Oz* screenwriters were poking gentle fun at the author, the movie also presented the perfect framing of Trine's metaphysics, which echoed and augmented the popular spiritual vision of the nation itself: belief in the innocence of the individual, the capacity to break through to other realms, and the transcendent promise of self-improvement.

Indeed, many of Trine's phrases and themes entered the lexicon of American spirituality. The term "Higher Power"—central to Alcoholics Anonymous (AA) and the 12-step movement—probably came from *In Tune With the Infinite*, where Trine repeatedly used the phrase with particular reference to alcohol: "In the degree that we come into the realization of the higher powers of the mind and spirit . . . there also falls away the desire for the heavier, grosser, less valuable kinds of food and drink, such as the flesh of animals, alcoholic drinks . . ." Trine's book was in the personal library of AA cofounder Dr. Bob Smith.* (AA is considered in detail in chapter XII.)

Trine helped popularize the term "Law of Attraction," which until his book was a little-known phrase from deep within the folds of meta-

---

* *Dr. Bob and His Library*, third edition by Dick B. (Paradise Research Publications, 1998).

physical culture (and was only just coming into coinage for the concept of like thoughts attracting like circumstances).* Many writers, including Neville Goddard, explored in chapter XIII, adopted Trine's term "enter the silence" to signal communion with the infinite. William James ranked Trine among the nation's most laudatory New Thought figures in his 1899 essay *The Gospel of Relaxation*. Henry Ford called *In Tune With the Infinite* a major factor in his success and pressed copies on friends and visitors to his office. Even pioneering televangelist Oral Roberts (1918–2009), met in chapter XIX, echoed Trine, encouraging congregants to reflect: "I am in tune with God."**

The man who started it all was born in Northern Illinois in 1866, the same year as the death of mental-healing pioneer Phineas Quimby. Ralph Waldo Trine, named for Transcendentalist philosopher Ralph Waldo Emerson, studied history and political science at Johns Hopkins University and later won a $100 prize for an essay on "The Effects of Humane Education on the Prevention of Crime."

Little is known about Trine personally, including the mystical influences that led to his signature work soon after he turned thirty-one. What is evident is that beneath the placid, almost priestly exterior that appears in his photographs burned a desire to unite mysticism and social reform. A 1902 profile in the New Thought magazine *Mind* said that Trine believed in the cooperative ethos of socialism and that

---

* The term "law of attraction" began in the work of influential nineteenth-century medium Andrew Jackson Davis (1836-1910), who in 1855 produced a six-volume treatise on metaphysical laws, *The Great Harmonia*. In volume IV, Davis defined the Law of Attraction not as a principle of cause-and-effect thinking but as a cosmic law governing the cycles and maintenance of life. Prentice Mulford also popularized the term, using it in 1892.

** Trine's career is explored in *The Positive Thinkers* by Donald Meyer (Pantheon, 1965, 1980, 1988) and *History and Philosophy of Metaphysical Movements in America* by J. Stillson Judah (The Westminster Press, 1967). Oral Roberts is quoted from *All Things Are Possible: The Healing and Charismatic Revivals in Modern America* by David Edwin Harrell (Indiana University Press, 1975).

he planned to write a book "from the viewpoint of a socialist who is such because of his New Thought philosophy."

It is not clear that Trine ever wrote such a book, but something very close appeared under his byline in 1906: *In the Fire of the Heart*. While *In Tune With the Infinite* employed a gentle, folksy tone emphasizing gratitude and generosity, *In the Fire of the Heart* revealed different colors. The New Thought pioneer summoned a "great people's movement to bring back to the people the immense belongings that have been taken away from them," calling it "the supreme need of our time." Trine inveighed against "predatory wealth," advocated busting up monopolies, striking for higher wages, and placing essential utilities and industries into public hands.

This was one book that Henry Ford didn't give away to friends. In fact, *Fire in the Heart* and Trine's 1910 follow-up *Land of Living Men* seemed to make little impact at all on his followers. By 1928, the spiritual writer was an honored guest in Ford's office, where he engaged in an almost fawning interview with the automaker. Their conversation was turned into a popular book, *The Power That Wins*, which ranged in observation from Ford's love for avocados to his belief in reincarnation. Whatever Trine's innermost commitments, he would never again be seen, nor succeed as, a political Jeremiah.

The power of *In Tune With the Infinite* rests on two counts. The first is that Trine created not the earliest but possibly the most effective and widely accessible iteration of the New Thought gospel that *thoughts are causative*. Trine's popularization remained unmatched until Norman Vincent Peale published *The Power of Positive Thinking* more than fifty years later. But Trine's book was something that Peale's was not—and this forms the second basis of its achievement. Although Trine's reference points are chiefly Christian, *In Tune With the Infinite* is one of the first widely popular works of *religious universalism.*

Peale's book was explicitly Christian; the Dutch Reform minister reimagined New Thought in language that was reassuringly familiar to the church-going public. (Although even in this regard Peale snuck in some radically mystical concepts and references.) Trine, by contrast, incorporated principles, if not always language, from broad-spanning religious traditions. In some respects, *In Tune With the Infinite* is as much a popularization of New Thought as it is of Hermetic philosophy. Hermeticism is a late-ancient Greek-Egyptian mystical school that taught that the individual is an extension of a higher mind, or *Nous*, and possesses the same creative potentials. You'll see this on display in chapter three, "The Supreme Fact of Human Life," where Trine talks about the nature of the "God-man." In chapter four, "Fullness of Life—Bodily Health and Vigor," Trine remakes the core Hermetic dictum "As above, so below" into "As within, so without; cause, effect." The Hermetic outlook is likewise present when Trine talks about a "divine inflow" into the individual. This also echoes eighteenth-century mystic Emanuel Swedenborg's concept of a "Divine influx."

Trine, for all his folksy language, was a radical thinker. And *In Tune With the Infinite*, a book that ultimately sold more than two million copies when the nation itself was far less populous than today, brought everyday Americans ideas that were jarring, fresh, anti-mainstream, and transcendent. That such themes of spiritual possibility sound so familiar to us today is testament to the author's legacy.

Chapter III

When Medicine and Metaphysics Got Along: Richard C. Cabot and the Emmanuel Movement

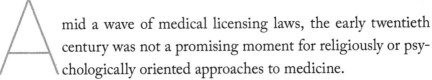 mid a wave of medical licensing laws, the early twentieth century was not a promising moment for religiously or psychologically oriented approaches to medicine.

Most physicians regarded any form of mind or faith-based methods, even when used as complementary treatments, as smacking of Christian Science, a philosophy they considered cultish and dangerous, a reactive summary judgment.

Protestant churches took a similar view. While Catholicism had long maintained measured faith in healing miracles and shrines, most Protestant seminaries and pulpits saw religious healing as something that had ended with the apostolic era. Indeed, during the Reformation, Protestant movements often cast aspersions on the healing claims of the Catholic Church, considering talk of medical miracles as nothing more than the church's attempt to shore up its role as the exclusive organ of God's word on earth. That attitude more or less prevailed at the start of the twentieth century.

A few early twentieth-century physicians grudgingly used bread pills or sugar remedies to placate hypochondriacal patients, and some doctors recognized the usefulness of hypnosis as an analgesic. But any talk of using mental or faith-based treatments was considered heresy in the medical community.

Richard C. Cabot (1868–1937), a young, Harvard-educated physician at Massachusetts General Hospital, had a different take.

Born in Brookline, Massachusetts, in 1868, Cabot, from his earliest years, inhaled the atmosphere of New England Transcendentalism. His father, James, was an intimate friend of Ralph Waldo Emerson's, to whom he served as editor, literary executor, and early biographer. The Cabot family attended a liberal Unitarian church, and Richard studied at Harvard under William James and idealist philosopher Josiah Royce. (Source notes appear at the end of this chapter.)

William James was already devising the principles of the philosophy called pragmatism. The heart of James's pragmatic outlook is that the measure of an idea's value is its effect on conduct. On this, James was uncompromising. To speak of allegiance to one creed or another was meaningless, he reasoned, unless you could demonstrate its impact on human behavior, "its *cash-value*, in terms of particular experience," James wrote in 1898.

Such thinking gave Cabot a framework for his own radical inquiries. He decided to become a medical doctor—but, crucially, he held to the belief that healing, like all facets of life, *must be a composite*. He believed that biologic cures in no way precluded, and often were aided by, the confidence of the patient, which could be fortified by faith, suggestion, and realistic, healthful self-belief.

Taking a leaf from James's pragmatism, Cabot insisted that if a method healed, it was valid, whether the treatment was allopathic, alternative, spiritual, emotional, or any combination. While Cabot firmly believed that "spiritual healings" were really mental in nature, he conceded that the faculties at work were sometimes inscrutable and warranted further study.

"It is a thousand pities that these dissensions—these sectarian dissensions—have occurred in medicine as well as in religion," Cabot wrote in 1908. "We ought to get together. There is truth in all the schools; indeed there is nothing more characteristic of the American spirit than the realization of that fact."

Cabot was a brilliant laboratory researcher—at age twenty-eight in 1896 he wrote the first English-language textbook on hematology. Yet he turned down an opportunity to become the first bacteriologist at Massachusetts General Hospital; two years later he accepted a less prestigious position in the outpatient department.

Cabot was more interested in face-to-face treatment than in lab research. He believed that physicians were assuming an inappropriately distant and inflated role in the new century, and were neglecting the experience, emotions, social problems, and fears of the patient. In response, Cabot hired the nation's first medical social worker at Massachusetts General in 1905. The hospital administration disapproved of the move and refused to pay her. Cabot paid the salary himself.

The following year, Cabot joined forces with a controversial and intriguing healing program, which emerged from an Episcopal church in Boston's Back Bay. Called the Emmanuel Movement, for Emmanuel Church which housed it, the project was a psycho-therapeutic clinic, presided over by the church's Reverend Elwood Worcester and his associate rector, Samuel McComb. The men sought to aid patients through prayer, support-group meetings, affirmations, hypnotic suggestion, and medical lectures delivered by Boston physicians.

The Emmanuel Movement sharply distanced itself from both Christian Science and mind-cure, insisting that its focus was limited to "functional nervous disorders," such as alcoholism, depression, migraines, chronic aches and pains, and digestive and bowel ailments. (This focus on "functional disorders" became a point of controversy, however, as the Emmanuel Movement also treated patients for tuberculosis, an infectious disease that then had no cure.)

Further distinguishing itself from the mind-cure field, the Emmanuel clinic would see patients only on referral and diagnosis of a physician. Reverend Worcester framed the clinic's activities not as an alternative to medicine but as a complement. The Emmanuel group received enormous, and often positive, media exposure, frequently from the nation's largest magazines, such as *Ladies' Home Journal* and *Good Housekeeping.*

Cabot became the Emmanuel Movement's chief medical advisor in 1906. He was intrigued not only by the relief that its methods seemed to bring, but by how the movement addressed a large number of ailments that, while real enough, didn't necessarily belong in the physician's examination room.

"Now, without trying to limit the field precisely," Cabot wrote in 1908, "I should say that the diseases which are essentially mental or moral or spiritual in their origin should be treated (in part at least) by mental, moral and spiritual agencies. Cases of this type constitute in my experience about two-fifths of all the cases that come to an ordinary physician . . ."

To Cabot, the complementary approach was suited to disorders such as insomnia, digestive and bowel problems, and phantom aches and pains.

He felt, furthermore, that American medicine blinded itself with its specialized divisions. Every healer, from an osteopath to an allopath to a Christian Science practitioner, could speak of cure rates for those diseases that *came to them*, but not to the field of ailments in general. As Cabot saw it, medical professionals' frame of reference was too narrow, their willingness to collaborate too limited. *Share patients and share data*, he urged.

Although Cabot believed in the efficacy of faith-based or mind-cure treatments, his support rested upon a strict distinction between "functional" and "organic" ailments. The mind-healing movements, he insisted, were highly capable of treating the kinds of functional diseases seen at the Emmanuel program—that is, bodily discomfort and stress-related disorders—which were not bacterial or structural. However, organic disease—biologic and organ-centered disorders—absolutely required standard medical care.

"Our friends the Christian Scientists," he wrote, "entirely ignore the distinction between organic and functional disease. I believe that organic disease is not helped to any extent by mental means, while functional disease has been helped a great deal by this means. Hence, there is nothing more important than to make clear this distinction."

Cabot's reasoning squares with the findings of today's most well-regarded placebo studies. The director of Harvard's Program in Placebo Studies and the Therapeutic Encounter, Ted J. Kaptchuk, told the *Wall Street Journal* in 2012: "Right now, I think evidence is that placebo changes not the underlying biology of an illness, but the way a person experiences or reacts to an illness." (It should be noted that Cabot considered placebos deceptive and he explicitly opposed their use; Kaptchuk's contemporary research, by contrast, centers on "transparent placebos," in which a patient knows he is receiving an inert substance.)

For all the possibilities, Cabot and the Emmanuel Movement had limited success in winning the support of mainstream medicine.

Cabot produced case studies and statistics showing traceable benefits from the Emmanuel program of prayer, encouragement, and religious counseling. Most medical professionals, however, turned up their noses. In journals and talks, physicians often complained that Emmanuel conflated the activities of doctors and clergy, and confused the public. (Cabot himself was never fully satisfied with the completeness of Emmanuel's record keeping.)

"The Emmanuel movement," wrote physician Charles Dean Young in 1909 in the *Boston Medical and Surgical Journal*, "was and is, unquestionably well meant"—mental and spiritual healers had by this time come to realize that praise for good intent lined the steps to the guillotine—"but its originators are powerless to confine it within its legitimate bounds as the medical profession is powerless to prevent quackery, and, for some reason, the dear public does so love to be humbugged."

That same year Sigmund Freud visited America and, while he acknowledged knowing little about Emmanuel, the psychoanalyst told the *Boston Evening Transcript* on September 11: "This undertaking of a few men without medical, or with very superficial medical training, seems to me at the very least of questionable good. I can easily understand that this combination of church and psychotherapy appeals to the public, for the public has always had a certain weakness for everything that savors of mysteries . . ."

Ironically, the Emmanuel Movement, and other early strains of mind-cure, whetted the American appetite for Freud's theories of the unconscious. William James, who had contemporaneously labored to track the existence of a "subliminal mind," was dismayed by Freud's certainty that his psychoanalytic movement alone had science at its back. James wrote a colleague on September 28 that Freud had "condemned the American religious therapy (which has such extensive results) as very 'dangerous because so unscientific.' Bah!"

The controversies were no help to Cabot's career. In 1912, in what must have been a significant personal disappointment, Cabot was passed over for his expected appointment as Harvard's Jackson Professor of Medicine, one of the university's oldest medical professorships. Harvard instead opted for a professor who was more active in laboratory science.

Cabot continued an important medical career, including as a director of battlefield medicine in France during World War I.

Following the war, Cabot launched a new campaign to urge American seminaries to train clergy in clinical and patient counseling. In 1925, he partnered with Anton Boisen, a minister who recovered following his institutionalization in a mental hospital to become one of the most eloquent voices for training seminary students in pastoral therapy. Cabot and his supporters met with measured success, helping to start pastoral training programs at Massachusetts General Hospital and Worcester State Hospital.

While widely copied in its early years, the Emmanuel Movement reached its end in 1929 with Reverend Worcester's retirement. There were no ready successors to his leadership.

Indeed, none of Emmanuel's imitators were active for more than a few years. Emmanuel and its offshoots had petered out for reasons foreseen by Cabot: Ambitious clergy may have been willing to assume a counseling role, but they lacked training to sustain rigorous, ongoing programs.

"The average clergyman," wrote Carl J. Scherzer, a hospital chaplain who had studied Emmanuel, "was not academically trained to undertake such a healing program even though he possessed a personality that might predict a reasonable amount of success in it."

Cabot died in 1939, ten years after Emmanuel closed its doors.

Although Cabot and Emmanuel failed to win over mainstream physicians, the movement proved a greater impact on the churches themselves. In a national survey of liberal Protestant ministers in the early 1950s, more than one-third of respondents reported using methods of spiritual healing, which included affirmations, individual and group prayer, and acts of forgiveness—all elements of the Emmanuel program.

This was a marked change from Protestant clergy's indifference toward such measures at the start of the century. And Cabot's calls for pastoral clinical training found new champions in the next generation.

Notes on Sources

On the career of Richard C. Cabot, I benefited from Ian S. Evison's doctoral dissertation, *Pragmatism and Idealism in the Professions: The Case of Richard Clarke Cabot* (University of Chicago Divinity School, 1995). In an age when academic specialization has sequestered too much scholarship behind inscrutable terminology and ever-narrowing topic areas (trends that Cabot himself foresaw), Evison's study is a marvel of clarity across a wide breadth of subjects. Also of significant help were "The Conceptual Underpinnings of Social Work in Health Care" by Sarah Gehlert from *Handbook of Health Social Work* edited by Sarah Gehlert and Teri Arthur Browne (John Wiley & Sons, 2006); "The Emmanuel Movement, 1906–1929," by John Gardner Greene, *New England Quarterly*, September 1934; "'A Bold Plunge into the Sea of Values', The Career of Dr. Richard Cabot" by Laurie O'Brien, *New England Quarterly*, vol. 58, no. 4, December 1985; "Richard Cabot: Medical Reformer During the Progressive Era" by T. Andrew Dodds, M.D., M.P.H., *Annals of Internal Medicine*, September 1, 1993; and

"Clinical Pastoral Education" by Rodney J. R. Stokoe, *Nova Scotia Medical Bulletin*, vol. 53, 1974. William James's statement on the "*cash-value*" of an idea is from his "Philosophical Conceptions and Practical Results," *University Chronicle*, vol. 1, no. 4, September 1898. James's article is the text of a talk he delivered on August 28, 1898, at the Philosophical Union of UC Berkeley, where he outlined his philosophy of pragmatism; the event is worthy of a book in itself. Cabot's statement on "a thousand pities" is from Evison (1995). Cabot's statements on "moral or spiritual" diseases, and his passage on "functional" versus "organic" disease, are from his *Psychotherapy and Its Relation to Religion* (Moffat, Yard & Company, 1908). Cabot's book was one of a series of titles on medicine and religion published as a project of the Emmanuel Movement. Ted J. Kaptchuk is quoted from "Why Placebos Work Wonders" by Shirley S. Wang, *Wall Street Journal*, January 3, 2012. Charles Dean Young is quoted from his article "The Emmanuel Movement," *Boston Medical and Surgical Journal*, February 18, 1909. Both Freud and William James are quoted from Nathan G. Hale's *Freud and the Americans* (Oxford University Press, 1971). On Cabot's advocacy of pastoral clinical training, I benefited from Stokoe (1974) and from the outstanding dissertation *From Jewish Science to Rabbinical Counseling: The Evaluation of the Relationship Between Religion and Health by the American Reform Rabbinate, 1916–1954,* by Rebecca Trachtenberg Alpert (Department of Philosophy, Temple University, 1978). Carl J. Scherzer is quoted from his article, "The Emmanuel Movement," *Pastoral Psychology*, vol. 2, no. 11, February 1951. The survey of healing practices among Protestant ministers is detailed in Charles S. Braden's "Study of Spiritual Healing in the Churches," *Pastoral Psychology*, May 1954.

Chapter IV

Working Class Mystic: James Allen

n a writing career that lasted only a decade, the English essayist, moralist, and mystic James Allen (1864–1912) revolutionized the field of modern inspirational literature and provided an example of dramatic personal progress in the story of his own advancement from factory orphan to literary lion.

Before Allen's death from tuberculosis at age forty-seven, he produced the enormously popular meditation *As a Man Thinketh* and combined themes of social reform, Victorian self-reliance, and New Thought metaphysics like no author before or since.

Allen's few years of output, ranging from the publication of his first book in 1901 to his death in early 1912, resulted in nearly twenty books, the launch of two magazines, and a countless range of letters, poems, and articles. The British seeker drank deeply from Eastern spirituality (he was among the first Westerners to popularize principles of Buddhism), American motivational and mind-power philosophy, and the rock-ribbed moralism of Victorian England, where he grew up in the shadow of factories and poverty.

His era was one in which Victorian readers were inspired by works like "Invictus" by William Ernest Henley (1849–1903), who was twenty years Allen's elder:

> It matters not how strait the gate,
> How charged with punishments the scroll,
> I am the master of my fate:
> I am the captain of my soul.

Allen possessed the ability to combine the ideal of the British "stiff upper lip" with the insights of New Thought, Buddhism, Confucianism, and Mystical Christianity. He may be the only writer for whom this is true. Allen was also a social reformer: he was a vegetarian (an influence from Buddhism), an early advocate for humane treatment of animals, and a supporter of laws protecting workers and promoting social equity.

All this arose from the brief career of a man who lost his father at age fifteen and had to quit school for factory work to ensure his family's survival. As important as anything that he wrote, Allen provided a living example of his philosophy of moral and material progress. That is why I have titled this chapter "Working Class Mystic." That is what Allen is to me—and his life story should be better known to the millions of readers who swear by his signature book, *As a Man Thinketh*.

James Allen was born to a laboring household on November 28, 1864, in the industrial town of Leicester, in central England. His mother, Martha, could neither read nor write. She signed her marriage certificate with an X. His father, William, was a factory knitter who maintained a small manufacturing business. The eldest of three brothers,

James was a bookish and gentle boy, doted upon by his father, who cultivated his taste in books and philosophy. (Source notes appear at the end of this chapter.)

A downturn in the textile trade drove William out of business, and in 1879 he traveled to New York City to look for new work. His plan was to get settled and pay for the rest of the family to join him. But the unthinkable occurred. On the brink of Christmas season, just after James had turned fifteen, word came back home that its patriarch was dead. William had been found robbed and murdered two days after reaching New York. His battered body, with its pockets emptied, lay in a city hospital.

James's mother, Martha, found herself in charge of James and his two younger brothers. The family had no means of support. "Young Jim" would have to leave school and work as a factory knitter if the Allens were to survive and remain intact.

The teenager had been his father's favorite. An avid reader, James had spent hours questioning his father about life, death, religion, politics, and Shakespeare. "My boy," William told him, "I'll make a scholar of you." Those hopes were gone.

James took up employment locally as a framework knitter, a job that occupied his energies for the next nine years. He sometimes worked fifteen-hour days. But even amid the strains of factory life, he retained the dignified, studious bearing that his father had cultivated. When his workmates went out drinking, or caught up on sleep, Allen studied and read two to three hours a day. Coworkers called him "the Saint" and "the Parson."

Allen read through his father's collected works of Shakespeare, as well as books of ethics and religion. He grew determined to discover the "central purpose" of life. At age twenty-four he found the book that finally seemed to reveal it to him: *The Light of Asia* by Edwin Arnold. The epic poem introduced Allen, along with a generation of Victorians, to the ideas of Buddhism. Under its influence, Allen came to believe that the true aim of all religion is self-development and inner refinement.

Shortly after discovering *The Light of Asia*, Allen experienced a turning point in his outer life, as well. Around 1889, he found new employment in London as a private secretary and stationer—friendlier vocations to the bookish man than factory work. In London, he met his wife and intellectual partner, Lily Louisa Oram. They wed in 1895. The following year, Lily gave birth to the couple's daughter and only child, Nora.

By this time, Allen had developed an impassioned interest in the world's spiritual philosophies, poring over the works of John Milton, Ralph Waldo Emerson, Walt Whitman, and early translations of the *Bhagavad Gita, Tao Te Ching*, and sayings of Confucius and Buddha. He marveled over the commonalities in the world's religions. "The man who says, 'My religion is true, and my neighbor's is false,' has not yet discovered the truth in his own religion," he wrote, "for when a man has done that, he will see the Truth in all religions."

He soon grew interested in the ideas of America's burgeoning New Thought culture through the work of Ralph Waldo Trine, Orison Swett Marden, and Christian D. Larson, who is met in chapter IX. His reading of New Thought literature sharpened his spiritual outlook—in particular, his idea that our thoughts are causative and determine our destiny.

By 1898, Allen found an outlet for his spiritual and social interests when he began writing for the magazine, *The Herald of the Golden Age*. The journal was a pioneering voice for vegetarianism and humane treatment of animals (a cause he discovered in Buddhism), and also highlighted metaphysics and practical spirituality. Allen's writing for

The Herald of the Golden Age commenced a period of feverish creative activity.

By 1901, he published his first book of spiritual philosophy, *From Poverty to Power*. The work extolled the creative agencies of the mind, placing an equal emphasis on Christian-based ethics and New Thought motivation. In 1902, Allen launched his own spiritual magazine, *The Light of Reason*—a tribute to Arnold's title—later redubbed *The Epoch*.

The following year, Allen produced the book that made his name known worldwide: the short, immensely powerful meditation, *As a Man Thinketh*. The title came from Proverbs 23:7: "As he thinketh in his heart, so is he." In Allen's eyes, that brief statement laid out his core philosophy—that a person's thought, if not the cause of his circumstances, is the cause of *himself*, and shapes the tenor of his life.

As the book's popularity rose, the phrase "as a man thinketh" became the informal motto of the New Thought movement, adopted and repeated by motivational writers throughout the century. Indeed, twentieth-century New-Thoughters frequently borrowed, cross-referenced, and repurposed one another's language—sometimes to the point where an original reference, or its meaning, got lost. This was the case with Allen's title phrase. Read in context in Proverbs 23:6–7, the precept "as a man thinketh" is not a principle of cause-and-effect thinking, but rather a caution against covetousness and hypocrisy:

> Eat thou not the bread of him that hath an evil eye, neither desire thou his dainty meats: For as he thinketh in his heart, so is he: Eat and drink, saith he to thee; but his heart is not with thee.

This kind of misunderstanding was common in New Thought. The early positive thinkers were passionate to describe their ideas as the fulfillment of ancient doctrines. Hence, they tended to retrofit the positivity gospel to Scripture and other antique sources, sometimes ignoring the context of favored passages.

Regardless, Allen's book was otherwise marked by memorable, aphoristic passages, which have withstood the march of time. *As a Man Thinketh* defined achievement in deeply personal terms: "You will become as small as your controlling desire; as great as your dominant aspiration." Toward the end of *As a Man Thinketh*, Allen wrote in a manner that amounted to autobiography:

> Here is a youth hard pressed by poverty and labor; confined long hours in an unhealthy workshop; unschooled, and lacking all the arts of refinement. But he dreams of better things: he thinks of intelligence, of refinement, of grace and beauty. He conceives of, mentally builds up, an ideal condition of life; vision of a wider liberty and a larger scope takes possession of him; unrest urges him to action, and he utilizes all his spare time and means, small though they are, to the development of his latent powers and resources. Very soon so altered has his mind become that the workshop can no longer hold him.

Although I grew up in circumstances hardly comparable to the brutalities of England's "dark Satanic mills," I, like many readers, knew struggle and felt that Allen's pen expressed the progress of my own life.

The same year that he wrote *As a Man Thinketh*, 1903, Allen produced another book—less well known but equally powerful in scope and practicality: *All These Things Added*.

All These Things Added is consummate James Allen, and deserves special mention. The concise work encapsulates an entire philosophy of life. In *All These Things Added*, Allen created a method of day-to-day living designed to bring personal fulfillment and self-realization. He based it on his interpretation of *Matthew* 6:33: "But seek ye first the kingdom of God, and his righteousness; and all these things shall be added unto you."

The book captures Allen's struggle to live by the principle of reaching beyond one's grasp. And of seeking to produce more than one grabs. Perhaps more than any other book, *All These Things Added* reflects the personal search that marked Allen's life.

With the publication and success of these two books, the Allen family moved to the southern English coastal town of Ilfracombe, where Allen spent the rest of life. He produced books at a remarkable pace—often more than one a year.

With Lily as his partner, Allen hosted discussion groups on metaphysical themes, continued publishing *The Epoch*, and spent long periods in nature, taking early morning walks and exploring the coastal highlands. His life assumed a meticulous routine of meditating, writing, walking the coast, and gardening. His work habits never flagged. "Thoroughness is genius," he wrote in 1904. Friends sensed that he was living out the simple, ascetic ideal of one of his literary heroes, Leo Tolstoy.

For all the vigor of his output, Allen was in fragile health. Lily wrote of her husband's health faltering in late 1911. On January 24, 1912, Allen died at home in Ilfracombe at age forty-seven, probably of tuberculosis. His body was cremated—a funerary choice that was then unpopular in the West but reflected the seeker's fealty to Eastern traditions.

Lily continued to publish her husband's remaining manuscripts, to work on her own books, and to edit and publish *The Epoch*. She also founded her own New Thought-oriented society, the Union of Right Thinking. She died on February 14, 1952. The Allens' daughter, Nora, a Spiritualist and later a devout Roman Catholic, died July 18, 1976.

The true legacy of James Allen is that the British author established a philosophy of self-advancement set within a framework of Eastern mysticism, Christian asceticism, and American motivation. He combined these elements like no other writer. His values were simple, clear traits of thrift, reliability, hard work, respect of one's neighbor and employer, along with a deeply held belief in the unseen power of the individual who, through the proper exercise of thought, could radically transform his circumstances.

Allen was simultaneously the Victorian moralist and the searching mystic. The path to personal greatness, he believed, appears in eschewing self-indulgence, pursuing a modest existence of basic needs, and tirelessly exercising the control of your thoughts to minimize what is cruel and petty, while cultivating ideals of tolerance, generosity, kindness, and, above all, belief in self. Through these methods, Allen insisted, you can realize untapped powers and resources. This is the path he walked from factory orphan to internationally known writer.

Although Allen loved the greenery of the British landscape, his work found its greatest popularity outside his native land. In an obituary of January 27, 1912, the *Ilfracombe Chronicle* noted: "Mr. Allen's books . . . are perhaps better known abroad, especially in America."

Indeed, the twentieth-century's leading American writers of motivational thought—from Napoleon Hill to Norman Vincent Peale— read and noted the influence of *As a Man Thinketh*. Dale Carnegie, author of *How to Win Friends and Influence People*, said the book had "a lasting and profound effect on my life." The cofounder of Alcoholics Anonymous (AA), Bob Smith, called it a favorite. Black-nationalist pioneer Marcus Garvey embraced the book's do-for-self ethic and adapted the slogan "As Man Thinks So Is He" on the cover of his newspaper, *Blackman*. In years ahead, the book's influence showed up in myriad places: an adolescent Michael Jackson told a friend that it was his "favorite book in the world;" NFL Hall-of-Famer Curtis Martin credited *As a Man Thinketh* with helping him overcome pain and injury; businessman and Oprah Winfrey partner Stedman Graham said Allen's work helped him attain "real freedom."

The full impact of *As a Man Thinketh* and Allen's work in general can best be seen in the successive generations of readers who embraced his aphoristic lessons in directing one's thoughts to higher aims and to understanding success as the outer manifestation of inner development.

"Men do not attract that which they *want*," Allen told readers, "but that which they *are*."

In that sense, Allen attracted a vast following who mirrored the ordinary circumstances from which he arose—and whose hopes for a better, nobler existence were redirected back to them in writing that bore the mark of his experience.

In 1913, Lily Allen summarized her husband's mission in a preface to one of his posthumously published manuscripts, *Foundation Stones to Happiness and Success*:

> He never wrote *theories*, or for the sake of writing; but he wrote when he had a message, and it became a message *only when he had lived it out in his own life, and knew that it was good.* Thus he wrote *facts*, which he had proven by practice.

Notes on Sources

Key sources on James Allen are "James Allen: A Memoir" by Lily L. Allen, *The Epoch*, February–March 1912 (this was the magazine that the Allens originally published as *The Light of Reason*); and *James Allen & Lily L. Allen: An Illustrated Biography* by John Woodcock

(Sun Publishing, 2007), a valuable codex to Allen's life. William Allen ("I'll make a scholar of you") is quoted from *The Epoch* (1912). Allen's quote "The man who says, 'My religion is true' " is from his posthumous 1912 work, *Light on Life's Difficulties*. Lily Allen's statement "He never wrote *theories*" is from her introduction to Allen's posthumous 1913 work, *Foundation Stones to Happiness and Success*. Allen's statement "thoroughness is genius" is from his 1904 *Byways of Blessedness*. The quote from the *Ilfracombe Chronicle* obituary is from Woodcock (2007). Dale Carnegie is quoted from *How to Stop Worrying and Start Living* (Simon & Schuster, 1944). Bob Smith's interest in *As a Man Thinketh* is noted in *Dr. Bob and His Library* by Dick B. (Paradise Research Publications, 1992, 1994, 1998). For Marcus Garvey's interest in New Thought see my *Occult America* (2009). Michael Jackson's comment is from "Radnor Family Had Inside Look at Michael Jackson" by Patti Mengers, *Delaware County Daily Times* (PA), June 28, 2009. Curtis Martin's reference to Allen appeared in "Hobbled Martin Practices and Is Probable for Patriots," by Gerald Eskenazi, *New York Times*, September 14, 2002. Stedman Graham is quoted from "Stedman Graham Tells How to Achieve Personal Freedom" by Shannon Barbour, *New Pittsburgh Courier*, June 12, 1999.

A work as famous as *As a Man Thinketh* would seem to have an easily verifiable date of first publication, but sources conflict. Various records use the years 1902 or 1904. I have cited 1903, which represents the earliest verifiable year of publication based on records from the James Allen Archive at the Ilfracombe Library in Devon, England. Savoy Publishing Company of London issued the book that year. Another historical complexity in Allen's life is the precise date when his father, William, reached New York. Lily Allen pegged William's arrival, and subsequent murder, to when James was age fifteen, which he turned on November 28, 1879. Passenger ship records show two men named William Allen reaching New York from the United Kingdom in that year: one, age forty, arrived from Liverpool on April 28, and another, age forty-seven, arrived from ports in Scotland and Ireland on November 1. The latter arrival better fits the time frame that Lily provided. The matter of exactly when William arrived requires further historical research.

Chapter V

Heaven Is a Place On Earth: The Revolutionary Vision of Wallace D. Wattles

The mind is its own place, and in it self
Can make a Heav'n of Hell, a Hell of Heav'n.
—PARADISE LOST

t began as the bleakest of Christmases at the Wattles home. In the Indiana winter of 1896, the family patriarch, Wallace, a rake-thin Methodist minister with a passion for defending workers and the poor, had been away in Chicago at a conference of social reformers. A Christian socialist, Wallace D. Wattles was already irritating the more conservative members of his congregation, some of whom were eyeing his dismissal.

Back home in La Port, Indiana, his family could not afford a Christmas tree; all they could muster was an evergreen branch decorated with a few smudgy tallow candles and strung with popcorn. Gifts were meager—the family spent the last of its holiday savings on a cuff box which waited for Wattles under the branch.

"Finally father came," his daughter Florence recalled in a 1911 letter to his publisher, Elizabeth Towne. "With that beautiful smile he praised the tree, said the cuff box was just what he had been wanting—and took us all in his arms to tell us of the wonderful social message of Jesus."*

It was a critical turning point for Wattles. In Chicago, he had met a radical minister, George D. Herron (1862–1925). An ardent purveyor of the "social gospel," Herron gained national prominence using the message of Christ to condemn the cruel mechanisms of an economic system that sent children to work in cotton mills. He impressed upon Wattles that Christ's vision of social justice must be at the heart of the pastorate's mission.

For Wattles, born in 1860 on an Illinois family farm, where he was still laboring at age nineteen in the rural Nunda Township, it was the final stroke in a spiritual philosophy he was developing himself.** The minister had been imbibing metaphysical ideas that were bubbling up around him and combining them with his own experiments into the creative powers of thought.

As Wattles saw it, the individual was a prisoner to outer circumstance only to the degree that he or she was a prisoner of circumstance within. *Free the mind*, he concluded, and outer circumstance will follow. Reading Eastern philosophies along with Descartes, Spinoza, Leibnitz, Schopenhauer, Hegel, and Emerson, the seeker reasoned that if the mind—this magical, ethereal "thinking stuff" that molded the surrounding world—could be properly harnessed, there was no limit to what a person could achieve.

---

* The recollections of Florence Wattles appear in a letter that publisher Elizabeth Towne included in a reprint of Wallace D. Wattles' *The Science of Being Great* (1911), which Towne retitled *How to Be a Genius*.

** United States Federal Census, 1880. Wattles' birthdate is sometimes given as 1861 ("abt 1861" the census document reads, identifying him as a nineteen-year-old "farm laborer" born in Illinois). Consensus is 1860, hence I have used that date.

America in the late-nineteenth century was suffused with influences from Spiritualism, Mesmerism, Christian Science, and Theosophy. Each, in its own fashion, imbued the nation's spiritual culture with the conviction that divine mysteries exist not at the top rung of a cosmic ladder but within the settings of ordinary life.

And ordinary life was undergoing remarkable changes. As the nineteenth century closed, the fruits of modern science appeared everywhere: telegraphs, motor engines, electricity, wireless signals, X-rays, and automated production. In medicine, Pasteur's germ theory was explaining illnesses that for years had resisted understanding. In biology, Darwin had theorized a gradual order in the development of all forms of life. In politics, Marx and Engels had classified economics as a matter of "science," in which inevitable outcomes could be foreseen. In psychology, Freud had begun to codify childhood traumas that triggered adult neuroses while William James and F.W.H. Myers postulated the existence of a "subliminal mind" (later called the subconscious or unconscious) as the driving engine of emotional life. Along with other luminaries, the pair founded the British and American Societies for Psychical Research, which sought to scientifically test clairvoyance and mediumship. Hypnotists (more respectable versions of Mesmerists) claimed the power to alter behavior through autosuggestion and conditioning.

Caught in this onrush of currents, intellectual leaders from all walks of life—academia, clergy, business—reasoned that scientific principles were applicable to every aspect of existence. Why couldn't there be a "science" of success, or even a "science" of religion—that is, a protocol of definable, rational steps that would produce a desired result?

Inspired by the possibilities, a group of religious thinkers and impresarios formed a loosely knit spiritual movement around this "scientific" religious concept. Thoughts, they argued, could be seen to produce actual events, such as health or sickness, wealth or poverty. They claimed Ralph Waldo Emerson as their founding prophet: "We know," the Concord mystic wrote in "Spiritual Laws" in 1841, "that the ancestor of every action is a thought." The Bible, in their reading, seemed to agree, particularly the Proverb: "As a man thinketh in his heart, so is he." In an enthused leap of reasoning, the movement that came to be called New Thought maintained that the individual's creative mind is synonymous with the creative force called God. As such, a person could literally think his dreams to life. It was America's boldest—and most influential—attempt at what religious scholar John B. Anderson called "a practical use of the occult powers of the soul."*

The metaphysical dimensions of New Thought could seem so magical, so unrestrained in their promise of limitless potential, that a 1926 bestseller by publisher Robert Collier (1885–1950) deemed New Thought, *The Secret of the Ages*.

Many of the movement's most popular writers and sermonizers re-imagined worldly acquisition as the very exercise of God's will. In their hands, it was as if the entire object of Transcendentalism that is, transcendence of earthly bonds and distractions—had been turned on its head. And here New Thought's sense of ethics and seriousness as a religious movement fell open to question: What was to finally separate this philosophy from being anything other than a tool for pursuing one's most random drives and selfish wants? Was this the endpoint of American religious innovation—the vaunted "secret of the ages?"

On this question hung the dilemma of Indiana minister Wattles. Although his books became central to a twenty-first-century New

---

* *New Thought, Its Lights and Shadows* (Sherman, French & Company, 1911).

Thought revival and served as a major influence behind the mega-selling book and movie *The Secret*, the social-gospel advocate had wanted the "occult powers of the soul" to serve a different end than worldly gain, or that alone.

It wasn't that he eschewed New Thought's emphasis on wealth building—indeed, he embraced such aims in his 1910 guide *The Science of Getting Rich*. But there was a critical difference in Wattles' approach, one overlooked by those who later embraced his work: Wattles believed in using mind-power to wipe away barons of industry and overthrow the prevailing social order. Rather than a narrowly conceived iteration of success, *The Science of Getting Rich* was, in fact, a guidebook to personal utopia, where state and corporate dinosaurs are predicted to wither away, replaced by a cooperative system of widespread wealth and beneficent anarchy. The author taught that by "thinking in a Certain Way" you can at once personally succeed and counter oppressive economics, writing with emphasis in the original:

> You are to become a creator, not a competitor; you are going to get what you want, but in such a way that when you get it every other man will have more than he has now.
>
> I am aware that there are men who get a vast amount of money by proceeding in direct opposition to the statements in the paragraph above, and may add a word of explanation here. Men of the plutocratic type, who become very rich, do so sometimes purely by their extraordinary ability on the plane of competition . . . Rockefeller, Carnegie, Morgan, et al., have been the unconscious agents of the Supreme in the necessary work of systematizing and organizing productive industry; and in the end, their work *will contribute immensely toward increased life for all. Their day is nearly over; they have organized production, and will soon be succeeded by the agents of the multitude, who will organize the machinery of distribution.*

If Wattles' more careful readers detected a tinge of socialist language, they were right. The author saw New Thought as a means to the kind of leisurely socialist utopia that had enthralled legions of readers of Edward Bellamy's Victorian-era futuristic novel, *Looking Backward* (1888). In *A New Christ*, published the same year as *The Science of Getting Rich*, Wattles envisioned a marriage of New Thought—America's homegrown success philosophy—and Christian Socialism:

> As we approach socialism, the millions of families who are now propertyless will acquire their own beautiful homes, with gardens and the land upon which to raise their food; they will own horses and carriages, automobiles and pleasure yachts; their houses will contain libraries, musical instruments, paintings and statuary, all that a man may need for the soul-growth of himself and his, he shall own and use as he will.

It was as though Karl Marx had imbibed the mother's milk of American metaphysics. Within Wattles existed a struggle to unite two mighty currents that were sweeping early twentieth-century America: social radicalism and mind-power mysticism. Was it possible, as Wattles dreamed, that these movements could be united into one radical whole? Could there be a revolution by mental power?

By the time he emerged as a New Thought leader, Wattles had already been forced to resign from his Methodist pulpit in North Judson, Indiana, in 1900.* He had gone too far in his social radicalism, at one point insisting that churches should refuse monetary offerings

---

* "Leaves the Methodists," *Fort Wayne Sentinel*, June 27, 1900.

from businessmen who profited off sweatshop labor. Soon after, he announced his departure from Methodism and grew active in the more progressive environs of Quakerism.

Wallace gained allies in mind-power circles—particularly his trailblazing publisher Elizabeth Towne (1865–1960), a Massachusetts suffragist who ran his work in her New Thought journal, *Nautilus*. Towne began the magazine in 1898, as a single mother with two children to support. Her marriage—which began when she dropped out of school at age fourteen—finally ended in divorce in 1900.*

Relying on temporary financial backing from her father of $30 a month for six months, Towne built *Nautilus* into a relative powerhouse of up to 90,000 monthly subscribers with some of her own books surpassing sales of 100,000 copies. Towne ran the journal until age eighty-eight in 1953, making it one of the longest-running spiritual magazines in American history. Her career played out in the political arena, as well. In 1926, Towne was elected the first female alderman in Holyoke, Massachusetts. Two years later she mounted an unsuccessful independent bid for mayor. Towne and her second husband, William, were also active in Theodore Roosevelt's 1912 Progressive Party campaign for president.

Taking inspiration from the presidential runs of socialist leader Eugene V. Debs (1855–1926), Wattles made his own upstart bids for public office, each time on Debs' Socialist Party of America ticket. In his home state of Indiana, Wattles first campaigned for Congress in the Eighth Congressional District in 1908.

After distantly trailing, he ran the following year for mayor of his hometown of Elwood, Indiana, where he placed a surprisingly close

---

* Sources on Towne include "What Women Are Doing Today" by Lucie M. Yager, *The Business Woman's Magazine*, Vol. 4, May 1905; "Elizabeth Towne, Author, Leader in Religion, Dies," *North Adams Transcript*, June 1, 1960; *Mind Cure in New England: From the Civil War to World War I* by Gail Thain Parker (University Press of New England, 1973); and "Pioneering Woman in Publishing and Politics" by Tzivia Gover, *Historical Journal of Massachusetts*, Vol. 37, Spring 2009.

second. Finally, in 1910 he ran for Prosecuting Attorney for Madison County, Indiana, coming in third.

During his 1909 mayoral campaign, the delicate-framed man stood before 1,300 striking workers during a heated showdown at a local tin mill and pledged them his support.*

Seen in a certain light, these were heterodox activities, not only for Towne as a woman, but for both she and Wattles as New Thought leaders. The movement emphasized the ideal of action *from within*. Although several early New Thoughters, including author and publisher Helen Wilmans (1831–1907) and, as seen, British writer James Allen (1864–1912), were active in reformist politics—pioneering Black nationalist Marcus Garvey (1887–1940) himself sounded New Thought themes—too much notice of tragedy, poverty, or injustice, so went the New Thought gospel, served only to perpetuate such things.

Hence, Wattles could sometimes sound at war with himself. In one stroke, he urged readers, "do not talk about poverty; do not investigate it, or concern yourself with it," and at other times he spoke passionately before audiences of the squalor of Chicago tenements and the hopelessness of immigrant children living there. He admiringly quoted from the social-reform journalism of Elbert Hubbard (1865–1915), who had exposed child-labor abuses in turn-of-the-century cotton mills. Hubbard, as it happened, was another success prophet with a taste for social protest.

Hubbard was famous for his 1899 motivational essay, *A Message to Garcia*, in which he extolled the can-do heroics of a U.S. soldier during the Spanish-American War. Business leaders loved it. Yet

---

* "Trouble at Elwood," *Fort Wayne Sentinel*, July 12, 1909.

Hubbard lost his life while hoping to end another war. In 1915, Hubbard and his wife Alice, a suffragist and New Thought enthusiast, died with nearly 1,200 civilians when a German U-boat torpedoed the passenger ship Lusitania in the waters off Ireland. Hubbard boarded the ship in New York on a self-styled peace mission to Europe where he declared plans to interview the German Kaiser and inveigh against the carnage of the Great War.

"Big business has been to blame for this thing," wrote the motivational hero before he left, ". . . let it not escape this truth—that no longer shall individuals be allowed to thrive through supplying murder machines to the mob."*

As we've seen, even the most popular New Thought prophet of the day, Ralph Waldo Trine (1866–1958), nursed a passion to unite mysticism and social reform. Trine gained a legion of followers through his 1897 mind-power book, *In Tune With the Infinite*. It was the book that every New Thought minister and writer seemed to have read and borrowed from. Industrialist Henry Ford kept copies in his office to giveaway. But beneath Trine's serene persona burned the fires of another social radical.

A 1902 profile in the New Thought magazine *Mind* said Trine believed in the cooperative ethic of socialism, and that he planned to write a book "from the viewpoint of a socialist who is such because of his New Thought philosophy."** Something similar appeared under his byline in 1906: *In the Fire of the Heart*. While *In Tune With the Infinite* employed a mollifying tone emphasizing gratitude and generosity, *In the Fire of the Heart* showed different colors. The New Thought pioneer called for a "great people's movement to bring back to the people the

---

* Elbert Hubbard is quoted from his 1914 essay, "A Peace Picnic," reprinted in *Selected Writings of Elbert Hubbard* (Wm. H. Wise & Co., 1922). Also see "Love and Glory in East Aurory" by Stefan Kanfer, *City Journal* (Spring 2007). Other sources include *Art & Glory: The Story of Elbert Hubbard* by Freeman Champney (The Kent State University Press, 1968, 1983).

** The career of Ralph Waldo Trine is explored in *The Positive Thinkers* by Donald Meyer (Pantheon, 1965, 1980, 1988) and *History and Philosophy of Metaphysical Movements in America* by J. Stillson Judah (The Westminster Press, 1967).

immense belongings that have been taken away from them," calling it "the supreme need of our time." Trine condemned "predatory wealth," advocated ending monopolies, striking for better wages, and nationalizing essential utilities and industries.

In 1911, in what was to be Wattles' last book, *The Science of Being Great*, he offered tribute, probably the only in all of motivational literature, to his socialist hero Debs, a fellow Hoosier who later went to federal prison for opposing U.S. entry into World War I:

> To rid yourself of the old false ideas you will have to think a great deal about the value of men—the greatness and worth of a human soul. You must cease from looking at human mistakes and look at successes; cease from seeing faults and see virtues. You can no longer look upon men and women as lost and ruined beings that are descending into hell; you must come to regard them as shining souls who are ascending toward heaven. It will require some exercise of will power to do this, but this is the legitimate use of the will—to decide what you will think about and how you will think. The function of the will is to direct thought. Think about the good side of men; the lovely, attractive part, and exert your will in refusing to think of anything else in connection with them.
>
> I know of no one who has attained to so much on this one point as Eugene V. Debs, twice the Socialist candidate for president of the United States. Mr. Debs reverences humanity. No appeal for help is ever made to him in vain. No one receives from him an unkind or censorious word. You cannot come into his presence without being made sensible of his deep and kindly personal interest in you. Every person, be he millionaire, grimy workingman, or toil worn woman, receives the radiant warmth of a brotherly affection that is sincere

and true. No ragged child speaks to him on the street without receiving instant and tender recognition. Debs loves men. This has made him the leading figure in a great movement, the beloved hero of a million hearts, and will give him a deathless name. It is a great thing to love men so and it is only achieved by thought. Nothing can make you great but thought.

Wattles' daughter, Florence, a budding socialist orator in her own right, insisted that her father's earlier mayoral vote got rigged and the election had been stolen. "They voted not only the dead men in the cemeteries, but vacant lots as well," twenty-three-year-old Florence said in her 1911 address to a socialist convention in Kokomo, Indiana. "We were robbed of the election, but in 1912 we will carry the election. Mark that. And we'll get the offices, too. We mean to do it through a thorough and completely effective organization."*

On the stump, Florence exuded the same sense of biblical justice as her father, the man who told of the social gospel and the metaphysical powers of the mind. "We don't want to vote merely because it is our right . . . ," she said in a 1916 speech in Indianapolis. "We don't want to vote merely to get into practical politics. We don't want to vote in order to sit in the legislature or on the bench. We want to vote on behalf of the struggling masses, and to do good for those about us."**

With Florence at her father's side, her spirits fresh and ready for a fight, anything seemed possible. Yet within a week of Florence's Kokomo speech, Wattles was dead. Though his writings had extolled the curative powers of thought, he had always been physically frail. His health collapsed on February 7, 1911, when he died of tuberculo-

---

* "Says Even Dead Voted in Recent Elwood Election," *Indianapolis Star,* January 29, 1911.

** "Biographical Sketch of Florence A. Wattles Bowers," by Noelle Fenwick, *Part III: Mainstream Suffragists,* National American Woman Suffrage Association.

sis at age fifty while traveling to Ruskin, Tennessee, which had been home to the Ruskin Commonwealth Association, a socialist commune from 1894 to 1901. In addition to his numerous books and articles on mind metaphysics, Wattles left behind a sole novel published in 1910, *Hell-Fire Harrison*, about the adventures of an independent-minded American tobacco farmer and congressman in late-eighteenth-century England.

The Fort Wayne Sentinel, knowing the local author and organizer mostly as a political figure, noted "he was one of the best known socialists in Indiana." And, almost as an afterthought, "He also wrote several books on scientific subjects."*

For her part, Florence moved in 1917 to New York City, where she worked for publisher E.P. Dutton, becoming director of publicity in 1925. Losing none of her old fire, she wrote to Debs' brother, Theodore, on company letterhead on January 30, 1930, addressing him as "Dear Comrade," and seeking his input and records for a potential biography she hoped would be published on his brother.

"You will recall my father," she wrote. "He was W.D. Wattles. And is buried in Elwood, Indiana. He and Comrade Hollingsworth"—Indiana social gospel minister J.H. Hollingsworth—"were very dear friends. Comrade H. knew father much better than you and 'Gene ever knew him, but even you know of him and his work . . . He was a remarkable personality, and a beautiful spirit, which, to me, at least, has never died . . ."**

---

* "Indiana Socialist Dies," *Fort Wayne Sentinel*, February 8, 1911.

** Florence's letter appears in the Eugene V. Debs Collection, Special Collections Department. Indiana State University Library.

Wattles' reputation and works experienced an extraordinary rebound nearly a century following his death. In 2007, word spread that *The Science of Getting Rich* was a source behind *The Secret*. The book began to hit bestseller lists. I published a paperback edition myself that reached number-one on the *Bloomberg Businessweek* bestseller list. My audio condensation later hit number-two on iTunes.

But what many of Wattles' new generation of readers missed was his lifelong dedication to the ethic of collective advancement and creativity above brutal or underhanded competition; and his belief that competition itself was an outmoded idea, soon to be supplanted by the creative capacities of the mind. Once unlocked, he taught, these greater faculties would grant working people the keys to a life of prosperity for themselves and all around them.

Was Wattles' vision of New Thought and social reform really so utopian? We live in an age of remarkable new discoveries of the mind's power: physicians have performed successful placebo surgeries* and demonstrated the placebo response in weight loss** as well as in

---

* In July 2002, researchers in the *New England Journal of Medicine* reported the effectiveness of placebo surgery: participants from the Houston Veterans Affairs Medical Center received mock arthritic knee operations—involving a benign incision—and experienced substantially similar rates of relief, and vastly reduced recovery time, as patients who received standard invasive arthritic knee surgery. (Researchers have speculated that the placebo response may be the only cause for reported relief in such operations.) See: "A Controlled Trial of Arthroscopic Surgery for Osteoarthritis of the Knee" by J. Bruce Moseley, Kimberly O'Malley, Nancy J. Petersen, et al., *The New England Journal of Medicine*, July 11, 2002.

** In a 2007 study, Harvard psychologist Ellen Langer reported that hotel maids experienced weight loss and reduced blood pressure when taught to understand that their daily work routine had significant aerobic benefits. Once these facts were established, within four weeks subjects lost weight without altering their work habits or personal lives and compared to no such changes in a control group. See: "Mind-set matters: exercise and the placebo effect" by Alia J. Crum, Ellen J. Langer, *Psychological Science*, February 18, 2007. In other studies by Langer (these subject to later controversy but their results never fundamentally refuted*), elderly subjects experienced physical and mental improvements—including increased strength and flexibility, recovered memory and cognitive function, and improved mood and vitality—when immersed in nostalgic settings filled with stimuli from their youth, including vintage books, music, and movies. Settings that evoked feelings of youth actually seemed to summon the reappearance of youthful traits, extending even to improved eyesight. (I venture that novelty itself may have been the triggering factor.) See "What If Age Is Nothing but a Mind-Set?" by Bruce Grierson in *The New York Times Magazine*, October 22, 2014. (*Researchers often dispute older studies, such as Langer's 1981 aging study, based on newer standards of methodology. But this phenomenon affects our view of all past clinical work, as it will affect how future researchers view today's practices, since methods inevitably progress.)

instances where placebos are transparently administered;* in the field called neuroplasticity, brain scans reveal that the brain's neural pathways are actually "rewired" by thought patterns—a biological act of mind over matter;** quantum physics experiments pose extraordinary questions about causality between thought and object, with implications extending to the perceptual basis of reality itself;*** and academic ESP research repeatedly demonstrates the nonphysical conveyance of data across boundaries of time, space, and mass in laboratory settings.**** Wattles' mission, now more than a century old, was to ask whether these extraordinary possibilities, which were only hinted at in the science of his day, can be applied and experimented with on the material and social scales of life.

Wattles did not live long enough to see the enduring influence of *The Science of Getting Rich*. But his calm certainty and profoundly confi-

---

* In 2010, Harvard Medical School researchers conducted an unprecedented "honest placebo" study in which an openly sham pill brought lasting relief to sufferers of Irritable Bowel Syndrome. Subjects knew they were receiving an inert substance, yet 59 percent reported relief (compared to 35 percent in the control group). It may be that a patient's belief in the very possibility of mental therapeutics is sufficient to enact the self-healing response. See: "Placebos without Deception: A Randomized Controlled Trial in Irritable Bowel Syndrome" by Ted J. Kaptchuk, et al., *PLoS ONE*, December 2010, Volume 5, Issue 12. In a 2016 follow-up study, collaborating researchers published a second paper on the transparent placebo, this time among ninety-seven sufferers of lower-back pain in Portugal. Once more, the subjects, seventy-six of whom completed the trial, were divided into two groups: a no-treatment or control group and a group administered a transparently inert substance with the understanding that a placebo response was being tested for. "There was," researchers wrote, "a clinically significant 30% reduction in both usual and maximum pain in the placebo group compared to reductions of 9 percent and 16 percent in usual and maximum pain, respectively, in the continued usual treatment group." Moreover, "honest placebo" subjects reported a 29 percent reduction in "pain-related disability" compared to near-zero in the control group. See: "Open-label placebo treatment in chronic low back pain: a randomized controlled trial" by Cláudia Carvalho, et al., *Pain*, December 2016, Volume 157, Number 12.

** For a detailed analysis by one of the pioneers in the field, see *The Mind and the Brain: Neuroplasticity and the Power of Mental Force* by Jeffrey M. Schwartz, M.D. and Sharon Begley (HarperCollins, 2002).

*** The literature in this field is vast. For a useful overview see *Quantum Enigma: Physics Encounters Consciousness*, 2nd Edition, by Bruce Rosenblum and Fred Kuttner (Oxford University Press, 2011).

**** For a comprehensive analysis of psychical research and its replications, see Etzel Cardeña's article in *American Psychologist*, the flagship journal of the American Psychological Association: "The Experimental Evidence for Parapsychological Phenomena: A Review," 2018, Vol. 73, No. 5.

dent yet gentle tone as a writer suggest that he understood the portent of what he was conveying.

Although *The Science of Getting Rich* will always be his classic, a core runner up is his widely read *The Science of Being Great*. The final line of his opening chapter is: "You can become what you want to be." That statement forms the heart of his career. Moreover, it is, in a sense, an encapsulation of American metaphysical ideals—the outlook of a still-young nation when Wattles wrote his books. His vision harmonized with the sense of limitless possibility that many Americans felt in the early twentieth century when the nation's growth and expansion seemed endless. This ethic still inspires people today.

Wattles' work can bridge the divisions some seekers feel between pursuit of self-betterment and aspiration to something greater; for him, the two were synonymous. He believed, with no sense of personal conflict, that the potential of the individual must be expressed both socially and materially. "Man is formed for growth," Wattles wrote in *The Science of Being Great*, "and he is under the necessity of growing. It is essential to his happiness that he should continually advance. Life without progress is unendurable."

If you venture into his 1910 and 1911 books, I think you will discover Wattles' complete philosophy of life: namely, that each person is run through by a capillary of immaterial influx—call it God, *Nous* (Ancient Greek for over-mind), or nonlocal intelligence—which can raise the individual to extraordinary heights of personal excellence, acts of creativity, and skills marked by virtuosity. But to fully place him or herself within this eternal, creative current, Wattles wrote, the individual must first be in alignment with generativity and reciprocity to other, like-created beings. (A different view of the author's model, which I explore in *The Miracle Club* and *Daydream Believer*, is that the psyche is capable of *selecting*—a term I prefer to manifesting—among different intersections of time, a concept considered by some quantum and string theorists.)

Self-refinement, Wattles concluded, is the key to transforming oneself into a vehicle for this Greater Principle of life, which yearns for expression through individual beings.

Everything that this good and thoughtful man believed necessary for a powerful life appears in these short and compelling books. He wished them to deliver readers to their greatest heights of achievement—and deepest sense of responsibility.

Chapter VI

New Thought Reimagined: The Kybalion *and* William Walker Atkinson

Truth embodied in a tale shall enter in at lowly doors.
—ALFRED, LORD TENNYSON, IN MEMORIAM A. H. H., 1850

Recent to this writing, I was privileged to work on the feature documentary *The Kybalion* with director Ronni Thomas. Ronni's dedication to this movie, which released in 2022—and surprised us by premiering as the number-three documentary on iTunes—was nothing less than heroic. The artistic vision that emerged from it, I hope viewers will agree, justifies his dedication.

The documentary is, of course, based on the classic 1908 occult text, *The Kybalion*, which purported to be a commentary on a work of late-ancient Greek-Egyptian Hermetic wisdom and, hence, a retention of Hermetic tradition itself. In actuality, the book was written by an energetic Chicago publisher, lawyer and writer named William Walker Atkinson (1862–1932) who used the pseudonym Three

Initiates. In the early twentieth century, Atkinson ran an innovative esoteric publishing house called the Yogi Publication Society from Chicago's Masonic Temple Building. His company issued a wide-ranging catalogue of highly recognizable, diminutive blue hardcovers from the publisher's offices in the twenty-one-story skyscraper, which couched Masonic meeting rooms at the top. It was built in 1892 and demolished in 1939, seven years after Atkinson's death.

Atkinson wrote prolifically under many pseudonyms. Three Initiates has proven his most enduringly popular but he also used names including Yogi Ramacharaka, Theron Q. Dumont, and my personal favorite, Magus Incognito. Atkinson was a prodigious writer and aficionado of New Thought and the mind-power metaphysics that were sweeping the Western world at the time and have since become deeply entrenched in American spiritual life.

Atkinson's writing exposed thousands of early twentieth-century readers to ideas of an esoteric nature, which they might not have had other opportunities to encounter. He wrote at least thirteen books under the byline Yogi Ramacharaka alone. Some observers look back and say that was just ersatz Vedism, novelty yoga, it wasn't the real thing. And there is, of course, truth to that verdict. Yet it is also true that this enterprising man introduced many people to variants of Vedic and yogic ideas, which would not explode across the American scene until probably the late 1960s. Traditional gurus, such as Swami Vivekananda (1863–1902), had visited America prior to Atkinson's calico adaptations. But his popular work helped prime Americans for the wave of spiritual teaching from the East that was soon to come.

When Maharishi Mahesh Yogi (1917–2008), for example, traveled to the United States in 1959 to teach Transcendental Meditation—an authentic teaching from Vedic tradition—large swaths of the public, and certainly those within the metaphysical culture, were able to receive and understand what Maharishi and others who followed him were offering, and to contextualize it, thanks, in part, to Atkinson's little blue hardcovers. Never underestimate the power of novelty to open doors, whet appetites, and prime interest.

Working on *The Kybalion* film was really a dream come true for me. Yet it was an unlikely dream. Because when I first discovered the book more than fifteen years ago, I almost wrote it off. I did not take it seriously. I thought, well, here is a novelty of early twentieth-century occultism written by someone who married certain Hermetic and New Thought themes and draped them in faux Egyptian garb. I looked askance at the drama Atkinson cultivated around the book by likening it to an ancient work of Greek-Egyptian wisdom and using the sensationalistic byline, Three Initiates.

For years, the internet buzzed with debate over the identity of the Three Initiates. Most documentary and contextual evidence supports that it was Atkinson writing alone. Atkinson acknowledged his sole authorship in an entry in *Who's Who in America* in 1912. American occultist Paul Foster Case (1884–1954) is sometimes identified as one of the Three Initiates, and he appears to have told as much to some of his colleagues.* But Case would've been just twenty-four when the book appeared in 1908, also at a time that he had just arrived in Atkinson's hometown of Chicago, so I consider the collaboration unlikely, although it's possible that they corresponded about some of the book's concepts.

Around the time I first read the book, I was speaking with a scholar of religious studies—a well-known man whose name I won't mention because this was a private conversation—and I remarked on my misgivings about *The Kybalion*. He got a gleam in his eye and said, "You know, there are some good ideas in that little book." That haunted me.

---

* See *Paul Foster Case: His Life and Works* by Paul A. Clark (OHM, 2013).

I thought, perhaps I was in a hurry to deem to myself too serious for *The Kybalion*. Again, I had thought, it's not *real* Hermeticism. I wanted the real thing. But looking back, I realize that that was not the right framing.

Until recently, Hermeticism itself was widely considered an ersatz philosophy, which many scholars of religion viewed as a faux antique "mutt" of pseudo-Egyptiana and Neoplatonism. Since the 1980s, that view has shifted with Hermeticism now better understood as an authentic retention of aspects of Egyptian antiquity, a point to which I return. *The Kybalion*, while it certainly is a twentieth-century novelty, combines insights from Hermeticism with modern metaphysics. The better part of seriousness is not insisting on binary divisions between "real" and "fake" (indeed the original Hermetica proffered its own conceits of deep antiquity)—rather, it is understanding context.

I decided to suspend judgment and revisit the book. I fell into it. One summer vacation, I read *The Kybalion* five times consecutively, which may or may not make you want to join me on vacation. Maybe I was just ready to receive it at that point because my own studies in Hermeticism had gone further. In 1711, Alexander Pope famously wrote in *An Essay on Criticism*: "A little learning is a dangerous thing." Perhaps the more you get to know, the less seriously you take yourself. And maybe because my own Hermetic studies had deepened at that point, I was able to pause and realize that Atkinson had done a fairly remarkable job of mining, selecting, and cultivating some of the psycho-spiritual ideas from Hermetic tradition.

Although Atkinson was relying on several sources, including the work of occult writer Anna Kingsford (1846–1888)*, he was probably drawing upon a Hermetic translation that appeared two years before *The Kybalion*. In 1906, a scholar of the occult and esoteric antiquity,

---

* Credit is due historian Mary K. Greer for this insight. Important documentary forensics have also been contributed by scholars Philip Deslippe (*The Kybalion: The Definitive Edition*, TarcherPerigee, 2011) and Richard Smoley (*The Kybalion: Centenary Edition*, TarcherPerigee, 2018).

G.R.S. Mead (1863–1933), produced a three-volume set called *Thrice Greatest Hermes*—referring to Hermes Trismegistus, the Greek appellation for the Egyptian god of intellect, Thoth.

Mead had been secretary to the world traveler and occult philosopher Madame H.P. Blavatsky (1831–1891). Among Blavatsky's remarkable roles on the world stage, she served as a kind of patron and source of encouragement to Mead, who produced one of the first truly serviceable English translations of Hermetic literature. Historian of esotericism Wouter J. Hanegraaff makes an important note in his 2022 study *Hermetic Spirituality and the Historical Imagination*: "One may add that while G.R.S. Mead's edition and translation (1906) was universally ignored by scholars because of the author's Theosophical commitments (see Hanegraaff, 'Out of Egypt'), he sometimes saw more clearly than his learned despisers . . ." It wasn't until several generations later, in 1992, that scholar and translator Brian P. Copenhaver produced a wonderful translation, *Hermetica*, through Cambridge University Press, which surpasses Mead but also stands on Mead's shoulders.

I believe it is important in terms of historicism and the search itself that we understand our history but not get excessively partisan about what constitutes authenticity in spiritual literature. Perhaps it violates our sense of seriousness that Atkinson used histrionic bylines like Three Initiates, or one hears strange (and sometimes exaggerated) stories or shorthand accusations around Madame Blavatsky. It was her secretary, Mead, who produced a translation that at least made these ideas serviceable, useful, and available to English-speaking people and gave indirect birth to works like *The Kybalion*, which ultimately deepened my own study. I doubt I am alone in that.

I must say that at this point in my search, I take religious novelty seriously. In my experience, many people embark on significant personal journeys thanks to what might be considered novelty. We see this everywhere. When the Catholic Church, for example, newly beatifies saints it is creating a kind of doorway through which contemporary people can enter new ideas or modes of worship. New doorways represent a furtherance, a possibility. We find seekers who might begin their studies with ideas or figures that lack ancient or scholarly vintage, but an antecedent of something truthful is present and a door gets opened and you never really know where it's going.

The Hermetic literature grew from Ancient Greece's encounter with Ancient Egypt. In the latter stages of Ancient Egyptian civilization, after Alexander the Great's invasion and conquering of Egypt in 332 B.C., the Pharaonic system was abolished. Thereafter, Egyptian rulers were often called Ptolemies, a term for general or military commander in Alexander's armies. A Greek ruling class and administrative apparatus took over Egypt for much of the remainder of its ancient history culminating in Roman governorship and military domination.

The Alexandrian era spelled the decay of Egypt's temple orders and religious systems—until the reign of Cleopatra in 51–30 B.C. The name Cleopatra has, of course, reached us through myriad dramas, plays, movies, and popular references. But who was Cleopatra from a historical perspective? She was an Egyptian ruler of Greek descent. In the wake of Alexander's armies, the Greek administrative class was, more or less, Philo-Egyptian; rulers often admired and adopted Egyptian culture. But they also intermarried to preserve their Alexandrian bloodline. As a result, and despite their cultural admiration, the ruling class often had a distant relationship to the millions who made up Egyptian civilization. Cleopatra was different. She was more than just a Philo-Egyptian installed on a Hellenic throne. She cared about and aimed to revive Egypt's esoteric tradition. She did so primarily from the cultural and economic seat of Alexandria where she funded restoration of Egypt's monuments, priesthoods, and temple orders.

Roughly concurrent to Cleopatra's efforts, and particularly in the decades immediately following the death of Christ, there arose in Alexandria a cohort of Greek-speaking scribes, also of the administrative class. This cohort hit upon a simple but revolutionary idea. They began writing down elements of Egyptian esoteric tradition in the Greek language. This undertaking proved enormously significant for the West in future centuries because it served to preserve and translate some of Egypt's esoteric philosophy into an expository literary form that modern Westerners could grasp. The timing of this record, of when it was produced, later became a source of controversy, a point to which I also return.

Ancient Egypt, of course, had its own language of hieroglyphs; but it was a symbolic language, a characterologically based language, and it did not have the kind of straight-forward, expository qualities to which we as Westerners have grown accustomed. Ancient Egypt also used Demotic, a reformed and streamlined hieroglyphs adapted for official business or documents, but it wasn't really a literary-descriptive device. Indeed, the West could not even begin to decipher hieroglyphic language itself until after the discovery of the Rosetta Stone by Napoleon's armies in 1799.

These Greek scribes also wrote down ideas that had been previously passed on through oral tradition. Indeed, most of our religious and philosophical ideas began as oral tradition and only later got committed to writing by figures who we call by names like Homer or Plato or Pythagoras, or in the last case by his students. In actuality, we know little about the personhood or even the veritable existence of such figures. In fact, it was common in the ancient world that scribes—we wouldn't consider them authors in our modern sense—affixed the name of a venerated or legendary figure to their writings in order to lend them gravity. It's a modern innovation that a writer or author has an individual identity. In antiquity in Egypt, in the Mediterranean, in the Biblical lands, in Hindustan or Ancient India, in the Far East in

China and Japan, it was common that a scribe functioned on behalf of a government, army, empire, academy, or royal court. In many cases, we do not know if authorial names used for attribution represented single, distinctive personas. For example, we do not know the identity of Lao Tzu, the legendary author of the *Tao Te Ching*. We do not know with any certainty the identity of Sun Tzu, the author of *The Art of War*, whose authorship was not credited until several centuries after the death of the dynastic general who bore that name. Nor do we really know who Homer was, or if he existed as a singular being.

Likewise, this late-ancient Greek-Egyptian literature was often attributed to Hermes or Hermes Trismegistus, an appellation of honor that the Greco-Egyptians bestowed upon Thoth, Egypt's god of writing and intellect, who they saw as "three-times greater" than their own god of intellect, Hermes. Hence, Greek scribes and builders termed this being "thrice-greatest" or Hermes Trismegistus.

There existed many diffuse Hermetic tracts. Some were ceremonial or magical in nature, oriented toward specific spells, prayers, or alchemical operations; these are sometimes called technical Hermetica. Other writings were more philosophical and existential in nature. Within these tracts, one can discover a common philosophical core. The outlook that animates the philosophical Hermetica can more or less be put this way: All of creation emanates from one great higher mind or life force, which the Greeks called *Nous*. And this higher mind creates through the exercise of thought. Creation expands outward through concentric circles of reality and humanity appears within one of these concentric circles.

One work of Hermetic literature, which was probably written in very late antiquity, is called *The Emerald Tablet*. It was first translated from Latin into English by Sir Isaac Newton (1643–1727). In this work appears the famous dictum, "as above, so below," which I think parallels the Western Scriptural precept, "God created man in his own image." Among the ideals within philosophical Hermetica is that just as humanity was created by an infinite mind, *Nous*, so can we create within our own sphere of existence. The secret of human development is to discover one's creative dimensions and the expansion to which they point. Yet there also exists a tension between man's self-actualization—a process that makes him greater than the gods who are fixed in existence ("ye are gods," reads Psalm 82)—and the physical limitations man suffers in his sphere of existence ("ye shall die as princes," the Psalm continues).

What I've just described is one of the areas where Hermetic literature becomes deeply important for contemporary seekers. I mentioned that William Walker Atkinson was interested in New Thought and the mind-power metaphysics sweeping the Western world in the late nineteenth and early twentieth centuries. The principle of New Thought, which grew from the transcendentalist ferment of New England in the mid-to-late nineteenth century, is that mind creates or selects all experience. Within New Thought, the individual is viewed as a conveyance of a higher creative force or God. This metaphysics grew extremely popular throughout Western life. And yet this outlook can also be profoundly frustrating for those of us who take it seriously, as I do. Because many of us on the path, certainly speaking for myself, peer into New Thought literature and feel instinctively, *there's truth here, there's innate truth here*, yet its extreme idealism does not account for all the observed and probed complexities and sufferings of life.

Indeed, as noted in the introduction, modern New Thought lacks a theology of suffering. It does not adequately account for mass crises throughout the world. We experience many different laws and forces, including physical forces, such as geography, seismic shifts, tidal waves, hurricanes, famines, and volcanoes, not to mention warfare and all the inhumanities that we inflict upon one another sometimes as a result of varying other forces. New Thought, as a spiritual culture, has historically offered little response to criticism other than to insist critics "don't get it" or to borrow and append ideas from other religious outlooks. It is insufficient, in my view, to repair gaps in a philosophy by clipping from another and saying, in effect, well, it's karma or it's the mass of historical human consciousness weighing on events, which really becomes an argument on behalf of randomness, the very thing from which New Thought is supposed to deliver us. Rather, I think we must sometimes stand bare in front of ideas we love and acknowledge that something in this philosophy, truthful and valuable as it is, is not fully working, is not covering all the bases of life.

I believe Hermetic literature can provide distinct help in this regard. One of the ideals in the Hermetica, and you'll find this reflected in *The Kybalion*, is that the mind is a veritably creative force; the mind is a causative force; but we human beings are far from the center of cosmic reality. Hence, we must suffer the framework that we occupy, even if we have the potential of transcending it, and the physical limits it places on us, including mortality itself.

These bodies are going to decay and there exists inexorable suffering and tragedy in our world. I often say that while it may be true that mind or psyche is the ultimate arbiter of reality, we *experience* many different laws and forces. A law is, by definition, universal; but that does not mean its effects are consistently felt. The impact of the psyche may be conditioned by circumstance, much like gravity, which responds to mass. H_2O is always water but it may be experienced as solid, vapor, or liquid. Natural laws are conditional. Why would a law of mind differ? An ancient antecedent for this outlook, later popularized in *The Kybalion*, is found in Hermetic literature.

I believe that New Thought can refine itself by revisiting the modern marriage to Hermeticism that William Walker Atkinson sought to foster.

Let me return to a question I touched on earlier. If we possess this sup-posed retention of ideas from Ancient Egypt, preserved in the exposi-tory language of Greek, why is this literature not more widely known? Why are there not more serviceable translations? And why did we as a civilization pass across centuries without better translations, which would make these ideas more accessible to modern seekers?

The West's encounter with this literature certainly has vintage. It began when a core of Hermetic writings, later called the *Corpus Hermeticum*, got rediscovered during the Renaissance around the year 1460 (the record sometimes shows 1462), and were translated from Greek into Latin. Latin was, of course, the language used by edu-cated people who composed Europe's ruling structure. For centuries, English speakers had to rely upon a not wholly accurate translation produced in 1650 by John Everard from the Renaissance Latin. Yet after that the scent trail goes largely cold. Why did this work suffer relative neglect by translators and scholars?

Several factors were at play. Study of the esoteric started to get derailed at the end of the Renaissance, more or less in the lead up to the Thirty Years War, a devastating conflict that decimated Central Europe beginning in 1618. The war was, in part, a reaction against some of the occultic and religious liberalism that had marked the era. But more specifically, the Hermetic literature fell into disrepute due to a groundbreaking textual analysis by a linguist named Isaac Casa-ubon (1559–1614). In a work published in 1614, Casaubon determined that the Hermetica was produced in late antiquity, specifically in the generations following Christ. This revelation eventually proved deflat-ing to many educated people of the era and in the decades ahead. (It should be noted that—as with much of intellectual history—Casau-bon's analysis was preceded by decades of fragmentary effort by other linguists who raised related questions.) Yet herein lies a strange histor-ical wrinkle, which runs into the present day.

During the Renaissance, numerous seekers, translators, benefac-tors, and clerics—people who had charge of culture—held to a hope or ideal that there existed somewhere in the mists of deep antiquity a pristine, primeval theology; there was, so the thinking went, an incep-tive theological outlook older than everything else—older than Chris-tianity, older than Judaism—and that if man could rediscover this primeval theology, or *prisca theologia*, he could peer into the workings of the universe. This hope seemed poised to come true when, around 1460, a Byzantine monk, probably employed as an antiquity seeker, entered the court of Florentine ruler Cosimo de' Medici (1389–1464) with the Greek-Egyptian manuscripts later called *Corpus Hermeticum*. Cosimo was so enthralled—and eager to read the material before his death that he directed his court translator, Marsilio Ficino (1433–1499), to suspend work translating Plato and direct his attention to the philosophy of Hermes.* Many believed that the discovery of the *prisca theologia* was at hand.

Along with this outlook, a belief also circulated among cultured people in the Renaissance that the figure of Hermes Trismegistus was perhaps a real historical being: a psychopomp, a man-god—and that Hermes Trismegistus may have been contemporaneous to Abraham or tutored Moses when the future Hebrew liberator dwelt in Egypt.

These dreams receded after Casaubon's textual analysis demon-strated that the Hermetic literature dated to late antiquity, in the decades following Christ. Along with these withered hopes, another kind of viewpoint settled over the Western cultural scene in the dawn-ing Age of Enlightenment. The viewpoint was that because the wished-for vintage of these philosophical tracts had been dispelled, there was

---

* Ficino in 1463 originally translated fourteen of seventeen tracts, which he printed in 1471. In 1482, Italian scholar and Hermeticist Lodovico Lazzarelli (1447–1500) translated three additional treatises.

something compromised, fraudulent, and corrupted about the Hermetic literature itself. Other theological statements, both Abrahamic and Eastern, were spared this judgment. This intellectual leap represented an error in the development of the modern Western mind.

The summary judgment of the Hermetica's "illegitimacy" grew from a deeply ingrained malady of Western intellect—which is that we are habituated to "either/or" or "take it or leave it" thinking. This might also be called "black and white" thinking or "binary thinking." Reaction to the Hermetic literature is a case in point. Because the Hermetic literature, so the reasoning went, proved not as old as acolytes and historians believed, it follows that the project of its revival, and even the literature itself, is compromised, sullied, and counterfeit. Natural philosopher Sir Thomas Browne (1605–1682) was left to write in his 1643 tract *Religio Medici*, "The severe Schools shall never laugh me out of the Philosophy of Hermes, that this visible World is but a Picture of the invisible wherein . . ."

Left out of this debate was a historical principle, alluded to earlier, that is as critical to our understanding of the value of the Hermetica as it is to contextualizing nearly any ancient text. Simply because we determine the date when a text was produced—sometimes through contemporaneous comparisons, analysis of vernacular, and other historical markers—*that does not mean that the text's ideas started then*. Not only were texts copied and recopied, sometimes among different languages, but *the story of humanity is itself the story of oral tradition*. The human story mirrors itself on both a macro and micro scale. When a baby is born that child possesses only the expressive ability of sound. The infant can cry to indicate he or she is hungry or that there's something wrong. Eventually, that child develops motor skills and later speech. Later still, speech becomes writing. What else is writing but an approximation of speech?

The development of human history mirrors that of the individual. It is a fact of history that much of our religious and parabolic literature began as oral tradition. This is so whether we are referencing Scripture or Homer or the teachings of Pythagoras. Indeed, most of the ideas attributed to Pythagoras were not written down, in this case by his students, until centuries after the Greek sage died. Why would the cultural scene be any different for Greek-Egyptian antiquity? Hence, I view the Hermetic literature as a deeply valuable time capsule of a very distant, ancient past to which we possess a frayed thread of connection; that thread has gotten broken, that thread has intermingled with other related or unrelated ideas, that thread has, at times, gotten interrupted. But it persists. It may not be tidy but it is present. To assume that the Hermetic literature is not reflective of a much older oral tradition is to assume that it is an exception to the history of ideas itself.

In any case, as the Age of Enlightenment proceeded, the Hermetica was written off and, at times, even mocked. In Mary Shelley's *Frankenstein*, published about two centuries after Casaubon, some of her characters—this wasn't Shelley's point of view but she was depicting it—debase Hermetic tradition and ridicule the tragic figure of Victor Frankenstein for reading its tracts. Recent to this writing, I encountered a blog that studies the anthropology of texts whose writer, while offering many erudite insights on early Christian texts, reflected on "Casaubon and the exposure of the Hermetic corpus," noting that, "I knew that the 'Hermetic corpus' was bogus, but not why"—conflating the redating (and contending the texts themselves intentionally clouded the matter) with a revelation of philosophical or textual illegitimacy.*

Due to this leap in thinking, the Hermetic literature was mostly excluded from the ancient philosophical and spiritual corpus. Eventually, the Hermetica fell into near obscurity. Indeed, after the 1650

---

* For the blog, see: roger-pearse.com/weblog/2011/05/12/casaubon-and-the-exposure-of-the -hermetic-corpus/. One of the texts in the *Corpus Hermeticum*, book XVI, asserts its own linguistic antiquity, a case I explore further in *Modern Occultism* (2023).

English translation and some errant literary references, the trail goes largely cold. There appeared, thanks to the late-nineteenth-century occult revival instigated by Madame Blavatsky, some less-than-satisfactory Victorian translations. As noted, it was only in 1992 when Copenhaver's translation emerged—and I cannot recommend it highly enough—that we came to possess what I think can be considered the first truly creditable English translation.*

In sum, the dismissal of the Hermetica cost us centuries of progress in our ability to peer into the existential outlook of our ancient ancestors. As alluded, this was due, in large measure, to a misunderstanding of how ideas get passed on and to the thought habit of binary thinking. In *The Kybalion* film, author, researcher, and clinician Raymond Moody, M.D., who coined the term Near-Death Experience (NDE), makes the valuable observation that in the West most of us are educated to think in *opposites*—to understand that truth is composed of polarized absolutes. This stems largely from the influence of Aristotle. But Moody points out that such an outlook is incomplete. A third option exists. There is *true*, there is *false*—and there is *unintelligible*. This is a critical insight, especially in our era when we are, for example, witnessing the mainstreaming of the UFO thesis, throwing modern culture into an indeterminant or uncertain place. Yet we experience hobbled intellectual capacities, often with "believers" off to one side and rejectionist "skeptics" off to another. Our culture is poorly suited to sustaining uncertainty and thus pursuing questions in a non-polemical manner. This also weakens our policy-making apparatus in areas ranging from healthcare to climate change. I've often said that

---

* I should add a further word about the historically important 1906 translation by G.R.S. Mead. If you read it, or parts of it, I think you'll see that it is rendered in almost leaden Victorian prose, which seems to adopt the language of the King James Bible. I think Mead, a truly gifted scholar and translator, miscalculated that this literary device would bring gravity to the text. He was a great intellect but his translation proved impersonal, difficult to read, and somewhat violative of the spare language of the original. Mead was, I believe, among the sources Atkinson (himself an acolyte of Theosophy) drew upon—and from this turgid translation he mined certain gems, which he combined with his own interest in New Thought.

the ability to sustain paradox is perhaps the chief marker of maturity on the spiritual or ethical path.

In some ways, discussion around *The Kybalion*, much like the Hermetica itself, provides a perfect exposition of this predicament. Contemporary commentators who wish to demonstrate their hold on seriousness will sometimes opine that the book is "crap." That epithet appears popular among seekers and skeptics wishing to signal no-nonsense bona fides. A journalist who follows spiritual topics recently wrote me: "I loathed *The Secret* and think the Law of Attraction is crap." (I agree that such popularizations are flawed; they also contain instincts for potentials inherent in human nature. Hence, I criticize but do not dismiss them.)

Along similar lines, people sometimes debate, often vociferously, whether *The Kybalion* is "real" or "fraudulent" Hermeticism. But, as noted, I consider this the wrong framing. Here I want to quote scholar of Hermeticism Philip Deslippe from his 2011 introduction to *The Kybalion: The Definitive Edition*, which I was privileged to publish:

> Early Hermetic writings were often written anonymously and by small groups or unaffiliated individuals and, above all, well before the fascinations of Florentine nobility in the Renaissance or the high expectations of moneyed British occultists, the early Hermetic texts were popular. They were meant for subaltern people and marginal seekers, those outside established cults or places of power. To critique *The Kybalion* for being a type of unwashed, inauthentic spiritual teaching, or to be preoccupied by Atkinson's use of a pseudonym or to question the authority of the text, is to in some sense attack it for being traditionally Hermetic.

Again, *The Kybalion* is neither "real" nor "fake"—it is novel. It is contemporary. It is an adaptation. The book's dramatic excesses can be accepted or set aside while drinking from its deeper currents. Graduated versus absolutist thinking is required when approaching it.

I should note that Hermeticism itself, and its adaptation in *The Kybalion*, posits a reality composed of polarities: "as above, so below." Or as twentieth-century spiritual philosopher G.I. Gurdjieff put it: "every stick has two ends." But within this subtler schema of polarities there exist vastly graduated states. Gurdjieff, in what may reflect a deeper understanding of the Hermetic framework, further noted that the end of every stick itself branches off into polarities ad infinitum. Aristotle's view of absolutes may be useful and even compelling within limited equations; but it cannot serve as the uber-law of reality, a point all the more pronounced today with interpretations of quantum mechanics—in which a particle appears in a state of infinitude and endless outcomes coexist—and postulations of string theory and the existence of infinite dimensions.

As mystic Neville Goddard, encountered in chapter XIII, noted, "Beginnings and ends are all dreams."

With regard to understanding and contextualizing the Hermetica, we have, as suggested, experienced real progress in our era. Overall, this literature is less controversial and better understood today than it was a generation ago. In the 1980s, many scholars continued to dismiss the Hermetica as little more than warmed-over Neoplatonism. They treated Hermetic literature much as I had once treated *The Kybalion*. But as we've learned more and uncovered other texts of deep antiquity from Egypt, we find correspondences between the Hermetica and Ancient Egyptian esoteric thought. This turnaround began, in part, through a remarkable book, first published by Cambridge University Press in 1986, *The Egyptian Hermes* by Garth Fowden.

Likewise, certain Hermetic texts, including *The Emerald Tablet* itself, were once considered works of pseudo-Hermetica. Until at least the 1920s, and for several decades beyond, *The Emerald Tablet* was deemed a medieval fakery written in Latin. But since the 1920s, we have discovered progressively earlier fragments of the work.* The earliest reference that we now have to *The Emerald Tablet* is from the eighth century A.D. in Arabic. Hermetic works got translated not only into Latin but also into Arabic, which likewise served as a source of retention.

This is another of the reasons I discourage "high horse" thinking around esoteric or occultic texts or concepts: we learn more as time passes and assessments of a work's vintage or centrality may change. Indeed, the term Gnosticism, at its scholarly inception in the seventeenth century, was used pejoratively. At this stage of my search, I have come to regard ersatz seriousness as among the chief barriers to intellectual development and authentic exchange.

It is really extraordinary to me that in our search today—and I hope you'll permit me a little idealism—the ancients still have help to provide us. I do not think I'm putting it in too dramatic a way when I note that.

In our generation, we possess the first really quality English translations of the Hermetica. I've mentioned Copenhaver but there is also another translator, Clement Salaman, who with a team of collaborators published a wonderful translation in 2000, *The Way of Hermes*, with Inner Traditions. And there exist other important translations,

---

* This history is well summarized in "Historical Note Concerning *The Emerald Tablet*" in *Meditations on the Tarot* written anonymously by Catholic scholar and traditionalist Valentin Tomberg (1900–1973). The posthumous work is thought to date to 1967 with its first publication in French in 1980 and its English publication five years later. I published a 2002 edition at Penguin Random House, which includes the translator's corrections and an afterword by Cardinal Hans Urs von Balthasar.

including of the technical Hermetica, such as *Greek Magical Papyri in Translation* by Hans Dieter Betz (University of Chicago Press, 1996). Hence, this material has become available to us in ways that it wasn't to previous generations. That's profoundly exciting. Similar developments are occurring through Project Hindsight and other efforts relating to the new translation of previously unknown or untranslated Hellenic works of astrology.*

In light of all this, I honor the work of William Walker Atkinson. Yes, he used dramatic pseudonyms and, yes, he employed histrionic and occasionally strained, fanciful language. All that is true. But he also did the work of ploughing an overgrown field to discover, adapt, and distill certain ancient or esoteric ideas, which I believe have proven deeply valuable, certainly to my search.

When viewing Atkinson's work, it is, as noted, the wrong framing to ask, "Is it or isn't it real Hermeticism?" Hermeticism has always been a patchwork; it has always been controversial; it was long neglected. It is only within recent decades that observers would even pose the question of whether something constituted "real" Hermeticism because a generation or so ago, the dominant scholarly culture did not even think in terms of there being a "real" Hermeticism. This was at one time true of Hermeticism's distant cousin, Gnosticism.

Our thread of connection to Hermetic literature was maintained by a handful of outsider thinkers—including occult scholar Manly P. Hall (1901–1990) in *The Secret Teachings of All Ages*—who had the instinct, since validated by time, that something of deep value and historical worth appeared in this esoteric writing.

The Kybalion itself was based upon that instinct. And I hope that the documentary we were privileged to make both honors that instinct and weds it to certain contemporary innovations, ideas, and practices, just as Atkinson attempted in his era. Comparing ancient and modern

---

* E.g., see: astro.com/astrowiki/en/Project_Hindsight.

insights sometimes requires selecting among recent ideas in spirituality, psychology, and the sciences that are, in themselves, not part of
Hermeticism but that run parallel to its philosophical instincts, which
is a rich area of study in itself. Parallel insights, i.e., insights that may
be separated by vast stretches of time, language, culture, and geography but that vector in similar directions, point us, in my view, toward
a scent trail of universal truth.

Above all else, let us value the verity that we are not alone on
this path today. We have systems of retention, we have the group
exchange, and we have the distant voices of the ancients, incomplete
but precious, to help us on our way.

Chapter VII

The Splendor of Florence Scovel Shinn

What makes a "serious writer"? In the final book of metaphysical author Florence Scovel Shinn, *The Secret Door to Success,* venerable New Thought minister Emmet Fox (1886–1951) wrote in his 1940 foreword:

> One secret of Shinn's success was that she was always herself...
> colloquial, informal, friendly, and humorous. She never sought to be
> literary, conventional, or impressive. For this reason she appealed to
> thousands who would not have taken the spiritual message through
> more conservative and dignified forms, or have been willing to read . . .
> at least in the beginning . . . the standard metaphysical books.

Fox's comments were as much tribute as eulogy: the illustrator and author Shinn died that year, 1940, at her home in New York City.

I quote from Fox's elegy with a tinge of hesitancy. There is, I think, something of a backhanded compliment, or even veiled putdown, in his assessment that Shinn's books are for seekers who might not have taken her teachings on mind-power metaphysics through more "dignified forms."

A thought habit of today's spiritual and intellectual culture, and many who seek their place in it, is suspicion of *simple ideas and methods*. In Shinn's outlook—always proudly direct visualizing, decreeing, and emoting are all means of causation: "Continually 'making believe' impresses the subconscious," she wrote in her 1925 perennial *The Game of Life and How to Play It*.

I had this exchange in 2017 with filmmaker David Lynch, the whole of which appears in my 2022 book *Uncertain Places*:

Mitch: I think part of the problem with our spiritual and intellectual culture today is that if something works, we are immediately suspicious of it. We're suspicious of simple things. Which I think is a problem.

David: Well, it is a big problem. The proof is in the pudding, in the tasting. So, it's difficult to describe the beautiful experience, the bliss of transcending to people who haven't experienced it. But it's true that there is a treasury within each one of us human beings.

The director was specifically referencing Transcendental Meditation, but I see a more general critique in his remarks, one that applies to Shinn and other artists who sing the song of the practical.

Shinn's methods, including her technique of "speaking the word"—of placing faith in greater spiritual channels and announcing the arrival of that which is needed—either work or do not. If her ideas work—and I warrant from experience that, in some measure, amid a complexity of forces, they do and challenge readers to consider their own applications—where is the need for more "dignified" framings to which Fox alludes?

I believe that readers and seekers must never feel embarrassed or sheepish over an idea because it is simple in rendering or *hoi polloi* in appeal.

As alluded, the only proving ground of a religious, self-developmental, or therapeutic method is *efficacy*. That may be why Shinn is far more widely read today than Fox and many of her contemporaries. The work of the New Thought icon remains a formative influence on readers touched by her chin-out message that *thoughts are causative*.

Shinn is best known for her 1925 classic *The Game of Life*. While Shinn deemed life a "game," her own existence was not easy—nor did she pursue ease.

Born Florence Scovel in Camden, New Jersey, in 1871, she took a rare path as a female artist, attending the Pennsylvania Academy of the Fine Arts. There "Flossie," as friends knew her, met a fellow student she later wed, realist painter Everett Shinn (1876–1953).

Married in 1898, they moved to New York's Greenwich Village, where the couple collaborated on stage plays and became part of the Ashcan School of American artists, a cohort known for depicting street scenes, tenements, and the immigrant experience. Shinn also illustrated popular children's and adult literature.

In 1912, Flossie and Everett divorced at the latter's urging, according to Ira Glackens (1907–1990), a family friend and memoirist who recalled Everett's temperament as "volatile and inconstant." Everett went on to three more busted marriages before his death in 1953.

Writing in vivid, Capotesque tones in his 1957 book about his artist father and cohorts, *William Glackens and the Ashcan Group*, Ira recounted:

He [Everett] finally told Flossie that he wanted a divorce. Little Flossie, "the pocket Venus," took some time to recover from the blow, and when she did she embarked on an entirely new career and seems never to have drawn again. She got religion, but in a way all her own. I believe Flossie's religion was what was known as New Thought or Unity. It was a religion of success.

Flossie worked out her own philosophy and then wrote a book with a sure-fire title: The Game of Life and How to Play It. No publisher would touch it. So she sold her old Biddle silver . . . and published it herself, in 1925. The last I heard, it had gone into forty editions.

Shinn often spoke at New York's Unity Truth Center but also delivered lectures independently at Steinway Hall near Times Square. For his part, Everett remained in touch with his ex-wife, a well-loved, even bon vivant presence, as Ira somewhat cheekily recalled:

Flossie could not be dull if she tried, and her own book, along with its inspiration, always brings laughs. She became a widely known speaker and her talks were always bright and lively . . . She rented a large apartment on Fifth Avenue, overlooking Central Park, as her religion required her to "affirm" wealth—her basic thesis—so that it would "manifest." Somehow, it always did.

Shinn provided a role model for many independent seekers not only by how she expressed principles of protean selfhood but also, as Ira implied, by her do-it-yourself ethic. When no publisher would take a chance on *The Game of Life*, the middle-aged divorcee, writing in an era when women had just won the right to vote, sold the family silver—the sole remaining asset from her blue-blooded Biddle ancestry—and published the book herself.

It became one of the most popular works of practical metaphysics of the next hundred years and remains widely read, appearing today in myriad editions in print, digital, and audio, as well as anthologies—this for a public-domain volume that can be freely downloaded.

Shinn achieved comparable success in self-publishing her follow-up, *Your Word Is Your Wand,* in 1928, and her coda, *The Secret Door to Success,* in 1940. The final books that bear Shinn's byline are *The Power of the Spoken Word,* issued posthumously in 1944, and the short work *The Magic Path of Intuition,* published in 2013, apparently from a newly discovered manuscript, as explained by the press Hay House.

Following "an illness of several weeks," reported the *New York Times,* the writer and illustrator died at home in Manhattan at age seventy on October 17, 1940. Her death certificate identifies only "natural causes." She was cremated. As Ira Glackens recounted:

> Finally one day Flossie went into her living room, sat down and died. Not long afterward her effects were sold in a dingy auction room. E.G. [Edith Glackens, Ira's mother] did not learn of the auction until too late. Hurrying there, she found Flossie's goods and chattels had been sold and carted away. Only a few of her old drawings were scattered on the floor, not yet having been swept up, and the attendant said she might have them. So E., faithful to her old friend, picked her drawings off the floor and carried them home. No one else had cared. One or two of those rescued drawings are now in the Library of Congress.

Shinn and her contemporaries interpreted the Bible as a psychological blueprint of individual development and personal excellence. Although she avowedly admired the 1908 occult classic *The Kybalion*, which the author references in *The Secret Door to Success*, Scripture was Shinn's chief resource, reflecting a common tenet of New Thought tradition.

Indeed, Shinn influenced some of the most powerful and varied voices in positive-mind culture, from the intellectually vibrant mystic Neville Goddard (1905–1972) to the folksy, mega-selling Reverend Norman Vincent Peale (1898–1993), author of *The Power of Positive Thinking*, both of whom adopted Shinn's phraseology in their work.

In 1995, two years after Peale's death, an article in the summer edition of *Lutheran Quarterly*, "Peale's Secret Source" by George D. Exoo and John Gregory Tweed, sought to expose the All-American pastor's "unsettling theological secret," namely that his writing "shows a startling similarity to the writings of an obscure teacher of Occult [sic] science named Florence Scovel Shinn."

Seizing upon a cover endorsement that Peale provided for an anthology of Shinn's work issued by his publisher Simon & Schuster in 1989, the writers concluded that the Protestant minister and popularizer of positive-thinking did more than clip-and-paste Shinn's work but practiced her "Occult science" himself, pointing to the ninety-year-old Peale's statement: "*The Game of Life* is filled with wisdom and creative thoughts. That its teachings work I know to be a fact, for I've long used them myself."

Although the writers outlined Peale's "remarkable structural and thematic similarity to the writings" of Shinn, I find their connections overstated. While Peale demonstrably adopted phrasing, techniques, and ideas from the mystical ethers of New Thought—a practice common to nearly all writers in the genre—the correspondences resulted more from widespread popularity of New Thought lingo and concepts across the modern scene than of untoward borrowing on Peale's part.

Shinn also impacted more recent spiritual and social voices, including New Age writer-publisher Louise Hay (1926–2017), founder of Hay House, and activist-actress Yolanda King (1955–2007), eldest daughter of Martin Luther King, Jr., who told me of her affinity for Shinn in a 2005 interview for *Science of Mind* magazine, probably King's last before her untimely death two years later, at age fifty-one, from heart failure.

Shinn's natural, practical voice touched a wide range of seekers and metaphysical ministers and writers. In so doing, she contributed to New Thought's popular tone: one of encouragement, experiment, boldness, and boundless possibility.

If New Thought cuts corners philosophically—I have critiqued it as such and return to this—it also opens doors, urging readers toward further search rather than, as some critics generalize, ruinous behavior or delusion.

In her books, Shinn attained a goal that most authors reach for but rarely grasp: leaving a testament that conveys something of the woman herself.

Chapter VIII

Better Every Day: Émile Coué

One of the most significant names in modern psychological and motivational philosophy will evince blank looks from most people today: French mind theorist Émile Coué (1857–1926).

Yet Coué, who earned both adulation and jeers during his lifetime, devised a simple, mantra-based method of self-reprogramming that has recently been validated across a wide range of disciplines, often by researchers unaware of the inceptive insights upon which their studies rest. I believe that Coué's approach not only deserves new credit and respect, but also holds promise for anyone in pursuit of practical therapeutic methods.

Coué proposed a simple formula of using mantras or affirmations to reprogram your psyche along the lines of confidence, enthusiasm, and wellness. His methods prefigured the work of self-help giants like Napoleon Hill, Anthony Robbins, and Maxwell Maltz—the last met in chapter XVIII—as well as recent clinical developments in sleep, neurological, placebo, and psychical research.

Indeed, at one time, thousands of people in the U.S. and Europe swore by Coué's approach. His key mantra—"Day by day, in every way, I am getting better and better"—was repeated by the Beatles, along with a wide range of therapists and spiritual writers. In rediscovering Coué, you will be able to determine for yourself if his simple approach works.

Before exploring Coué's method and its application, it is useful to understand his unusual background. Born in Brittany in 1857, Émile Coué developed an early interest in hypnotism, which he pursued through a mail-order course from Rochester, New York. Coué studied hypnotic methods more rigorously in the late 1880s with French physician and therapist Ambroise-Auguste Liébeault. Liébeault was one of the founders of the so-called "Nancy School" of hypnotism, which promoted hypnotism's therapeutic uses. Leaving behind concepts of occultism and cosmic laws, many of the Nancy School hypnotists saw their treatment as a practical form of suggestion, mental reprogramming, relaxation, and psychotherapy.

This was Coué's view, bolstered by personal experience. While working in the early 1900s as a pharmacist in Troyes, in northwestern France, Coué made a startling discovery: patients responded better to medications when he spoke in praise of the formula. Coué came to believe that the imagination aided not only recovery but also a person's general sense of well-being. From this insight, Coué developed his method of "conscious autosuggestion." This was essentially a form of waking hypnosis that involved repeating confidence-building mantras in a relaxed or semiconscious state.

Coué argued that many of us suffer from poor self-image. This becomes unconsciously reinforced because your willpower, or drive to achieve, is overcome by your imagination, by which he meant one's habitual self-perceptions. In 1922, he wrote in *Self Mastery Through Conscious Autosuggestion*, "When the will and the imagination are opposed to each other, it is always the imagination which wins." By way of example, he asked people to think of walking across a wooden plank laid on the floor—obviously an easy task. But if the same plank is elevated high off the ground, the task becomes fraught with fear, even though the physical demand remains the same. This, Coué asserted, is what we are constantly doing on a mental level when we imagine ourselves as worthless or weak.

These insights drove the autosuggestion pioneer toward his signature achievement. Coué believed that through self-suggestion or autosuggestion, any individual, with nearly any problem, could self-induce the same kinds of positive results he had observed when working in Troyes. In pursuit of an overarching method, Coué devised his self-affirming mantra: "Day by day, in every way, I am getting better and better." Although few people today have heard of Coué, many still recognize his formula. The mind theorist made his signature phrase famous through lecture tours of Europe and the U.S. in the early 1920s.

To critics, however, Coué reflected everything fickle and unsound about modern mind metaphysics and motivational philosophies. *How, they wondered, could anyone believe that this little singsong mantra— Day by day, in every way, I am getting better and better—could solve anything?* But in a facet of Coué's career that is often overlooked, he demonstrated considerable insight, later validated by sleep and placebo researchers, into *how* he prescribed using the formula.

Coué explained that you must recite the "day by day" mantra just as you're drifting to sleep at night when you're hovering within the very relaxed state between wakefulness and slumber. Sleep researchers now call these moments hypnagogia, an intriguing state of mind during which you possess sensory awareness, but your perceptions of reality bend and morph, like images from a Salvador Dalí painting.

During hypnagogia, your mind is extremely supple and suggestible. Coué understood this by observation and deemed it the period to gently whisper to yourself twenty times: "Day by day, in every way, I am getting better and better." He didn't want you to rouse yourself from your near-sleep state by counting, so he recommended knotting a small string twenty times and using this device like rosary beads to mark off your repetitions. He also said to repeat the same procedure at the very moment you wake in the morning, which is a state sometimes called hypnopompia. It is similar to the nighttime state insofar as you are occupying a shadow world of consciousness, yet possess sufficient cognition to direct your mental workings.

Coué insisted that his mantra-based routine would reprogram your mind and uplift your abilities. Was he correct? There's one way to find out, at least for your own private purposes: *Try*. We must never place ourselves above what are perceived by some as "simple" ideas. I have been influenced by the spiritual teacher Jiddu Krishnamurti (1895–1986), who emerged from the Vedic tradition but was an unclassifiable voice. Krishnamurti observed that the greatest impediment to self-development and independent thought is the wish for respectability. Nothing does more to stunt personal experiment, he taught, than the certainty that you must follow the compass point of accepted inquiry. Once you grow fixated on that compass point, nearly everything that you read, hear, and encounter gets evaluated on whether it moves you closer to or further from its perceived direction. This makes independent experiment extremely difficult. But if you're unafraid of a little hands-on philosophy, Coué presents the perfect opportunity with his original mantra, intended to serve all purposes and circumstances. Of course, you can also craft your own simple mantra that reflects a specific desire, but you might want to start with Coué's original version to become comfortable with the practice.

If you need further encouragement to self-experiment, it may help to realize that Coué's influence traveled in many remarkable directions. The Beatles tried Coué's method and apparently liked it, as references to Coué appear in some of their songs. In 1967, Paul McCartney used Coué's mantra in the infectious chorus of *Getting Better*, "It's getting better all the time . . . ," and the lyrics paid further tribute to the healer: "You gave me the word, I finally heard / I'm doing the best that I can." John Lennon also recited Coué's formula in his 1980 song *Beautiful Boy*, "Before you go to sleep, say a little prayer: Every day, in every way, it's getting better and better."

Beyond the Fab Four, placebo researchers at Harvard Medical School recently validated one of Coué's core insights. In January 2014, clinicians from Harvard's program in placebo studies published a paper reporting that migraine sufferers responded better to medication when given "positive information" about the drug.* This was the same observation Coué had made in the early 1900s. Harvard's study was considered a landmark because it suggested that the placebo response is always operative. It was the first study to use suggestion, in this case, news about a drug's efficacy, in connection with an active rather than inert substance, and hence, found that personal expectation impacts how, and to what extent, we experience an active drug's benefits. Although the Harvard paper echoed Coué's original insight, it made no mention of him.

I wondered whether the researchers had Coué in mind when they designed the study and asked one of the principals, who did not respond. So, I contacted the director of Harvard Medical School's program in placebo studies, Ted J. Kaptchuk, a remarkable and inquis-

---

* "Altered Placebo and Drug Labeling Changes the Outcome of Episodic Migraine Attacks" by Slavenka Kam-Hansen, et al, *Science Translational Medicine*, January 8, 2014, Vol. 6, Issue 218.

itive clinician who also worked on the study. "Of course I know about Coué," Kaptchuk told me, "'I'm getting better day by day.'" He agreed that the migraine study coalesced with Coué's observations, though the researchers had not been thinking of him when they designed it.

Coué's impact appears under the radar in an unusual range of places. An influential twentieth-century British Methodist minister, Leslie D. Weatherhead, looked for a way that patients and seekers could effectively convince themselves of the truth and power of their affirmations, especially when such statements chafed against circumstantial reality, such as in cases of addiction or persistently low self-worth. Weatherhead was active in the Oxford Group in the 1930s, which preceded Alcoholics Anonymous (AA) in its pursuit of religious-therapeutic methods, as later explored in chapter XII. In using suggestions or affirmations to improve one's sense of self-worth and puncture limiting beliefs, the minister was, in his own way, attempting to update the methods of Coué.

Weatherhead understood that affirmations—such as "I am confident and poised"—could not penetrate the "critical apparatus" of the human mind, which he compared to "a policeman on traffic duty." Other physicians and therapists similarly noted the problem of affirmations lacking emotional persuasiveness. Some therapists insisted that affirmations had to be credible in order to get through to the subject; no reasonable person would believe exaggerated self-claims, a point that Coué had also made. While Weatherhead agreed with these critiques, he also believed that the rational "traffic cop" could be eluded by two practices. The first was the act of repetition: "A policeman on duty who refuses, say, a cyclist the first time, might ultimately let him into the town if he presented himself again and again," he wrote in 1951. Continuing the metaphor, Weatherhead took matters further:

I can imagine that a cyclist approaching a town might more easily elude the vigilance of a policeman if the attempt to do so were made in the half-light of early dawn or the dusk of evening. Here also the parable illumines a truth. The early morning, when we waken, and the evening, just as we drop off to sleep, are the best times for suggestions to be made to the mind.

As Weatherhead saw it, the hypnagogic state—again, the drowsy state between wakefulness and sleep, generally experienced when a person is drifting off in the evening or coming to in the morning—is a period of unique psychological flexibility, when ordinary barriers are down. This is pure Couéism. Moreover, this fact probably reflects why people suffering from depression or anxiety often describe the early waking hours as the most difficult time of day—the rational defenses are slackened. If the individual could use the gentlest efforts to repeat affirmations, without rousing himself fully to a waking state, the new ideas could penetrate, Coué and Weatherhead believed.

The mystical writer Neville Goddard (1905–1972), whose career is considered in chapter XIII, made a similar point about the malleability of the hypnagogic mind. So did the twentieth-century psychical researcher and scientist Charles Honorton (1946–1992), who used this observation as a basis for testing the potential for telepathy between individuals. Honorton considered a hypnagogic state "prime time," in effect, for extrasensory perception or ESP.

In the early 1970s, Honorton and his collaborators embarked on a long-running series of highly regarded parapsychology ("psi") experiments, known as the "ganzfeld" experiments (German for "whole field"). These trials were designed to induce a hypnagogic state in a "receiver." The subject was placed, seated or reclining, in a soft-lit or darkened room and fitted with eyeshades and earphones to create a state of comfortable sensory deprivation or low-level stimulation (such as with a "white noise" machine). Seated in another room, a "sender" would attempt to telepathically convey an image to the receiver. After the sending period ended, the receiver was asked to select the correct image from among four—three images were decoys, establishing a chance hit-rate of 25 percent. Experimenters found that receivers consistently made higher-than-chance selections of the correct "sent" image. Honorton collaborated with avowed skeptic and research psychologist Ray Hyman in reviewing the data from a wide range of ganzfeld experiments. The psychical researcher and the skeptic jointly wrote: "We agree that there is an overall significant effect in this database that cannot be reasonably explained by selective reporting or multiple analysis."* Honorton added, "Moreover, we agree that the significant outcomes have been produced by a number of different investigators."

Hyman insisted that none of this was proof of psi, though he later acknowledged that, "Contemporary ganzfeld experiments display methodological and statistical sophistication well above previous parapsychological research. Despite better controls and careful use of statistical inference, the investigators seem to be getting significant results that do not appear to derive from the more obvious flaws of previous research."** Although serious psychical research has come under withering, and often unfair criticism in recent years, the ganzfeld experiments have remained relatively untouched—and their methodological basis is derived directly from the insights of Coué. (I review this and other key parapsychology findings in my 2022 *Daydream Believer*.)

* "A Joint Communiqué: The Psi Ganzfeld Controversy" by Ray Hyman and Charles Honorton, *Journal of Parapsychology*, vol. 50, December 1986.

** "Evaluation of a Program on Anomalous Mental Phenomena" by Ray Hyman, *Journal of Parapsychology*, 1995, Vol. 59, No. 4.

Coué's presence also emerges in popular literature. One of the most enduring and beguiling pieces of popular metaphysics on the American scene is a twenty-eight-page pamphlet called *It Works,* written in 1926 by a Chicago ad executive named Roy Herbert Jarrett, who went under the alias "R.H.J." His widely used method is to write down and focus on your desires—first, you must clarify your need; second, write it down and think of it always; and third, tell no one what you are doing to maintain mental steadiness. Plain enough, perhaps, but the seeker's insights rested on the deeper aspects of Couéism.

In the early 1920s, Jarrett and many other Americans were thrilled by news of Coué's mantra. The "Miracle Man of France" briefly grew into an international sensation as American newspapers featured *Ripley's-Believe-It-Or-Not*-styled drawings of Coué, looking like a goateed magician and gently displaying his knotted string at eye level like a hypnotic device.

In early 1923, Coué embarked on a three-week lecture tour of America, with one of his final stops in Jarrett's hometown of Chicago, where the Frenchman addressed a packed house at Orchestra Hall. A raucous crowd of more than 2,000 demanded that the therapist help a paralytic man who had been seated onstage. Coué defiantly told the audience that his autosuggestive treatments worked only on illnesses that originated in the mind. "I have not the magic hand," he insisted. Nonetheless, Coué approached the man and told him to concentrate on his legs and repeat, "It is passing, it is passing." The seated man struggled up, haltingly walked, and the crowd exploded. Coué rejected any notion that his "cure" was miraculous and insisted that the man's disease must have been psychosomatic.*

---

* Coué is quoted in Chicago from "Coué Proves Theory Worth," *Los Angeles Times,* February 7, 1923. (I altered the article's amusing use of the phonetic "ze" for "the" in its attempt to capture his French accent.) Additional articles on Coué's first American tour, which he briefly reprised in 1924, include "Crowd in Orchestra Hall Cheers Coué as His First Attempt in Chicago to Effect Cure Seems a Success," *Chicago Daily Tribune,* February 7, 1923; "Youth's Tremors Quieted by Coué," *New York Times,* January 14, 1923; and "Emile Coué Dead, a Mental Healer," *New York Times,* July 3, 1926.

To some Americans, Coué's message of self-affirmation held particular relevance for oppressed people. The pages of Black nationalist Marcus Garvey's newspaper, *Negro World*, echoed Coué's "day by day" mantra in an editorial headline: "Every Day in Every Way We See Drawing Nearer and Nearer the Coming of the Dawn for Black Men." The paper editorialized that Marcus Garvey's teachings provided the same "uplifting psychic influence" as Coué's.*

Coué took a special liking to Americans. He found American attitudes a refreshing departure from what he knew back home. "The French mind," he wrote in 1923 in *My Method, Including American Impressions*, "prefers first to discuss and argue on the fundamentals of a principle before inquiring into its practical adaptability to everyday life. The American mind, on the contrary, immediately sees the possibilities of it, and seeks . . . to carry the idea further even than the author of it may have conceived."

The therapist could have been describing salesman-seeker Roy Herbert Jarrett and many others in the American positive-mind tradition. "A short while ago," Jarrett wrote in 1926, the year of Coué's death, "Dr. Emil [sic] Coué came to this country and showed thousands of people how to help themselves. Thousands of others spoofed at the idea, refused his assistance, and are today where they were before his visit."

Just as Coué had observed about the American mind, Jarrett sought to boldly expand on the uses of autosuggestion. Sounding the keynote of America's metaphysical tradition, Jarrett believed that subconscious-mind training did more than just recondition the mind: it activated a divine inner power that served to out-picture a person's mental images into the surrounding world. "I call this power 'Emmanuel' (God in us)," Jarrett wrote. In essence, the entirety of American positive-mind metaphysics rests on Coué-style methods.

---

* The *Negro World* headline appeared September 15, 1923. The editorial quote is from February 10, 1923.

Coué's instincts spoke to the individual's most profound wish for self-help and personal empowerment. It is my observation, as both a historian and seeker, that some people across generations have experienced genuine help through his ideas. So, once more, I invite you to self-experiment with Coué's method. We all possess the private agency of personal experiment; indeed, it may be the area in life in which we are most free. Yet we often get so wrapped up in the possibilities of digital culture and the excitement of social media that we neglect the technology of thought, through which we may be able to significantly reform some aspect of ourselves and our surrounding world.

You may find that the ideas of this mind pioneer, a figure so under-recognized in today's culture, offer the very simplicity and effectiveness that you have been seeking.

* * *

For a brief but complete explanation of how to use the mantra, I am providing the words of Émile Coué himself from his 1922 book, *Self-Mastery Through Conscious Autosuggestion:*

How to Practice Conscious Autosuggestion

Every morning on awakening and every evening as soon as you are in bed, close your eyes, and without fixing your attention in what you say, pronounce twenty times, just loud enough so that you may hear your own words, the following phrase, using a string with twenty knots in it for counting:

"DAY BY DAY, IN EVERY WAY, I AM GETTING BETTER AND BETTER."

The words: "IN EVERY WAY" being good for anything and everything, it is not necessary to formulate particular autosuggestions.

Make this autosuggestion with faith and confidence, and with the certainty that you are going to obtain what you desire.

Moreover, if during the day or night, you have a physical or mental pain or depression, immediately affirm to yourself that you are not going to CONSCIOUSLY contribute anything to maintain the pain or depression, but that it will disappear quickly. Then isolate yourself as much as possible, close your eyes, and pass your hand across your forehead, if your trouble is mental, or over the aching part of your body if physical, and repeat quickly, moving your lips, the words: "IT PASSES, IT PASSES," etc. Continue this as long as may be necessary, until the mental or physical pain has disappeared, which it usually does within twenty or twenty-five seconds. Begin again every time you find it necessary to do so.

Like the first autosuggestion given above, you must repeat this one also with absolute faith and confidence, but calmly, without effort. Repeat the formula as litanies are repeated in church.

Chapter IX

Resplendent Language, Ethical Compromises: Christian D. Larson

The famous coinages of inspirational giant Christian D. Larson (1874–1962) appear everywhere: "be all you can be;" "attitude of gratitude;" "live the simple life;" "make yourself over;" and "live in the present."

Today's culture would sound differently without the influence of the twentieth-century motivational icon.

While displaying a serene demeanor and relentlessly upbeat tone, however, Larson pursued a dual existence as both a visionary author who shaped the language of self-help and a sharp-elbowed businessman who violated ethical boundaries in his publishing empire.

Born to Norwegian immigrant parents in the near-wilderness of northern Iowa in 1874, Larson had planned on a career as a Lutheran minister. But after a year at a Lutheran seminary in Minneapolis in

1894, he grew interested in Unitarianism, Transcendentalism, and the new mind-power philosophies sweeping the Western world, particularly following an experience of "cosmic consciousness"—the state of inner awareness and elevated perspective described by Canadian psychiatrist Richard Maurice Bucke (1837–1902) and American philosopher William James (1842–1910). (Source notes follow this chapter.)

In 1898, Larson moved to Cincinnati where he began writing and publishing tracts in New Thought—newly popular as an umbrella term for the nation's positive-mind theologies—and quickly burgeoned into one of the field's most prolific and dynamic voices.

Some of Larson's earliest writing featured phrases so widely adopted in general culture that their pen of origin grew obfuscated. They include "attitude of gratitude," made famous fifty years after Larson's death by Oprah Winfrey. Larson also coined the term "be all that you can be" generations before it became the ubiquitous recruiting pitch of the U.S. Army, poised for a relaunch recent to this writing.

Larson's "Promise Yourself"—a verse meditation on the power of determined cheerfulness—gained worldwide notice in 1922 when it was adopted as the credo of Optimist International, a philanthropic club similar to the Jaycees or Rotarians. The verse work became known ever after as "The Optimist Creed." You can still find it today hanging in break rooms, gyms, and on fridges. It reads:

Promise Yourself

To be so strong that nothing can disturb your peace of mind.
To talk health, happiness, and prosperity to every person you
    meet.
To make all your friends feel that there is something in them.
To look at the sunny side of everything and make your
    optimism come true.
To think only the best, to work only for the best, and to
    expect only the best.

To be just as enthusiastic about the success of others as you
  are about your own.

To forget the mistakes of the past and press on to the greater
  achievements of the future.

To wear a cheerful countenance at all times and give every
  living creature you meet a smile.

To give so much time to the improvement of yourself that
  you have no time to criticize others.

To be too large for worry, too noble for anger, too strong for
  fear, and too happy to permit the presence of trouble.

To think well of yourself and to proclaim this fact to the
  world, not in loud words but great deeds.

To live in faith that the whole world is on your side so long
  as you are true to the best that is in you.

For a time, Larson was also enormously successful at publishing his own widely read books and magazines at his Chicago-based Progress Company. His monthly, *Eternal Progress*, launched in 1901, grew by the end of the decade into a handsomely produced, socially progressive journal that combined ideals of mind-power metaphysics with articles and photographs highlighting the nation's bounding growth.

Alongside articles heralding New Thought's emergence as "a universal religion," *Eternal Progress* featured reportage and illustrated spreads on great dams, railroads, skyscrapers, and other engineering marvels that fueled optimism about the future in the early twentieth century. A typical issue of *Eternal Progress* chronicled the rebuilding of San Francisco after the 1906 fire and earthquake, and the beauty and growing economy of the Pacific Northwest, with its logging and fishing enterprises. Larson also ran articles calling for universal suffrage and the creation of public programs to educate and reform prisoners.

Perhaps like no other magazine of the period, *Eternal Progress* captured the full-circle culture of the Progressive Era: bounding commerce, scientific advances, working-class struggles, social reforms, and the appeal of the new mental therapeutics. The zeitgeist of limitless potential appeared in Townsend Allen's poem "Eternal Progress" featured in the issue of March 1909:

> From the first primeval atom,
> Upward, upward is the trend;
> Greater out of lesser growing.
> Ever to the perfect end.
> Upward, onward, each to-morrow
> Should be better than the past;
> God's work in His creation;
> All who will may win at last.

To broaden the magazine's appeal beyond the metaphysical, the arriviste publisher shortened its name to *Progress* in June of that year, a decision he later reversed.

For all Larson's ideals, the visionary communicator displayed a pattern of tortuous and compromised business dealings.

On July 25, 1911, the U.S. District Court for Northern Illinois declared Larson's Progress Company in "involuntary bankruptcy" following complaints from creditors who were owed a whopping $300,000. The court ordered a receiver to take control of the company's plants and holdings, and suspended publication of Larson's 250,000-circulation magazine.

By August, Larson had left town for Los Angeles. He later told an interviewer that his Chicago printing plant had burned down and, rather than rebuild, he decided to follow the country's momentum and move West. At the time of the Progress Company's receivership in 1911, however, creditors estimated that the company continued to hold plant and printing assets of about $100,000—a surprisingly robust sum for a business that Larson said was lost in a fire. Closer to the truth may be that Larson, facing mountainous debt and scorned creditors, opted to act on his principle to "make yourself over" and left his liabilities behind to "reinvent" himself in Southern California.

Once in Los Angeles, Larson covered his tracks. He took one of the last books published in 1910 by his Progress Company, *Your Forces and How to Use Them*—his title was lifted without credit from the signature volume by essayist and New Thought acolyte Prentice Mulford (1834–1891), who died nearly twenty years earlier—and reissued it, switching the copyright year from 1910 to 1912 and changing the name of the copyright holder from the Progress Company to himself. He probably did this to shield the book from his Chicago creditors. This book contained Larson's "Optimist Creed." His switch in copyright dates, from 1910 to 1912, created the lasting misimpression that the world-famous meditation appeared two years later than it actually did.

Larson repeated this practice with several other works. In 1912, he reverted the name of his magazine back to its original title, *Eternal Progress*, and resumed publication. At least journalistically, Larson hadn't lost his taste for social justice, as he inaugurated the renewed publication with an essay contest offering $100 for the best article on "The Cure of Poverty."

Larson exemplified the conflicting ideals that could mark the early New Thought movement. Seen from one perspective, the prolific author meant what he wrote about the power of thought to impact events, which he articulated in more than forty books until his death in 1962.

In fairness, critics often failed to appreciate the depths of passion and sincerity necessary for any writer to energetically produce that kind of output—much of it, in Larson's case, appealingly readable. When Larson's message reached people who had been raised in religiously repressive settings, or amid the suffocating peer scrutiny of small towns, it could arrive as a vivifying gospel of self-will.

Yet Larson displayed a quality found in another mind-power pioneer and onetime securities fraudster who we next meet, Fenwicke Holmes (1883–1973)—Larson issued a correspondence course taken by Fenwicke and his better-known brother Ernest—who likewise made ethical compromises on the path to self-improvement. Simply put, this quality was Larson's *unnerving ability to avert his gaze so completely from the pale side of life*—as in his debt-ridden Chicago past—that *his sunny metaphysics concealed a lack of personal accountability*. This moral conundrum intermittently colored the positive-thinking movement for decades, as it does today.

The extent to which Larson was sincere is debatable. In that vein, he displayed an oddity of personality captured by author and editor Maude Allison Lathem in a 1940 interview for a class offered by the Science of Mind movement. "Innately," wrote Lathem, a collaborator to Ernest Holmes, encountered in the next chapter, "I believe that Mr. Larson is a timid man. He is quiet and reserved in manner and certainly conservative in his speech."

"Speaking of his conservative nature," Lathem continued:

when I went to interview him, I took with me a copy of "Practical Self-Help," a book that had helped me greatly almost twenty years ago. True, I didn't expect him to autograph it, "With love and kisses," as some professionals might do. I have only known him personally a few years, but he has written many things for our Science of Mind Magazine and lectures weekly at the Institute of Religious Science. But all that he put in my autograph was: "Christian D. Larson, March 6, 1940." Wouldn't *you* call him conservative?

Yes, I would. The writer's reserved character perhaps concealed a sharper and less idealistic core than the inspirational trailblazer wished the public to see.

Notes on Sources

The date of Larson's death is often reported as 1954. According to California state death records, the author was born on February 1, 1874, and died on June 10, 1962.

The phrases noted from Larson's work appear in *The Ideal Made Real* (Progress Company, 1909), with the exception of "be all that you can be," which appears in *Your Forces and How to Use Them* (Progress Company, 1910). This book should not be confused with Prentice Mulford's six-volume namesake, *Your Forces, and How to Use Them*, issued beginning in 1890.

For the relaunch of the Army's slogan, see "'Be All You Can Be,' Army to market for new recruits with old slogan," by Rose L. Thayer, *Stars and Stripes*, December 1, 2022.

Sources on Larson's background and career include the transcript of a 1940 interview/oral history that Larson gave to Maude Allison Lathem—a literary collaborator to Ernest Holmes—as part of an "Extension Course in the Science of Mind" offered by Holmes's Institute of Religious Science. Also helpful are two highly engaging profiles: "The Living Legacy of Christian D. Larson" by Mark Gilbert, *Science of Mind*, October 2011, and "*The Pathway of Roses* and Christian D. Larson's Journey in New Thought" by Jessica Hatchigan, which appeared in *Science of Mind*, April 2005, and was reprinted in a reissue of Larson's *The Pathway of Roses* the same year by DeVorss.

Also see "The Literature of 'New Thoughters'" by Frances Maule Björkman, *The World's Work,* January 1910. Progress Company's involuntary bankruptcy is reported in "Progress Company in Bankruptcy," *The Inland Printer* (Chicago), September 1911. In her history paper, Lathem reports that "the plant burned to the ground;" in the same oral history Larson described relocating to Los Angeles in August 1911. Also in that interview Larson identified the circulation of his magazine as 250,000—a remarkable figure but one that squares with the overall finances of his company.

Sorting through Larson's trail of copyright registrations and re-registrations entailed reviewing U.S. copyright data, library catalogue entries, publishing trade notices, and various editions of his books. In July 1912, *The Editor,* a literary trade journal, noted that Larson was restarting *Eternal Progress*; that article also reported his essay contest. Fenwicke Holmes discussed Larson's personal influence in his biography *Ernest Holmes* (Dodd, Mead, 1970). The note on the correspondence course appears in *Who's Who in New Thought* by Tom Beebe (CSA Press, 1977). For further background on Larson's "Optimist Creed" (originally published as "Promise Yourself") see my discussion of June 27, 2012, with journalist David Crumm at readthespirit. com and the Larson anthology *The Optimist Creed* (Tarcher/Penguin, 2011).

Chapter X

The Promise and Perils of Ernest Holmes

C ould twentieth-century America—the land of positive-thinking, recovery movements, and self-help—produce the morally persuasive, mass transcendental religion for which many seekers yearned?

The answer seemed to lie within one of the era's most unique and persuasive metaphysical thinkers: Ernest Holmes (1887–1960). In the early twentieth century, the stout, rotund Yankee journeyed from his native Maine to Los Angeles to spread his version of the positivity gospel. For a time, Holmes's Religious Science or Science of Mind movement showed promise of developing into the great American metaphysical faith.

In actuality, the last thing the intellectual and spiritual seeker wanted was to start a religion. From Holmes's early days on the metaphysical speaking circuit in the 1910s until his death in Los Angeles in April 1960, he mounted plaintive resistance to enthusiasts who transformed his mind-power philosophy into a network of churches replete with textbooks, rule-making bodies, and enough factional splits and infighting to populate a New Thought version of *I, Claudius*. At the January 1960 dedication of the ornate, domed Founder's Church in Los Angeles months before his death, Holmes gazed out over the crowded pews and said, "This church was not my idea."*

Whatever the reluctance of its founder, the Science of Mind movement, known more formally as the United Church of Religious Science, became the last—and in some ways the most influential—of all New Thought denominations.

Other ministries arrived earlier and claimed more members, such as Charles (1854–1948) and Myrtle Fillmore's (1845–1931) well-established Unity School of Christianity founded in Kansas City, Missouri, in 1889. But none had a twentieth-century figurehead quite like Ernest Holmes. Not only did Holmes, possessed of a ready smile and joie de vivre likability, devise a fully fleshed-out theology but he also inspired the most formative self-help philosophy of the twentieth century: the "power of positive thinking" of author–minister Norman Vincent Peale, who we further encounter in chapter XVI. In the end, Holmes proved a mighty catalyst, though his fame trailed far behind his influence.

Born in 1887 in a dingy Lincoln, Maine, farmhouse and never formally educated, the young Holmes devoured works on religious philosophy, physics, and the writings of Ralph Waldo Emerson; Christian Science founder Mary Baker Eddy; Eddy's brief protégé and later outcast student Emma Curtis Hopkins; Scottish evangelist Henry Drummond;

---

* Sources on Ernest Holmes include Neal Vahle's important biography *Open at the Top* (Open View Press, 1991), from which he is quoted; *Ernest Holmes: His Life and Times* by Fenwicke L. Holmes (Dodd, Mead, 1970); *In His Company: Ernest Holmes Remembered* by Marilyn Leo (M Leo Presents, 2006); Gordon Melton's biographical article in *Religious Leaders of America* (The Gale Group, 1999); and *Ernest Holmes: The First Religious Scientist* by James Reid (Science of Mind Publications, undated). For an overview of Holmes's religious development, see Arthur Vergara's series of historical articles published in the "Cornerstone" column of the 2011 and 2012 issues of *Creative Mind* magazine.

and British judge Thomas Troward, who published ambitious lectures on the logic behind creative-mind principles.

Holmes grew especially fond of Transcendentalism, particularly as expressed in Emerson's classic "Self-Reliance." Emerson's most famous essay was also his least understood. While some critics saw "Self-Reliance" as a paean to go-it-alone individualism, Ernest perceived its deeper currents: we all harbor a True Self, free of conformity and conditioning; to live from this core alone produces greatness. It set Ernest's mind on fire.

At the start of World War I, Ernest relocated from New England to Venice, California, where his older brother, Fenwicke (1883–1973), was already settled. Fenwicke shared his sibling's interests and became Ernest's intellectual partner. The two began filling lecture halls as early as 1916 with their metaphysical talks.

Roundish and twinkle-eyed, Ernest shined before audiences. He exuded unlikely charisma—as well as shrewd command of different spiritual philosophies and religious systems. He spoke with clarity and total confidence, rarely using notes. "As a speaker, a lecturer," Norman Vincent Peale recalled, "he was able to put together spontaneously a talk as airtight as a lawyer's brief, no loopholes, no perceived errors. It all held together."*

Holmes maintained that our mental images constantly outpicture into reality. We can direct the mind's forces and achieve our ideals—or we can succumb to the chaotic onrush of thoughts; either way, we dwell within the gravitational tug of our ideas. Whether Holmes adequately or consistently distinguished between

---

* Norman Vincent Peale discusses Homes in "The Pathway to Positive Thinking" by Elaine St. Johns, *Science of Mind* magazine, June 1987.

thoughts and emotions—the latter proving faster, wilder, and more triggering—is arguable.

The young metaphysician's following grew as he performed "treatments"—or prayer and mind-power healings—on visitors to the office where he worked as a purchasing agent and playground instructor for the city of Venice. After travels to New York and other cities, where he road-tested his message among different listeners, Ernest molded his ideas into the philosophy called Science of Mind or Religious Science. Beginning in 1926, his movement developed into a learning institute and later a thriving network of positivity-based congregations, formalizing in 1949 as the United Church of Religious Science. This proved an ill-fated choice of words, which in later decades confused Ernest's movement with the more visible and entirely unrelated Church of Scientology. (In 2011, the Holmes congregations reorganized under the anodyne name Centers for Spiritual Living.)

Holmes's comprehensive grasp of Scripture and world religious traditions, and his serious yet personable style, seemed, at least in his figure, to nudge New Thought into territory of intellectual and ethical solidity. His brother and collaborator Fenwicke, although civic-minded in his local campaigns against prize fighting, presented a shakier history.

In 1929, Fenwicke, then a Congregationalist clergyman and minister of Divine Science, another variant of mind metaphysics, came under investigation from the New York state attorney general for a stock-peddling scheme. Fenwicke purportedly pushed worthless mining stocks on congregants at his Divine Science congregation in New York as an adjunct to his prosperity teachings. The attorney general got an injunction barring Fenwicke and another Holmes sibling, William, from selling securities pending trial.

Watson S. Washburn and Edmund S. De Long, investigators for the attorney general, wrote about the Fenwicke Holmes affair in their 1932 book, *High and Low Financiers*:

> Five million dollars' worth of stock was sold by the Holmes brothers during the period commencing in 1920 and ending in 1929 when William and Fenwicke were enjoined from further stock-selling activities . . . a trial which has not yet been held. None of this stock ever paid a cent in interest or dividends.

The authors may have been exercising a certain degree of prosecutorial zeal. They worked for the man who pursued Fenwicke, New York State Attorney General Hamilton Ward, to whom their book is dedicated. Washburn and De Long were likely settling a score on a case that never made it through the courts. A trial had been scheduled for May 1930 but apparently never happened. State and federal court records show no decisions with Fenwicke's name attached. The likelihood is that a plea deal was struck, probably with Ward's successor, as Ward's term ended that same year.*

Fenwicke managed to escape the legal cloud. He became a formidable force in spreading the positive-thinking gospel, including to Japan, where it spawned a popular counterpart to Science of Mind: *Seicho-No-Ie,* or Home of Infinite Life, Truth, and Abundance. He also made a decisive impact on the influential mythologist Joseph Campbell, who attended Fenwicke's lectures in New York in the late 1920s. Campbell was uncertain about his direction in life. Fenwicke

---

* On Fenwicke's securities scandal see the *New York Times* articles: "Pastor Fights Suit to Stop Stock Sale," May 3, 1929; "Pastor Fights Ward Move," May 9, 1929; "Fenwicke Holmes Subpoena Vacated," May 15, 1929; "Court Finds Pastor Sold Bogus Stock," July 4, 1929; "Stock Fraud Bureau Finds W. H. Holmes," July 11, 1929; "Minister's Tactics in Stock Deal Told," February 1, 1930; "F. L. Holmes Church Loses 4 Trustees," February 6, 1930; "Pastor Is Indicted in Sale of Stock," March 19, 1930; "F. L. Holmes Leaves Church Pending Trial," March 24, 1930; "F. L. Holmes Case May 28," May 13, 1930. Also see "Pastor Grilled About His Stock Sales to Flock," *Chicago Daily Tribune*, February 1, 1930. *High and Low Financiers* was published by Bobbs-Merrill in 1932.

gave the young seeker an exercise to discover what he was looking for: "One should jot down notes for a period of four or five weeks on the things that interest one. It will be found that all the interests tend in a certain direction."* Campbell used this technique to reach his decision to become a scholar of myth. Fenwicke's advice seemed to echo in Campbell's famous maxim: "Follow your bliss."

Ernest Holmes narrowly eluded the vortex of his brother's legal problems. Investigators Washburn and De Long maintained that while Ernest was living in Venice Beach around 1917 he "was already engaged in a small way in the lucrative business of selling questionable stocks." They offered no evidence for the assertion and Ernest's name appeared in none of the news coverage that dogged Fenwicke. In fact, the younger brother had stopped working with Fenwicke in 1925— the reasons were never publicly discussed. They reunited in 1958, two years before Ernest's death, to collaborate on an epic poem, *The Voice Celestial*.

Holmes's command of Scripture and Yankee foursquare style seemed to move New Thought away from its fixation on personal gain. The possibilities appeared promising. Holmes stood at the center of Hollywood's mystical scene in the first half of the twentieth century, attracting admirers from Cecil B. DeMille to Elvis Presley. In the early 1950s, Holmes shared a congenial dinner with Albert Einstein at Caltech. Holmes said that Einstein agreed with his premise "that permanent world peace is not an illusion but a potential possibility and an evolutionary imperative, and that science will *aid* in that evolution."**

---

* Joseph Campbell's recollection is from *A Fire in the Mind: The Life of Joseph Campbell* by Stephen and Robin Larsen (Doubleday, 1991). For further perspective on Fenwicke see Jesse G. Jennings' article "Finding Fenwicke," *Science of Mind*, August 2008, and Jennings' introduction to *The Science of Mind: The Definitive Edition* (Tarcher/Penguin, 2010).

** Holmes's meeting with Einstein appears in Fenwicke's biography *Ernest Holmes* (1970).

The greater struggle for Holmes, in his writings and lectures, was to consistently wed a fundamentally success-driven theology to a primeval Christian ethic. Like his contemporaries, Holmes viewed the human mind as synonymous with what is called God and possessed of the same creative power. As such, he reasoned, this power is intrinsically good.

"Evil," Holmes wrote in his 1929 *The Bible in Light of Religious Science*, ". . . has no reality behind it or actual law to come to its support." It was similar in approach to Unity writer H. Emilie Cady, who wrote in her 1894 *Lessons In Truth*, "Apparent evils are not entities or things of themselves. They are simply an absence of good . . . But God, or Good, is omnipresent, so the apparent absence of good (evil) is unreal."

Most purveyors of New Thought described evil as darkness in a room once the light—or God Law—was closed out. But, unlike the Transcendentalists in their study of the cycles of nature, these enthusiasts made no allowance for the inevitability of night following day. They made no room for the balance of life and death, illness and health, that Emerson depicted in the essays they sometimes called inspiration. Nor did New Thought acknowledge Emerson's disdain for self-centered prayer. ("Prayer as a means to effect a private end is meanness and theft," he wrote in "Self-Reliance.") Hence, the movement embraced those facets of Transcendentalism that affirmed mind causation while overlooking or racing past counter-complexities.

And here we reach the ultimate dilemma of this most popular of American metaphysics. Unable to fully come to terms with tragedy or catastrophe in what believers considered a self-created world, New Thought lapsed into circular reasoning or contradiction. In one beat, Holmes described evil or illness as illusory. Yet in the next he cautioned: "The law [of mental creativity] is no respecter of persons and will bring good or evil to any, according to his use or misuse of it."

In what may have been a bitter irony of his life, the intellectual Holmes was on surer ground carrying out the practicalities of building a ministry than in confronting ultimate questions of human suffering. By the time of Holmes's death in 1960, his robust movement encompassed more than a hundred congregations exceeding 100,000 formal members. (A 2001 study found about 55,000 active congregants within the two main Holmes ministries.) Indeed, Holmes's legacy is considerable: His textbook, *The Science of Mind,* published in 1926 and extensively revised with editor Maude Allison Lathem in 1938, continues to sell thousands of copies across myriad editions a year; acolytes of his ideas number among the nation's most popular inspirational writers and speakers (such as Tony Robbins and Marianne Williamson); and his re-dubbed Centers for Spiritual Living actively ordains new ministers and practitioners.

Holmes, like Unity, successfully bridged the gap between New Thought as a loosely conceived idea and an organized religion. But his final years also saw his movement riven by a factional split. In a dispute over whether churches would be self-governed, a cluster of ministries broke away in 1957 to form their own organization, Religious Science International. (The rift was bridged in 2011.)

Indeed, Holmes often seemed happier delivering a lecture or completing a book than contending with the demands of organizational—or personal—life. In 1927, the metaphysician entered a marriage that friends considered warm but ceremonial: the West Coast transplant was widely known as a gay man—and, to his lasting credit, his congregations and those of others in the New Thought tradition were markedly welcoming of nonconforming congregants.

Just before Holmes's death, a student and protégé, Obadiah Harris (1930–2019), whom Holmes handpicked to preach at some of his leading churches, came to the mentor's bedside. Harris had to confess that he was leaving the movement to find his own path. "I wish I could go with you," the teacher replied.*

After Holmes's passing, seasoned minister and author Raymond Charles Barker (1911–1988) took the helm of his ministry. Whatever indifference Holmes harbored toward organizational politics was gone. Following the founder's memorial service, Barker approached Holmes's onetime mentee Harris and told him: "Obadiah, I am in charge of this movement and I intend to remain in charge for a long time. Now, tell me, is there anything I can do for you?"

Harris got the message. The younger man moved into academia and later assumed presidency of the esoteric learning center Philosophical Research Society in Los Angeles following the death of founder and occult scholar Manly P. Hall (1901–1990).

All this might sound the coda of Holmes's career but for his broadest, if least known, influence. The driving principle behind all the self-help movements of the late twentieth and early twenty-first centuries appeared in the title of Norman Vincent Peale's 1952 *The Power of Positive Thinking*. And here we reencounter the fingerprints of Ernest Holmes.

Raised in the Midwest, Peale took charge of an ailing and shrinking congregation on Manhattan's East Side during the Great Depression. Within twenty years, however, the Protestant minister reached into every corner of America—and many corners of the world—with his manifesto proclaiming the transformative power of positive imagery and self-affirmation.

His philosophy was core New Thought, though couched in terms to which the churchgoing public could easily relate. Peale eschewed

---

* Obadiah Harris's recollections are from personal interviews.

references to "magic laws" or "secrets of the ages," instead emphasizing traditional prayer, Bible reading, and healthy self-image. Nevertheless, careful readers might have wondered at the occultic tone of the minister's ideas about "the emanation of prayer power," specifically that "the human brain can send off power by thoughts and prayers. The human body's magnetic power has actually been tested."

In his thousands of articles, lectures, books, and homilies, Peale shared innumerable stories from his life, but he revealed relatively little about his influences or how he related to the spiritual and intellectual trends around him.

Peale and the Science of Mind founder met just once, in Los Angeles in the summer of 1940. At the time, each went to hear the other deliver a talk. But Holmes's work had already reached Peale when the bestselling minister was younger. "Ernest came into my life long before we actually met," Peale said. In a remarkable and overlooked interview given in 1987, six years before his death, to the magazine Ernest Holmes had started, *Science of Mind*, Peale recounted the direct influence he found in his older contemporary.

He experienced Holmes's outlook "before I even decided to be a minister, when I was a vacillating, insecure, twenty-year-old." These weren't empty words. Peale did suffer from a lifelong sense of inferiority, especially after his reputation as a minister of practical wisdom made him a target of mockery among critics and intellectuals, who saw him as a simplistic purveyor of feel-good nostrums. Yet this feeling of insecurity also proved his lifelong link to other people. What the doyens of lettered culture never understood is that only someone who knew what it meant to feel inferior could truly relate to people in need.

Peale recalled that when he worked as a cub reporter at a Detroit daily newspaper in the early 1920s, a tough-talking editor spotted his "paralyzing fear of inadequacy." As the minister recounted, "He took me aside and handed me a book, *Creative Mind and Success* by Ernest

Holmes." It was Holmes's second book, written in 1919. "Now I want you to read this," the editor told him. "I know this fellow Holmes. I've learned a lot from him, and so can you."

What did Peale learn? "Love God, love others, you can if you think you can, the proper control and use of the human mind, drop your limited sense of self and gain true Self-Reliance." Holmes's slender volume of essays and affirmations opened Peale to new possibilities of what a religious message could be. Peale entered Boston University Seminary soon after finding it. "There is no question in my mind that Ernest Holmes's teachings had helped me on my way," he said.

Three decades later, the ideas that Peale discovered in Holmes's short book—clearly broadened by his own life experiences—formed the basis for the most influential self-help philosophy of the twentieth century. While Peale was gracious in tone and lavish in praise when asked about Holmes in 1987, the minister otherwise appeared to go little out of his way to credit the California mystic. Biographies of Peale, including his personal memoirs, make no mention of Ernest Holmes. Ten years after Peale's death, a staff member giving me a tour of the minister's headquarters in upstate New York had never heard the name.

Chapter XI

The Enigma of Napoleon Hill

Few writers have made as deep an impact on the past century as Napoleon Hill (1883–1970). The Appalachian-born journalist virtually defined the field of motivational and success literature. His influence appears in the worldwide posterity of his most famous book, *Think and Grow Rich*, published in 1937.

Although you can certainly find more hallowed works of therapeutic and practical philosophy than *Think and Grow Rich*, few have attracted such sustained and varied readership.

And few, I believe, do more to hone your abilities and sense of purpose. My conviction grows from personal experience. Since I also write critically of Hill as a man in this chapter, I want to open with my reasons for enduring fealty to his work.

I write these words about ten years from when I returned to *Think and Grow Rich* with real commitment in 2013. Until then I had read dozens of self-help books (including Hill's), worked for years as a publisher in the field, and harbored something of a "been there, done that" attitude toward much of the genre.

However, in fall of 2013, believing that a corporate buyout jeopardized my longtime job as a publishing executive (it ended four years later), I revisited *Think and Grow Rich* with renewed vigor and urgency.

For the first time, I did every exercise as though my life depended on it, which I often call the "magic formula," if there is any, to unlocking the book's benefits. As I did this, my work as a writer, narrator, and lecturer dramatically expanded—work that is now my full-time vocation.

Writing these words at age fifty-seven, I can state plainly: I've never been happier waking in the morning. Rather than wring my hands over whether another writer would fulfill his deadline and do his work in a quality fashion, I now take those burdens wholly—and gladly—on myself. I owe that, in significant measure, to Hill's program.

I've heard similar stories from many readers. Indeed, in more than twenty years as a publisher of spiritual and self-help literature—and equal time as a writer in these areas—I have never encountered a sustained reader of Hill's work who was not changed by it in concrete, measurable ways. Just as I was completing this chapter, a reader wrote me: "My husband and many clients of mine credit that book to their spiritual awakening. I was skeptical of it because of the title but once I began to read I couldn't believe the gems inside!"

Hill's success philosophy is not just for those who desire material wealth or that alone. It is for anyone possessed of any wish—whether student, soldier, teacher, artist, entrepreneur, or activist—that he or she hungers to actualize. That said, Hill's unsentimental attitude toward money-getting resonates with many readers.

Hill's work tends to polarize. I mentioned the dedication it evokes, including my own. In recent years, however, journalists have sharply questioned Hill's biography. I've likewise written critically of Hill, including in my 2014 history of the positive-mind movement, *One Simple Idea*, a point to which I return.

I have also encountered culture critics who blanketly deride Hill and related self-help authors. (Whether they've read them is questionable.) As I was working on this chapter, an academic tweeted at me about authors who "make money selling popular books about wishful thinking to people who don't know any better."

Such criticisms conceal subtle social snobbery (*people who don't know any better*) and, I believe, unacknowledged disdain for working and middle-class aspiration, not as politically idealized but as on-the-ground reality. Those unfamiliar with lack rarely understand, or interact with, the types of myriad and surprisingly varied readers who have brought greater sales to Hill's book in the twenty-first century than during his lifetime.*

In adulthood, I've met people—literally from movie producers to career military officers—who hit a dead end in life only to immerse themselves in *Think and Grow Rich* and discover a new set of practical, actionable possibilities—of transforming fallow prospects into progressive ones. Indeed, I am continually touched by how regional, cultural, lifestyle, and political differences melt away when enthusiastic readers of Hill encounter one another.

Since I count myself among such readers—and venture that their experiences likely intersect with mine—I will briefly share my own story.

---

* A reissue edition of *Think and Grow Rich* that I published in 2004, when the book was otherwise languishing on backlists, gradually netted about a million copies, renewing Hill's sales worldwide in myriad editions.

When I grew up in Queens in the 1970s, my father was a Legal Aid Society attorney who defended the poorest of the poor. For factors I deem outside his control, he lost his job and profession, leaving us to consider applying for food stamps and warming our always-unaffordable home with kerosene heaters. We wore used clothes and scraped together change and coupons to buy weekly groceries. There were no Hanukkah, Christmas, or birthday gifts. My older sister and I would buy them with our own money, earned from odd jobs, and pretend to friends that they came from our parents. In the words of The Notorious B.I.G., "Birthdays was the worst days."

One night, in desperation, my father stole my mother's engagement ring to pay debts, over which he may have been physically threatened. (He had started carrying pepper spray.) They divorced. My sister and I got by through after-school jobs, student loans, and precious availability of health benefits through my mother's labor union, the 1199 hospital workers. Given the economic devastation visited on many American households, both during the lockdown and the still-unhealed 2008 recession, I do not consider our story exceptional.

This sense of need is, quite simply, what got me on the scent trail of practical metaphysics. There is, of course, a strong mind-metaphysics component to *Think and Grow Rich*. But critics or passersby rarely realize that Hill's program is also, and above all, one of action. Anyone who begins his book without that commitment will almost certainly not finish it. Commonplace critical comparisons between *Think and Grow Rich* and *The Secret* reveal an observer's lack of familiarity with either.

In various books and articles, I have noted my refusal to regard inspirational figures—even those, like Hill, whose work has touched me—as agreeable cyphers devoid of ethical failures, corruption, or weaknesses.

Sycophancy does not honor the memories of people whose work we admire. Indeed, artists, writers, and activists—no less motivational figures—cannot be maturely understood from either the hagiographic haze of semi-worshippers (or franchisees) nor the vitriol of cultural detractors. I reject both approaches in considering Hill's life.

Oliver Napoleon Hill was born October 26, 1883, in a cabin in the Appalachian town of Pound in southwest Virginia. His mother died when he was nine. By the turn of the century, Hill began writing newspaper stories and embarked on a chequered business career as both a "man Friday" and entrepreneur.

In Hill's autobiographical writings, he displays a repugnant lack of moral feeling as a young man by helping local businessmen conceal the 1902 killing of a black bellhop in Richlands, Virginia. Less than ten years before, the southwestern town was the site of a lynching of five black railroad workers. The bellman died after a drunken bank cashier—an employee of Hill's boss Rufus Ayers, Virginia's former attorney general—dropped a loaded revolver, which went off, killing the attendant. Nineteen-year-old Hill sprang into action as the consummate fixer, coaxing local authorities to label the criminally negligent death as "accidental," he wrote, and getting the victim quickly buried. Ayers rewarded Hill by naming him manager of an area coal mine—the youngest such manager in the nation, Hill proudly reckoned.*

This incident reflected the troubling pattern of Hill's life: he identified with power so fully that he almost never questioned the decency, ethics, and general outlook of the man in the corner office (or, for that matter, of himself). Nowhere in Hill's accounts of high climbers is there any countervailing consideration of cunning, ruthlessness, or amorality—or of the kind of corrupt obsequiousness that Hill dis-

---

* The story of Hill covering up the bellhop's death is from *A Lifetime of Riches: The Biography of Napoleon Hill* by Michael J. Ritt Jr. and Kirk Landers (Dutton, 1995). The book is basically an authorized biography; it is to the authors' credit that the episode is included at all.

played in Richlands. Nor did Hill seem over-troubled by truthfulness when in 1914 he falsely claimed on his personal stationary to be a lawyer; he attended no law school.

It was not an isolated episode. In 1918, state authorities in Illinois accused the educational entrepreneur of fraudulently inflating the valuation of his Chicago success school to prospective investors.* With disturbing repetition in his early business record, Hill darted among experiences where either he or those around him were accused of fraud or malfeasance.** These episodes played out during periods when the writer claimed, without evidence, to have advised presidents Woodrow Wilson and Franklin Roosevelt.

Hill's interest in the "philosophy of success" seems to have emerged around 1908 while he was working as a reporter, including for *Bob Taylor's Magazine*. It was an inspirational and general-interest monthly published by the former governor of Tennessee who continued the enterprise as a U.S. senator.

As publisher, Taylor favored up-by-the-bootstraps life stories of business leaders. Through Taylor's connections, Hill was able to score

---

* "Two Warrants Out for Modest Napoleon Hill: 'Carnegie of Educational World' Accused of 'Blue Sky' Stuff," *Chicago Tribune*, June 4, 1918.

** "The Untold Story of Napoleon Hill, the Greatest Self-Help Scammer of All Time" by Matt Novak, *Gizmodo*, December 6, 2016. Novak's highly critical article is an important resource and cannot be discounted by any serious reader. That said, I have my criticisms of the piece. The writer displays intense interest in his subject for every reason but the one for which Hill is famous: his writing. Like journalist Albert Goldman in his "takedown" biographies of John Lennon and Elvis Presley, Novak appears so zealous to undo his subject's reputation that a reader could easily believe (as many probably did aforethought) that such an author has nothing to offer. Novak's research is laudable but his persistently caustic tone and frank unfamiliarity with Hill's key book detracts from an otherwise significant historical investigation. E.g., Novak's allegation that Rhonda Byrne's *The Secret* "essentially plagiarized" *Think and Grow Rich* is patently absurd and revealing of an insouciant lack of attention to the contents of either book; likewise offkey is his claim that Norman Vincent Peale's "ideas were borrowed heavily from Hill." Indeed, in an earlier version of the article, Novak confused the title of Peale's famous *Power of Positive Thinking* with an unrelated book by Hill and W. Clement Stone, *Success Through a Positive Mental Attitude*. New Thought has a long and diffuse history in America; Hill intersected with the philosophy considerably less than Byrne or Peale. These varying works, although nondescript to the ardent critic, are by no means interchangeable.

the ultimate "get": an interview with steel magnate Andrew Carnegie. Or so he said.

Hill described his encounter with Carnegie—"the richest man that the richest nation on earth ever produced," as he wrote in 1945 in *The Master-Key to Riches*—in terms that evoked Moses receiving the tablets on Mount Sinai. During their interview, Hill said, the industrialist gave him marching orders to codify a philosophy of success, which formed the basis for Hill's 1928 book *The Law of Success* and the wealth-building classic that followed nine years later, *Think and Grow Rich*.

Whatever impression Hill may have left on Carnegie, the industrialist made no mention of the younger man in his writings. Nor did Hill begin making references to their fateful meeting until nearly a decade after Carnegie's death in 1919, a story he related with greater drama and vividness as the years passed. (I must also note that the "tributes to the author from great American leaders" at the front of *Think and Grow Rich* are all from figures deceased by its 1937 publication.) Critics question whether the Carnegie encounter occurred at all. I am agnostic on the matter. *Bob Taylor's Magazine* featured how-I-did-it stories of millionaires—a staple of the day's popular literature—and the job (and Taylor's position) could have facilitated contact between journalist and subject.

In December 1908, under his birthname Oliver Napoleon Hill— one of the last times he used that byline—Hill produced for Taylor a regional essay on "Mobile and Southern Alabama," accompanied by an author photo of the bow-tied writer. No interview with Carnegie ever appeared, nor have I found further bylines for Hill in the magazine.

In any case, Carnegie's memoirs do paint the image of a man who enjoyed discussing the metaphysics of success. In his autobiography, published posthumously in 1920, Carnegie recalls that as an adolescent he "became deeply interested in the mysterious doctrines of Swedenborg," the eighteenth-century scientist-mystic. A Spiritualist aunt encouraged the young Carnegie to develop his psychical talents, or "ability to expound 'spiritual sense'."

Indeed, the industrialist was eager to be taken seriously as an author and reveled in probing whether there exist natural laws of money and accumulation. In June 1889, Carnegie published an essay "Wealth" for the *North American Review*, which might have been forgotten if not for its near-immediate republication by England's evening newspaper *The Pall Mall Gazette* under the more alluring title by which it won fame: "The Gospel of Wealth."

Taking a leaf from the neo-Darwinian views of philosopher Herbert Spencer, Carnegie described a "law of competition," which he believed brought a rough, necessary order to the world:

> While the law may be sometimes hard to the individual, it is best for the race, because it ensures the survival of the fittest in every department. We accept and welcome, therefore, as conditions to which we must accommodate ourselves, great inequality of environment, the concentration of business, industrial and commercial, in the hands of a few, and the law of competition between these, as being not only beneficial but essential for the future progress of the race.

Although contemporaneous success authors such as Ralph Waldo Trine and Wallace D. Wattles, whom we met earlier, extolled creativity above competition, Carnegie welcomed "laws of accumulation" as a necessary means of separating life's winners from losers. At his steel mills, the magnate sometimes backed his belief through ruthless and, by way of surrogates and business partners, brutal labor practices. Seven of his workers were killed by Pinkerton guards during the Homestead Strike of 1892.

Yet Carnegie's wealth essay contained a surprising wrinkle. He emphasized that great fortunes—which he saw emergent chiefly from production of raw materials, real estate, utilities, and inventions (the manufacturer disdained financial speculation)—are the product of the community. And should ultimately be returned to it. Wealth, Carnegie argued, is amassed as a passive result of an industrialist or investor benefiting from mass shifts in demography, migration, and public need. The world's reputedly richest man wrote that riches should be restored to the public rather than passed down through generations of family inheritance.

But in a sentiment that won jeers from contemporaneous radicals and reformers, Carnegie counseled that millionaires should electively dispense their money in acts of philanthropy during their lifetimes. He considered this disbursement the legitimate culmination of success, arguing that monopolistic capitalism must be leavened by voluntary largesse. The multimillionaire's sense of volunteerism had limits, however: should the rich not find ways to disperse their fortunes through philanthropy during their lifetimes, Carnegie called for a nearly 100 percent estate tax to settle the matter for them.

Whether one agrees with Carnegie on every point—and I do not—it is worth noting that he followed through on his statements with wide-ranging acts of structured philanthropy. In so doing, the industrialist helped presage the nonprofit field as it exists today.

It is this outlook—not the imaginary dialogues with Carnegie that Hill ploddingly devised in his 1948 *Think Your Way to Wealth*—that reflects the authentic Carnegie philosophy, at least as publicly stated.

Carnegie's counsel is for each individual to assess, but of one point he leaves no doubt—and it would've made him few friends among tech magnates of our era: great fortunes accrue not primarily due to the ability of their holders but to ancillary events and circumstances that emerge from public need and growth.

Back to Hill's version of events. As he tells it, at their 1908 meeting, the fetching reporter questioned Carnegie about his success-building secrets. The manufacturer urged Hill to speak with other captains of commerce to determine whether a definable set of steps led to their accomplishments. Carnegie offered to open doors for Hill.

Hill writes that he spent the next twenty years studying and interviewing businessmen, diplomats, generals, inventors, and other high achievers in an effort to map out their shared principles. He finally named seventeen traits (distilled to thirteen in *Think and Grow Rich*) that these outliers seemed to share. They included concentrating your energies on *one definite major aim*; doing more work than you are paid for; cultivating intuition, or a sixth sense; showing persistence; reprogramming your thoughts through autosuggestion; practicing tolerance of opinion; gaining specialized knowledge; and convening around you a collaborative Master Mind group, whose members could blend their mental energies and ideas.

As alluded, Hill's books never attracted critical attention other than to be dismissed or waved aside for shallow vulgarity. Indeed, New Thought and self-help literature became a category of book that went mostly unread by its detractors. But Hill was often subtler, shrewder, and surer in his understanding of human nature than many scoffers supposed.

I have written critically of Hill the man. But let me be clear—contradictions be damned—about the quality of Hill's program of achievement: it is, in my experience as a writer, publisher, and seeker, the finest that has emerged from the motivational field.

Whatever the source of Hill's inspiration, it is evident that the writer spent something like the twenty years claimed studying the lives of high achievers of all types—inventors, generals, diplomats, artists, statesmen—and cataloged their common traits into a step-by-step program. Hill was certain (as are many of his readers) that he created a model of *what exceptional people do* when translating an idea from conceptual to actual. I must add, crucially, that his written program is not one of trickery but of clean ledgers, ethical practices, and plain dealing. I have written disdainfully of popular books, such as *The 48 Laws of Power*, that counsel otherwise.

Can one finally distinguish between author and output? I have come to regard Hill in a similar vein to Carlos Castaneda (1925–1998), the self-made chronicler of indigenous North American magick: although his biography and encounters may be large parts fiction, Castaneda, like Hill, produced writing and insights that retain their hold on posterity due not to gullibility of audience but depth of insight. Critiques of Hill—while valid to varying degrees—are mitigated by the remarkable effectiveness of his program.

Wells either slake thirst or get abandoned.

Hill's career matters because of his work as a writer. In that vein, let me highlight several of the most impactful themes of his outlook:

1. **Definite Chief Aim.** If a reader takes away one idea from Hill's work, this should be it. In my experience, nothing does more to productively reorder your life than one penetrating, actionable, and obsessively felt aim to which all else is subordinated. The urge to this kind of exclusivity understandably evokes argument and pushback. Life places many demands on us—mustn't we meet each on its own terms? There is validity in that objection. But I consider it a tough truth of life that unitary focus affords the greatest likelihood of arrival. Think of your heroes. Whatever their myriad and private traits, they are known

for one core dedication. To clarify such an aim requires radical self-honesty. I should note that one well selected goal can cover many different bases and concerns in life.

2. **Reciprocity.** As noted, Hill's written program is ethical: he emphasizes transparency, non-prejudice, and delivering clear benefits to your end user, client, or employer. He stresses how gossip, trash-talk, and frivolous opining degrade you and deter your goals. As I've often written, people have no idea the extent to which they defile their sense of self-respect by indulging in meaningless vitriol; the shame one feels—or sublimates—is coped with by throwing another stone, creating an endless loop. Nothing will make you stand taller more quickly than desistance from the perverse and fleeting thrill of gossip, smears, and lowbrow sarcasm.

3. **Applied Faith.** I once defined faith as persistence; but Hill's work has taught me that faith is persistence combined with warranted confidence that you *will*, in some fashion, succeed based on immutable laws of effort and growth, which his program helps you identify. Rather than engage in toothless "wishful thinking," most people, in fact, grossly underestimate their abilities and hesitate to exercise them. Absent extreme countervailing measures—which, it must be noted, *do* exist—persistence avails some form of personal deliverance.

4. **Overcoming Procrastination and Fear.** These two traits are the same. Learning to control one controls the other. For practical purposes, begin your effort with overcoming procrastination, which is task-specific and thus easier to work on than fear in general. If procrastination proves an unyielding barrier, it may indicate that you're pursuing the wrong aim or one for which you're emotionally mismatched.

5. **Leadership.** Hill defines leadership as *initiative*: doing what's necessary without being told. You cannot claim leadership or have it bestowed on you. It is a form of behavior that stems from accountability and know-how. A real leader asks no one to do a task that he or she wouldn't—or is afraid to. Anyone else is just a boss.

6. **Master Mind.** A Master Mind is a harmonious support group of two or more people convened at least weekly to support each member's wishes. Hill taught that such a group pools and heightens each participant's insights, intuition, enthusiasm, and acumen. It is vital to his program.

7. **Sex Transmutation.** In a note resounding in esoteric spiritual traditions from Tantra and Kabbalah to Gnosticism and Hermeticism, Hill taught that sexual desire is the *force of life seeking expression*. When you place the sexual urge at the back of your efforts, he wrote, you heighten your abilities and insights. His formula is simple: upon feeling sexual desire *mentally shift* your attention away from physical satisfaction and toward the achievement of a vital task. Do this at times of your own choosing. Does it work? Yes, in my experience.

8. **Rebounding from Failure.** Rather than impeding growth, obstacles often facilitate it. Setbacks and failures frequently impel refining plans, abilities, ideas, and relationships. Without opposition we would remain mental and emotional children. Search every failure for commensurate seeds of compensation. Are there assholes in your life? If you cannot get away from them determine, at least for the time being, to use their provocations as inducements to refinement.

9. **Cosmic Habit Force.** Generative habits and natural rotations, Hill writes, like orbital movement of celestial objects, changing of seasons,

and cycles of birth and death, are the dynamic through which physicality maintains itself. This comports with ideas found in Taoism and Transcendentalism. When you dwell within the right personal habits and environment, Hill teaches, you merge, like a twig carried downstream, with waves or cycles of regenerative power and development.

Hill writes alluringly of a "secret" that runs throughout *Think and Grow Rich*. This secret, he says, appears at least once in every chapter and no less than one hundred times throughout the book. But he does not specifically name it. Hill writes that it is more beneficial for you to arrive at the secret yourself. Some readers, he says, grasp it almost immediately. For others, it takes multiple readings. Sometimes, right in the midst of a chapter, the secret may flash into your mind, he explains.

I have previously written that the secret of *Think and Grow Rich* can be put this way: "Emotionalized thought directed toward one passionately held aim—aided by organized planning and the Master Mind—is the root of all accomplishment." I stand by that. But a more basic conception of Hill's secret, comporting with point nine above, occurred to me during this writing: *the "secret" of* Think and Grow Rich *is to place yourself within the overall scheme of creation, obeying natural laws that inevitably and invariably beget growth, expansion, and renewal.*

Each step in Hill's work is designed to bring you into *natural alignment* with your surroundings. Once you are in this alignment and function within its flow—toward growth, utility, and regeneration—laws of creation appear at your back. You become like the seedling that eventually bursts through the soil. All of nature facilitates this process. Unlike the seedling or twig, however, a sentient being can consciously and selectively labor. Indeed, these laws possess greater potential for an aware being than for the seedling *because they not only aid expansion but also allow for dramatic re-creation of self.*

In that vein, I want to quote what I consider one of the most important passages in *Think and Grow Rich*. It appears in the chapter on "Imagination" and directly pertains to what I've been referencing:

You are now engaged in the task of trying to profit by Nature's method. You are (sincerely and earnestly, we hope), trying to adapt yourself to Nature's laws, by endeavoring to convert DESIRE into its physical or monetary equivalent. YOU CAN DO IT! IT HAS BEEN DONE BEFORE!

You can build a fortune through the aid of laws which are immutable. But, first, you must become familiar with these laws, and learn to USE them. Through repetition, and by approaching the description of these principles from every conceivable angle, the author hopes to reveal to you the secret through which every great fortune has been accumulated. Strange and paradoxical as it may seem, the "secret" is NOT A SECRET. Nature, herself, advertises it in the earth on which we live, the stars, the planets suspended within our view, in the elements above and around us, in every blade of grass, and every form of life within our vision.

Nature advertises this "secret" in the terms of biology, in the conversion of a tiny cell, so small that it may be lost on the point of a pin, into the HUMAN BEING now reading this line. The conversion of desire into its physical equivalent is, certainly, no more miraculous!

As Hill conveys, you can derive warranted confidence, realistic faith, renewed sense of self, and authentic help by placing yourself within the cyclical scheme of nature or creation.

After reading Hill and following his steps, I venture that you will approach your work (which is often the deepest part of a person's life, whether or not acknowledged) more effectively, fully, and successfully. By committing yourself to the ideas in *Think and Grow Rich* you will experience progressive change. This is my own critical testimony.

I also recognize that Hill's sometimes overwrought language, gee-whiz tone, outdated cultural references, ready use of spiritual metaphors, and even his title strike some readers as lowbrow, vulgar or gauche. I recognize that not every one of us feels at ease being judged by friends or peers for reading such literature. My advice: *get over it*. Ersatz seriousness is the greatest impediment to individual experiment and development. Most peer judgments are little more than personal taste informed by image-maintenance and the wish for security. If I've conveyed any sense that *Think and Grow Rich* may hold something for you, let no psychologized excuses deter you

I finally want to close with a word of exceedingly—and deceptively—simple advice that Hill delivered in a transcribed but undated and unpublished talk. His statement touches, indirectly but penetratingly, on everything I've tried to get across: "Avoid persons and circumstances which make you feel inferior."

Live with that for six months. See what occurs.

Chapter XII

Spiritus Contra Spiritum: The Mystic Roots of Alcoholics Anonymous

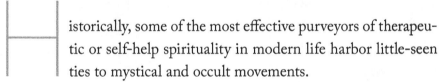istorically, some of the most effective purveyors of therapeutic or self-help spirituality in modern life harbor little-seen ties to mystical and occult movements.

Among such figures, the most consequential in shaping a persuasive, globally popular mental-therapeutic spirituality were Bill Wilson (1895–1971) and Bob Smith (1879–1950), cofounders of Alcoholics Anonymous (AA).

Nearly a century ago, AA arose, and continues, as the primary vehicle of *practical mysticism* in modern life, with spiritual sources as widespread as they are, in many cases, esoteric.

As tradition records, the Vermont-born men, Wilson and Smith, first met in May 1935 in Akron, Ohio. Bill was a newly sober alcoholic traveling on business from New York. Alone at a hotel, he was desperate for a drink. He thumbed through a local church directory seeking a minister who could help him find another drunk to talk to. Bill had the idea that *if he could locate another alcoholic to speak with, and to help, it might ease his pangs for booze.*

On that day, Bill found his way to Bob Smith, an area physician who had waged his own long and losing battle with alcohol. Both men had spent years vainly sampling different techniques and treatments. When they met in Akron, however, each discovered that his capacity to stop drinking *grew in proportion to his ability to counsel the other.* Wilson and Smith's friendship burgeoned into the founding of Alcoholics Anonymous and the modern twelve-step movement.

Bill and Bob appeared as all-American as their names. In their looks, dress, and politics, both men were as conservative as an old-fashioned banker, which, in fact, Wilson was.

But each was also a spiritual adventurer, committed to exploring the terrain of metaphysical experience, from Spiritualism and mediumship to positive-mind and Eastern metaphysics, in search of a workable solution to addiction. Together, they wove Christian, Swedenborgian, Jungian, Jamesian, Christian Science, mediumistic, and New Thought themes into the twelve steps of Alcoholics Anonymous, fostering perhaps the most *explicitly therapeutic* metaphysical movement in history.

Seen in a certain light, Alcoholics Anonymous had its earliest beginnings with Bill Wilson's marriage in January 1918 to his wife and intellectual partner, Lois Burnham (1891–1988).

Lois came from an old-line family with roots in Lancaster, Pennsylvania, and Brooklyn, New York. The Burnhams had a deep commitment to the Swedenborgian Church, the congregation founded on the mystical philosophy of eighteenth-century scientist-seeker Emanuel Swedenborg (1688–1772). The Swedish mage taught of an unseen spirit world whose forces and phenomena mirror our own, with thought the connecting tissue between the two.

Lois's paternal grandfather was among the nation's first Swedenborgian ministers. She and Bill were married at the Church of the Neighbor, a Swedenborgian congregation in Brooklyn. (Source notes appear at the end of the chapter.)

After that church's closing, Lois attended the New York New Church, a Swedenborgian congregation on Manhattan's East Side. Dating back to 1816, this congregation included Henry James, Sr., the father of William and Henry James, and Helen Keller. It continues today. Lois proved reticent about publicly expressing her Swedenborgian commitments: she wished to avoid any appearance of religious favoritism within AA.

Asked shortly before her death in 1988 whether Swedenborgianism had influenced the twelve steps, Lois replied that no particular faith should be singled out. "If there was a connection," she said, "I wouldn't tell you anyway, for that very reason."

The Swedenborgian commitment that ran through Lois's family appears to have impacted Bill, especially when his binge drinking drove him toward spiritual solutions. A key tenet of Swedenborgianism, later reflected in AA literature, is that the individual functions as a vessel for higher energies. Swedenborg described a "Divine influx" suffusing the material world. Popular early twentieth-century New Thought author Ralph Waldo Trine, who we met in chapter II, called it a "divine inflow."

This notion appears to have helped Bill define his personal "awakening experience." In December 1934, Bill was laid up in Towns Hospital in Manhattan, a tony, private sanitarium where he frequently retreated to recover from benders. He was trapped in a cycle of binge drinking, drying out, and drinking again. Bill was in agony over his inability to control the alcoholism that was driving him toward death, which he knew would arrive either from a drinking-related accident, illness, or indigence.

"Lying there in conflict," Bill wrote, "I dropped into the blackest depression I had ever known. Momentarily my prideful obstinacy was crushed. I cried out, 'Now I'm ready to do anything . . .'" What happened next completely reordered his life:

> Though I certainly didn't really expect anything, I did make this frantic appeal: "If there be a God, will He show Himself!" The result was instant, electric, beyond description. The place seemed to light up, blinding white. I knew only ecstasy and seemed on a mountain. A great wind blew, enveloping and penetrating me. To me, it was not of air, but of Spirit. Blazing, there came the tremendous thought "You are a free man."

Bill encountered something like the "Divine influx." His experience of religious awakening was confirmed for him several days later during a visit by his friend Ebby Thacher. Ebby was involved with a Christian evangelical fellowship called the Oxford Group. He handed Bill a book that became his closest companion and source of insight: *The Varieties of Religious Experience,* the 1902 classic of comparative religion by American philosopher and psychologist William James.

"I devoured it," Wilson recalled. In James's case studies, Wilson recognized his own epiphanic episode. The philosopher had termed it a "conversion experience." The realization of a higher power, James wrote, often struck a believer with such clarity and vividness that it objectively altered the circumstances of outer life. Bill's conversion experience had done so for him; he never drank again.

There is speculation that Bill's episode was produced or abetted by belladonna, a onetime botanical treatment for alcoholism known to induce hallucinations. Bill was untroubled by the prospect. In the late 1950s, he experimented under medical supervision with LSD, which he believed could induce rather than substitute for spiritual experience.

In the years immediately following his "white light" realization, Bill codified his awakening into the first three steps of the twelve-step program. The opening three steps reflected a kind of blueprint for a Jamesian conversion experience. They were written in such a way that the word *alcohol* could be replaced by any other compulsory fixation, such as *anger, drugs,* or *gambling*:

1. We admitted we were powerless over alcohol—that our lives had become unmanageable.
2. Came to believe that a Power greater than ourselves could restore us to sanity.
3. Made a decision to turn our will and our lives over to the care and direction of God *as we understood Him.*

Working as chief writer, Bill published the twelve steps in 1939 in what became known as the "Big Book," *Alcoholics Anonymous.*

Although James's work remained central to Bill, many other influences shaped his book. Bill tore through spiritual literature, reading and rereading Christian Science founder Mary Baker Eddy's 1879 *Science and Health,* alongside New Thought books such as Emmet Fox's 1934 *The Sermon on the Mount,* an interpretation of Christ's oration as a mental-manifestation philosophy. He also read Christian inspirational works, such as Scottish evangelist Henry Drummond's 1890 meditation on the transformative power of love, *The Greatest Thing in the World.*

In time, AA's written and spoken principles altered the lexicon of American life, giving rise to expressions such as "easy does it," "one day at a time," "first things first," and "let go and let God." Most significantly, its literature popularized an ecumenical term for God: *Higher Power.*

This phrase appeared in the group's core principle that the alcoholic's "defense must come from a Higher Power," as Bill wrote in the "Big Book." But Wilson and Smith also insisted that twelve-steppers must form *their own* conception of God *"as we understood Him,"* as the third step went. "Higher Power" neatly captured the radical ecumenism they were after. (I sometimes tell twelve-steppers today that if that term smacks too heavily of Abrahamic or monotheistic religiosity for their outlook, try substituting *Greater Force.*)

Higher Power probably entered AA's lexicon through Ralph Waldo Trine's 1897 New Thought bestseller, *In Tune With the Infinite,* a favorite of Bob Smith's. Trine repeatedly used the term, with particular reference to alcohol: "In the degree that we come into the realization of the higher powers of the mind and spirit . . . there also falls away the desire for the heavier, grosser, less valuable kinds of food and drink, such as the flesh of animals, *alcoholic drinks* . . ." (Emphasis mine.)

Bill's companion Ebby Thacher also brought him to two additional philosophies that deeply impacted AA's development: the teachings of a popular evangelical fellowship called the Oxford Group and the metaphysical outlook of psychologist Carl Jung. In a sense, all of these early influences—William James, the Oxford Group, and Jung—reflected vastly different thought systems. But their unifying kernel was the principle that the sensitive, searching mind could bring a seeker to the experience of a Higher Power.

The Oxford Group, initially launched as First Century Christian Fellowship, was an enterprising and profoundly influential religious lay movement in the first half of the twentieth century. Its teachings brilliantly distilled therapeutic and self-help principles from within traditional Christianity. So redubbed in 1929 because of its large contingent from Oxford University, the Oxford Group devised a protocol of steps and principles intended to awaken modern people to the healing qualities of God in a manner similar to that experienced by first-century Christians. The steps included radical honesty, stringent moral self-examination, confession, making restitution, daily meditation or "quiet time," and opening oneself to awakening or conversion experiences. Much of this was later reflected in the twelve steps.

To facilitate its program, Oxford's organizers pioneered the use of group meetings or "house parties." These took place in an encounter-group atmosphere of confession, shared testimonies, and joint prayer. Mutual help and peer therapy were central to Oxford's program, and gave rise to a similar structure in AA.

Yet for some Oxford members, eventually including Bill and Lois Wilson, the group-meeting atmosphere could deteriorate into a brow-beating, accusatory climate in which members were singled out for not sufficiently sharing intimacies or detailing moral failings. Oxford's internal culture demanded a gung-ho approach—converts were often coached to go "maximum" in their commitment.

This gung-ho style emanated from the group's founder, Frank Buchman, an American Lutheran minister who initiated its meetings in the early 1920s. Buchman was the organization's greatest asset—and gravest failing.

A shrewd and impassioned organizer, Frank Buchman built the group through a strategy of recruiting "key people." Such a figure might be a celebrity, banker, or, on a college campus, captain of the football team. A key person, in turn, attracted social admirers, sycophants, and aspirants into the fold.

Buchman often organized his Oxford meetings at posh hotels or homes of well-to-do members—again making the group attractive by its sheen of success. Mary Baker Eddy devised a similar strategy in building her Christian Science churches, schools, and reading rooms in high-tone neighborhoods. Even the Oxford Group's informal use of the august university's name—which it was later asked to discontinue—lent it an air of respectability and upward mobility.

In 1936, Buchman upset all of his carefully laid plans. The Lutheran minister ignited an international uproar when he apparently set his sights on attracting a unique key person: Adolf Hitler. During the 1930s, Buchman traveled to Germany, where he met with Heinrich Himmler, whose wife was reportedly in sympathy with the Oxford Group. Buchman vocally praised Hitler as a bulwark against atheistic Communism. ". . . think what it would mean to the world," he told a reporter for the *New York World-Telegram* in an interview published August 26, 1936, "if Hitler surrendered to the control of God. Or Mussolini. Or any dictator. Through such a man God could control a nation overnight and solve every last, bewildering problem." Similar statements had come from Glenn Clark, an inventive Presbyterian lay leader also active in New Thought. (Bob Smith attended retreats organized by Clark and praised him as one of his favorite authors.)

But Oxford's founder went further still, uttering his most notorious words: "I thank heaven for a man like Adolf Hitler, who built a front line of defense against the anti-Christ of Communism."

While Bill wanted to save drunks, Frank Buchman wanted to save "drunken nations." Buchman's maximalist worldview held no appeal for Bill and Lois, who, after distancing themselves for some months following Buchman's announcement, pulled away from Oxford entirely by 1937. By the end of the decade most of AA's groups had ceased all cooperation with Oxford, increasingly called Moral Re-

Armament (MRA). Around that time the Buchman organization also lost some of its most thoughtful ministers and organizers, including the Reverend Sam Shoemaker, an Episcopal priest at New York's Calvary Church, who was a major influence on Bill.

Yet Bill's friend Ebby had also introduced him to another, very different stream of ideas: the psycho-spirituality of Carl Jung. Bill said the psychologist's role was "like no other" in AA's founding.

At the same time, Bill also praised William James as "a founder of Alcoholics Anonymous." Bill may have eagerly emphasized AA's debt to respected figures like Jung and James as a means of exorcising the shadows of Frank Buchman. Yet all of these influences could not be easily separated out, one from the other. Ebby himself was first recruited to Oxford by a former patient of Jung's, a Rhode Island businessman named Rowland Hazard. Rowland's experiences, in turn, brought Jung's influence into AA.

Around 1931, Rowland visited the Swiss psychologist to seek help for his alcoholism. He reported leaving the doctor's care feeling cured, but suffered a relapse a few weeks later. Rowland returned desperate, pleading to know what could be done. Jung leveled with the American: He had never once witnessed a patient recover from alcoholism.

"I can do nothing for you," the psychologist concluded.

Rowland begged, surely there must be something?

Well, Jung replied, there may be one possibility: "Occasionally, Rowland, alcoholics have recovered through spiritual experiences, better known as religious conversions." Jung went on: "All you can do is place yourself in a religious atmosphere of your own choosing"—here was the AA principle of pursuing God *as we understood Him*—and "admit your personal powerlessness to go on living. If under such conditions you seek with all your might, you may then find . . ."

Jung's prescription matched what Bill had experienced at Towns Hospital. For Bill, it served as further confirmation of the urgency of a spiritual response to addiction.

Years later, Bill finally wrote to Jung, on January 23, 1961, in the last months of the psychologist's life. Bill wanted to tell him how his counsel to Rowland had impacted the AA program. He also wrote that "many AAs report a great variety of psychic phenomena, the cumulative weight of which is very considerable."

To Bill's delight, Jung replied with a long letter on January 30. The psychologist vividly recalled Rowland and what he had told him. Jung repeated to Bill his formula for overcoming alcoholism: *spiritus contra spiritum*. Jung's Latin phrase could be roughly translated as: *Higher Spirit over lower spirits*, or alcohol.

It was the twelve steps in a nutshell.

Following Bill's death in 1971, AA found compatibility with the dawning New Age movement of radically ecumenical and therapeutic spirituality, some of it supernatural in nature or at least perception. Indeed, the 1960s and '70s saw the emergence of a newly popularized mediumistic or "channeled" literature from higher intelligences such as Seth, Ramtha, the "Source" of early twentieth-century medical clairvoyant Edgar Cayce, and even the figure of Christ in *A Course in Miracles*.

The last of these was a profound and enduring lesson series, channeled beginning in 1965 by Columbia University research psychologist Helen Schucman. A concordance of tone and values existed between the work of psychic Edgar Cayce (1877–1945) and *A Course in Miracles*. In fact, Cayce's devotees and the *Course*'s wide array of readers discovered that they had a lot in common; members of both cultures blended seamlessly, attending many of the same seminars, growth centers, and New Thought churches.

Likewise, congruency emerged during Bill's lifetime between Cayce's world and followers of the twelve steps—extending to Bill himself. Starting in the 1970s, twelve-steppers of various stripes became a familiar presence at Cayce conferences and events. Cayce's universalistic religious message dovetailed with the purposefully flexible references to a Higher Power in the "Big Book," *Alcoholics Anonymous*. Indeed, Bill, Lois, and Bob, along with other early AAs were deeply versed in mystical and mediumistic teachings, extending to Cayce—and even the Wilsons' at-home Ouija board sessions and private seances.

In recently discovered correspondence, Bill wrote to the psychic's son and custodian Hugh Lynn Cayce, on November 14, 1951: "Long an admirer of your father's work, I'm glad to report that a number of my A.A. friends in this area [New York City], and doubtless in others, share this interest."

He went on to comment revealingly about contacts that Hugh Lynn had previously proposed between the Cayce organization and AA:

As you might guess, we have seen much of phenomenalism in A.A., also an occasional physical healing. But nothing, of course, in healing on the scale your father practiced it . . . At the present time, I find I cannot participate very actively myself. The Society of Alcoholics Anonymous regards me as their symbol. Hence it is imperative that I show no partiality whatever toward any particular religious point of view—let alone physic [sic] matters. Nevertheless I think I well understand the significance of Edgar Cayce and I shall look forward to presently hearing how some of my friends may make a closer contact.

All three works—the Cayce readings, *A Course in Miracles*, and *Alcoholics Anonymous*—demonstrated a shared sense of religious liberalism, an encouragement that all individuals seek their own conception of a Higher Power, and a permeability intended to accommodate the broadest expression of religious outlooks and backgrounds.

Although no vast religion of mental therapeutics ever appeared on the American scene, Alcoholics Anonymous, through its blending of ideas from Swedenborg, James, Oxford, Jung, Cayce, and New Thought, created a home for what James called the "religion of healthy-mindedness."

There exist myriad controversies over whether the AA program *works*. Clinicians have long noted the difficulty of studying the program: do its many dropouts constitute failures—or, in fact, is the program trackable *only* through those who remain for perpetuity?

Ebby Thacher, the man who ignited Bill Wilson's interest in spiritual self-help, repeatedly relapsed into drunkenness. After meeting Bill, Ebby spent much of his remaining life in a battle with alcohol, often ill and destitute. When Ebby died in 1966, he was sober but living as a dependent at a recovery center in upstate New York. Bill regularly sent him checks to keep him going.

Not that Bill's legs were always strong. Although he remained sober, Bill continually struggled with depression, chain-smoking, and extra-marital affairs. But he did attain his life's goal: until his death in 1971, he never drank again.

Why did one man remain sober and another fall down?

Bill's wife, Lois, in a passage from her 1979 memoir, *Lois Remembers,* explained, in an understated manner, the difference she detected between the two men. In so doing, Lois also illuminated a mystery, perhaps even *the* mystery, of human nature:

After those first two years . . . why did Ebby get drunk? It was he who gave Bill the philosophy that kept him sober. Why didn't it keep Ebby sober? He was sincere, I'm sure. Perhaps it was a difference in the degree of wanting sobriety. Bill wanted it with his whole soul. Ebby may have wanted it simply to keep out of trouble.

I dislike the term "soul" because it generally goes undefined, although Lois probably used it here as a figure of speech, like heart. In any case, I prefer *psyche*, which I see as a compact of thought and emotion. If one warrants, as I do, that the psyche possesses extra-physical capacities—as evidenced, for example, in academic psychical research—then then it follows that the two terms, soul and psyche, are, if not synonymous, then not at odds.

Language aside, let's revisit Lois's statement: *Bill wanted it with his whole soul.* Could that be the key? Within the parameters of physical possibility, you receive what you "want with your whole soul" (or psyche)—whether inner truth, personal accomplishment, relationships, whatever it is. Barring some great countervailing force, and for either ill or good, the thing that you desire above all else is, in some measure, *what you receive.*

Do you doubt that? Let me turn to a series of dialogues that twentieth-century spiritual teacher Jiddu Krishnamurti conducted with a group of young students in India, reproduced in the 1964 book *Think on These Things.* The teacher spoke of the pull of conformity and the need to develop a sense of inner freedom and direction.

A boy asked: "How can we put into practice what you are telling us?" Krishnamurti replied that if you want something badly enough, you know exactly what to do.

"When you meet a cobra on the road," the teacher said, "you don't ask 'What am I to do?' You understand very well the danger of a cobra and you stay away from it." Krishnamurti noted:

You hear something which you think is right and you want to carry it out in your everyday life; so there is a gap between what you think and what you do, is there not? You think one thing, and you are doing something else. But you want to put into practice what you think, so there is this gap between action and thought; and then you ask how to bridge the gap, how to link your thinking to your action.

Now, when you want to do something very much, you do it, don't you? When you want to go and play cricket, or do some other thing in which you are really interested, you find ways and means of doing it; you never ask how to put it into practice. You do it because you are eager, because your whole being, your mind and heart are in it.

What if someone doesn't possess an impassioned drive? This may be the meaning behind Revelation 3:16, which condemns those who are *lukewarm*: "So then because thou art lukewarm, and neither cold nor hot, I will spit thee out of my mouth." The hesitators, the undecided, those who cannot commit to a path—they receive nothing.

Life honors no halfway measures. This, ultimately, was Bill's discovery—on which stands the modern twelve-step movement.

Notes on Sources

A vast literature exists on the founding of Alcoholics Anonymous. It is a tribute to the integrity that Bill Wilson brought to AA that "approved literature" issued by the AA General Service Conference, rather than displaying the intellectual vacuity of most official publications, is surprisingly open about Wilson and Smith's spiritual experiments, including their forays into Spiritualism, seances, mysticism, and Bill's experiments with LSD. In her biography, *My Name Is Bill* (Washington Square Press, 2004), Susan Cheever ably notes elements of Bill's life that are absent from official literature, such as his depression and marital infidelity.

Key AA-approved literature includes *Pass It On: The Story of Bill Wilson and How the AA Message Reached the World* (Alcoholics Anonymous World Services, 1984), and *Dr. Bob and the Good Oldtimers* (Alcoholics Anonymous World Services, 1980).

Also helpful is the pamphlet "Three Talks to Medical Societies" by Bill W. (Alcoholics Anonymous World Services, undated), from which I quote Bill on his awakening experience from a 1958 address to the New York Medical Society on Alcoholism. This talk contains Bill's remark that he "devoured" the work of William James. Bill called James an AA founder in *Bill W.: My First 40 Years* (Hazelden, 2000). Bill references Jung's influence in his letter of January 23, 1961. On Bill's experience at Towns Hospital, also see "An Alcoholic's Savior: God, Belladonna or Both?" by Howard Markel, M.D., *New York Times*, April 19, 2010.

I have benefited from Lois Wilson's recollections in *Lois Remembers* (Al-Anon Family Group Headquarters, 1979), which is helpful on the Wilsons' split with the Oxford Group. Lois also notes that New Thought leader Emma Curtis Hopkins' family farm, High Watch in Connecticut, became an AA-based treatment center in 1940, a topic deserving further attention. Also helpful on Lois's upbringing in the Swedenborgian Church is *Wings & Roots: The New Age and Emanuel Swedenborg in Dialog* by Wilma Wake (J. Appleseed & Co., 1999), from which Lois is quoted on Swedenborg's influence.

The Oxford Group and, more particularly, Frank Buchman remain a source of controversy. An important critique of Buchman and Oxford appears in Tom Driberg's *The Mystery of Moral Re-Armament* (Secker and Warburg, 1964), which reprinted the 1936 *New York World-Telegram* piece containing Buchman's infamous quotes. Important as his book was, Driberg, a British Labour MP, was deeply critical of the Oxford Movement. Any writer or researcher approaching Buchman's life and Oxford's influence on AA must cast a broader net.

The works of Dick B., a historian who has doggedly cataloged the spiritual roots of AA, are a helpful window on Oxford's influence and its innovative spiritual program. Dick B.'s works include *Dr. Bob and His Library* (Paradise Research Publications, 1992, 1994, 1998); *The Books Early AAs Read for Spiritual Growth* (Paradise Research Publications, 1993, 1998); and the comprehensive *Turning Point: A History of Early AA's Spiritual Roots and Successes* (Paradise Research Publications, 1997), from which I quote Bill's recollections of the encounter between Rowland Hazard and Carl Jung. Also helpful on the Oxford Group is Charles Braden's *These Also Believe* (Macmillan, 1949).

I write further about Glenn Clarke in my *One Simple Idea* (2014).

Additional sources on the history of AA include *New Wine: The Spiritual Roots of the Twelve Step Miracle* by Mel B. (Hazelden, 1991); *Not-God: A History of Alcoholics Anonymous* by Ernest Kurtz (Hazelden, 1979, 1991); *AA: The Way It Began* by Bill Pittman (Glen Abbey Books, 1988); *AA's Godparents: Carl Jung, Emmet Fox, Jack Alexander* by Igor I. Sikorsky Jr. (CompCare Publishers, 1990); and *Ebby: The Man Who Sponsored Bill W.* by Mel B. (Hazelden, 1998). I benefited from the reissued 1939 first edition of *Alcoholics Anonymous*, published by Anonymous Press, and the fourth edition of the "Big Book" published by AA.

An archivist at the Edgar Cayce Foundation in Virginia Beach, VA, graciously sent me the recently catalogued letter that Bill Wilson wrote to Edgar Cayce's son, Hugh Lynn Cayce, on November 14, 1951.

Lois Wilson is further quoted from *Lois Remembers* (1979). Jiddu Krishnamurti is quoted from *Think on These Things* (Harper & Row, 1964). I write extensively about academic psychical research in my *Daydream Believer* (2022) and *Modern Occultism* (2023).

Chapter XIII

You Are As Your Mind Is: Neville Goddard

Although he died in relative obscurity in 1972, mystic Neville Goddard (1905–1972) now ranks among the twenty-first-century's most widely followed writers and lecturers in alternative spirituality.

Search results for the mononymous Neville's talks number in the millions. His books, once relegated to literature tables at New Thought churches (and even then difficult to find)—populate countless editions which, along with an expanding catalogue of anthologies, amass yearly sales of hundreds of thousands in print, audio, and digital.

Across Neville's vast range of lectures, which he freely permitted audience members to tape-record in a dawning age of portable technology—a foresight that secured his legacy in the digital era—the teacher contended with unfailing simplicity and elegance that everything you see and experience is the out-picturing of your emotionalized thoughts and mental images.

"The only God," the radical idealist told audiences, "is your own wonderful human imagination."

Neville's literary career began in 1939 with his slender, evocative volume, *At Your Command*. It is not only the mystic's first book but among his most elegant and powerful statements in a career that spanned more than ten volumes and thousands of lectures.

With disarming brevity, *At Your Command* presents Neville's full-circle philosophy: Your imagination is the creative force called God in Scripture; the Bible itself is neither historical nor theological but rather a symbolic blueprint of the individual's psychological development.

"Every man," Neville said in a lecture of October 23, 1967, "is destined to discover that Scripture is his autobiography."

It is idealist philosophy—or what might be called spiritualized objectivism—taken to the razor's edge, argued with jewel-like precision. However often Neville restated his basic premise, it always sounded fresh, reaching even repeat listeners and readers as though for the first time—a gift possessed by Ralph Waldo Emerson (1803–1882), Jiddu Krishnamurti (1895–1986), Vernon Howard (1918–1992)—the last of whom we meet in chapter XXI—and few others.

A British native of Barbados, Neville first ventured to the U.S. at age seventeen to study theater. He had never before left his island environs. Although the graceful, angular youth found some success on screen and stage, he radically changed directions in the early 1930s when he said he began studying under a mysterious teacher named Abdullah, a turbaned black man of Jewish descent. The seeker said they worked together in New York City for five years poring over Kabbalah, number symbolism, and Scripture.

Despite Neville's screen-idol looks, there exist few images of him. Some students thought him a man of mystery. One of Neville's most dedicated acolytes in the mid-1950s was Margaret Runyan (1921–2011), cousin of American storyteller Damon Runyon (1880–1946) and briefly wife to New Age icon Carlos Castaneda. Margaret recalled in her 2001 memoir, *A Magical Journey with Carlos Castaneda*:

> . . . it was more than the message that attracted Carlos, it was Neville himself. He was so mysterious. Nobody was really sure who he was or where he had come from. There were vague references to Barbados in the West Indies and his being the son of an ultra-rich plantation family, but nobody knew for sure. They couldn't even be sure about this Abdullah business, his Indian teacher, who was always *way back there* in the jungle, or someplace. The only thing you really knew was that Neville was here and that he might be back next week, but then again . . .

"There was," she concluded, "a certain power in that position, an appealing kind of freedom in the lack of past and Carlos knew it."

It is not a stretch to reckon that Neville's description of tutelage under an arcane teacher—a common theme in Western occultism since Madame H.P. Blavatsky's (1831–1891) late-nineteenth-century claims of guidance from hidden Masters—informed Castaneda's fanciful but indisputably penetrating narratives of mentorship to a Native American sorcerer.

At times, however, Neville opened up about his private life and how he responded to disappointing or bitter episodes.

In one instance, the lecturer recounted a painful incident from his drama school days, when he was fresh from the Caribbean and new to city life. In a late-career lecture of March 17, 1972, Neville described suffering humiliation by his acting teacher—but using the experience as a goad to something greater.

As you read his words, note that the youthful Neville probably spoke in a rounder, more rural Anglo-Caribbean accent—versus his later clipped and mellifluous diction—which his instructor deemed a career-killer:

My own disappointments in my world led up to whatever I am doing today. When the teacher in my school, I could ill afford the $500 that my father gave me to go to this small school in New York City, and she made me the goat. She called me out before an audience of about forty students. And she said, "Now listen to him speak. He will never earn a living using his voice."

She should not have done that, but she did it—but she didn't know the kind of person that she was talking about. Instead of going down into the grave and burying my head in shame, I was determined that I would actually disprove her. It did something to me when she said to me, "you will never earn" to the class—using me as the guinea pig to show them what not to do—and so, she said, I spoke with a guttural voice and I spoke with this very heavy accent, and I will never use my voice to earn a living.

We all went to this school and this teacher simply singled me out to make some little, well, exhibition of what I should not be doing in class. But I went home and I was so annoyed that I had lost my father's $500 or $600 that he gave me for the six-months course, but I was determined that she was false, that she was wrong. So, I went to the end. I went to the end and actually felt that I was facing an audience and unembarrassed that I could talk and talk and talk forever without notes, no notes.

By early 1938, Neville quit his theatrical career to dedicate himself to writing and lecturing on metaphysics. As noted, Neville is not only one of the most widely heard spiritual orators of the twentieth century but he spoke extemporaneously and elegantly across decades worth of lectures, without a note in sight.

Although Neville wrote fuller works with greater metaphysical exposition, *At Your Command* remains the perfect user's manual. What you experience, Neville told seekers, is not what you pray for but what matches your "awareness of being." Clarified desire, properly directed, he said, catalyzes a new state:

> For instance; if you were imprisoned no man would have to tell you that you should desire freedom. Freedom, or rather the desire of freedom would be automatic. So why look behind the four walls of your prison bars? Take your attention from being imprisoned and begin to feel yourself to be free. FEEL it to the point where it is natural—the very second you do so, those prison bars will dissolve. Apply this same principle to any problem.

Mere solipsism? The difference between a solipsist and an idealist is that the former burdens others to validate his self-image. Neville's system is fiercely independent. Wishful thinking? Neville's outlook evolved into what I consider the most elegant mystical analogue to quantum theory—and is increasingly recognized as such.

Speaking at a series of Los Angeles lectures in 1948, often published under the title *Five Lessons*, Neville announced: "Scientists will one day explain why there is a serial universe. But in practice, how you use this serial universe to change the future is more important."

In an era before the popularization of quantum theory, it was a striking observation. It was not until years later that quantum physicists began discussing the many-worlds theory, devised by physicist Hugh Everett III (1930–1982) in 1957.

For his part, Everett was attempting to make sense of some of the extraordinary findings emergent from about three decades in quantum mechanics. For example, scientists are able to demonstrate, through interference patterns, that a subatomic particle occupies a "wave state" or state of superposition—that is, an infinite number of places—until an observer or automatized device takes a measurement: it is only when measurement is taken that the particle collapses, so to speak, from a wave state into a localized one. Before measurement is taken the localized particle exists only in potential.

Some argue that the "wave state" is nothing but a probability formula—it is certainly that, too (extraordinary in itself)—but I believe I am accurately stating what has been observed in the last ninety-plus years of particle experiments.

Indeed, starting about twenty years ago, it became fashionable for New Agers and laypeople, like me, to put quantum theory at the back of cherished spiritual principles. It became equally fashionable for professional skeptics and mainstream journalists to pushback, crying *B.S.* and *sophistry*. That position, while still heard, has quieted. Not because skeptics have grown more pensive or attenuated to media-speak, but because the proposition of mind-over-matter, strange as it may seem, now resounds in debates on theoretical physics in mainline journals and magazines.

Since Neville exemplified his own philosophy, it is important to understand something about him personally. Let's pick up where we began earlier: the island of Barbados, where Neville was born in 1905. He was not a scion of the island's wealthy, landowning class. Rather, he was part of a large, somewhat scrappy family of British merchants. They ran a small grocery and provisions business.

Transplanted from his tropical home to the streets of New York City, Neville led a precarious financial life. When theater jobs ran dry, the actor and dancer found work as an elevator operator, shipping clerk, and department store salesman. He did land some impressive roles, including on Broadway. But most stage opportunities vanished with the onset of the Great Depression. He often wore the same suit of clothes and bounced around shared rooms on Manhattan's Upper West Side. Food was not a guarantee.

After Neville's speaking career took off, syndicated gossip columnist Jimmie Fidler reported on May 4, 1955, that the Barbadian came from an "enormously wealthy" family who "owned a whole island" in the Caribbean. This is invention—but over time, and in line with stories Neville told himself, the Goddard family did, in fact, grow rich.

The clan of green grocers expanded into Goddard Enterprises, which is now a publicly traded catering and food service employing about 6,500 people in the Caribbean and Latin America. Neville's father Joseph, called Joe, founded the business, and ran it with Neville's older brother Victor, of whom Neville spoke frequently in his lectures. Indeed, everything Neville related about the rise of his family's fortunes matches business records and reportage in Caribbean newspapers. But there is a more dramatic example of Neville's self-descriptions cleaving to fact.

In the years immediately before and after World War II, Neville lived in New York's Greenwich Village, a place he relished. He resided with his wife, Catherine Willa Van Schumus (1907–1975), nicknamed Bill, and daughter Victoria, or Vicky, at 32 Washington Square, a handsome, redbrick apartment tower on the west side of Washington Square Park. (The mystic's prospering family had since put him on a stipend.) Neville recalled many happy years in the building, which still stands.

Like millions, he was pulled away from home by the draft in late 1942, just under a year into America's entry to World War II. In lectures, however, Neville described using the powers of visualization to gain an honorable discharge a few months later and return home.

Why would the U.S. Army release a healthy, athletic man—Neville was lithe and fit as a dancer—at the height of the war effort when nearly every able-bodied male was mobilized? At age thirty-seven, he was a little old for the draft but well below the cutoff of forty-five.

In his accounts, the metaphysician wanted no part of the war. He was newly married with a four-month-old daughter and also had an eighteen-year-old son, Joseph, from a prior marriage. He had obligations most draftees did not. While stationed for basic training, the buck private requested a discharge—and was abruptly shut down.

Neville said he determined to use his methods of mental creativity. Each night, as he described it, he laid on his army cot and before drifting to sleep pictured himself home in Greenwich Village. He would see from the perspective of being in his apartment and strolling Washington Square Park. He continued, night after night, in this imaginal activity.*

After eight nights, Neville said, seemingly from nowhere, his commanding officer summoned him and asked, "Do you still want a discharge?" Neville said, "I do." The CO continued, "You're being honorably discharged."

I questioned this story and decided to verify it.

U.S. Army Human Resources Command provided Neville's service records. The one original document remaining is his final pay statement, which, along with digital archives, shows his enlistment from November 12, 1942 to March 1943 with the 490th Armored FA Battalion at Camp Polk, Louisiana. A spokesman for Army Human

---

* In lectures, Neville variously described his meditations lasting eight nights or as one vision on the first night of his request marked "approved" and then waiting nine days for his honorable discharge, which arrived on day ten.

Resources Command confirmed that Neville was honorably discharged in about four months in March 1943. The reason, as recorded by the military, is that the conscript was released "to accept employment in an essential wartime industry."

I asked: "This man was a metaphysical lecturer—how is that a vital civilian occupation?" The spokesman replied: "Unfortunately, Mr. Goddard's records were destroyed in the 1973 fire at the National Personnel Records Center," about a year after Neville's death.

On September 11, 1943, *The New Yorker* confirmed Neville being back on the lecture circuit in a surprisingly extensive profile, "A Blue Flame on the Forehead"—the last time mainstream letters took any note of the mystic.

I cannot say precisely what happened; I can only report that Neville described the logistics accurately. I must add that if any quotidian reason exists for Neville's honorable discharge, it may be a mistake in his draft records. Neville's Electronic Army Serial Number Merged File lists his marital status as "separated, without dependents." This is obviously incorrect. Yet the correction of this error does not mesh with official reasons for his discharge.

Across years, I've reviewed census data, citizenship applications, military documents, and other sources that track Neville's whereabouts and employment and can only say that his self-professed timelines and life details match the available record.

The one facet of Neville's career I have been unable to verify is his mentorship to the mysterious Abdullah, a man for whom there exists no definite paper trail beyond Neville's descriptions.

A commercial fortune teller called "Prof. Abdullah" occasionally appears in period newspapers but it is important to note that sundry "seers" widely populated the New York scene, often adopting Eastern or arabesque names. One or more "Abdullah" in the press does not make a match.

I have considered whether Neville's Abdullah may be found in the more impressive persona of a 1920s- and '30s-era Black-nationalist mystic named Arnold Josiah Ford. Like Neville, Ford was born in Barbados, in 1877, the son of an itinerant preacher. Ford arrived in Harlem around 1910 and established himself as a leading voice in the Ethiopianism movement, a precursor to Jamaican Rastafarianism.

Both movements held that the East African nation of Ethiopia was home to a lost Israelite tribe that had preserved the teachings of a mystical African belief system. Ford considered himself an original Israelite and a man of authentic Judaic descent. Like Abdullah, Ford was sometimes considered an "Ethiopian rabbi." Surviving photographs show Ford as a dignified, somewhat severe-looking man with a set jaw and penetrating gaze, sometimes wearing a turban, just like Neville's Abdullah, with a Star of David on his lapel. Ford himself cultivated an air of mystery, attracting "much apocryphal and often contradictory speculation," noted historian Randall K. Burkett in his *Garveyism as a Religious Movement* (Scarecrow Press, 1978).

Ford lived in New York City at the same time that Neville began his discipleship to Abdullah. Neville recalled his and Abdullah's first meeting in 1931, and U.S. Census records show Ford was living in Harlem on West 131st Street in 1930. In his study *The Black Jews of Harlem* (Schocken Books, 1964, 1970), historian Howard Brotz wrote of Ford: "It is certain that he studied Hebrew with some immigrant teacher and was a key link" in communicating "approximations of Talmudic Judaism" from within the Ethiopianism movement. This would fit Neville's depiction of Abdullah tutoring him in Hebrew and Kabbalah. (It should be noted that early twentieth-century occultists often loosely used the term *Kabbalah* to denote any kind of Judaic study.)

More still, Ford's Ethiopianism possessed a mental metaphysics. "The philosophy," noted historian Jill Watts in *God, Harlem U.S.A.*

(University of California Press, 1992), ". . . contained an element of mind-power, for many adherents of Ethiopianism subscribed to mental healing and believed that material circumstances could be altered through God's power. Such notions closely paralleled tenets of New Thought . . ."

Ford was also an early supporter of Black-nationalist pioneer Marcus Garvey and served as musical director of Garvey's Universal Negro Improvement Association. Garvey, as documented in my 2009 *Occult America*, suffused his movement with New Thought metaphysics and phraseology.

The commonalities between Ford and Abdullah are striking. Yet too many gaps emerge in Neville's and Ford's backgrounds to allow for a conclusive leap. Records of Ford's life grow thinner after 1931, the year he departed New York and migrated to Ethiopia, where he died in 1935. Ethiopian emperor Haile Selassie, after his coronation in 1930, offered land grants to any African Americans willing to relocate to the East African nation. Ford accepted the offer. The timing of Ford's departure is the biggest single blow to the Abdullah-Ford theory. Neville said he and his teacher had studied together for five years. This obviously would not have been possible with Ford, who had apparently left New York in 1931, the same year Neville said he and Abdullah first met.

Was there a real Abdullah? On this count, an enticing and notable testimony exists.

In the final year of his life, bestselling metaphysical author and minister Joseph Murphy (1898–1981), met in chapter XV, told an interviewer that he studied in the 1930s with the same teacher who tutored his friend and contemporary New Yorker, Neville. It was a turbaned man of black-Jewish descent named Abdullah.

In 1981, Murphy sat for a little-known series of interviews with French-Canadian writer Bernard Cantin, who in 1987 published the French language work *Joseph Murphy se raconte à Bernard Cantin* [*Joseph*

Murphy Speaks to Bernard Cantin]. It has never appeared in English. Murphy described his experience with Abdullah, as recounted by Cantin:

> It was in New York that Joseph Murphy also met the professor Abdullah, a Jewish man of black ancestry, a native of Israel, who knew, in every detail, all the symbolism of each of the verses of the Old and the New Testaments. This meeting was one of the most significant in Dr. Murphy's spiritual evolution. In fact, Abdullah, who had never seen nor known the Murphy family, said flatly that Murphy came from a family of six children, and not five, as Murphy himself had believed. Later on, Murphy, intrigued, questioned his mother and learned that, indeed, he had had another brother who had died a few hours after his birth, and was never spoken of again.

In a letter of June 1987, Murphy's second wife, Jean, told Cantin that his interviews with her husband were the only to have received the metaphysician's approval in the past thirty years.

Although he won audiences on both coasts by his death in 1972, it was difficult to fathom that the Barbadian's voice, persona, and ideas would resonate in future decades. Indeed, the Woodstock Generation displayed little interest in the silver-maned, tailored man who spoke of the promethean power of imagination.

Conflicting accounts exist around Neville's death. The most widely heard is that on October 1, 1972, Neville "collapsed and died of an apparent heart attack" at age sixty-seven in his West Hollywood home, as reported in *The Los Angeles Times* on October 4, 1972.

In actuality, Neville's death certificate from the state of California provides a different record, which squares with an account from one of his intimates, driver and friend Frank Carter, who was the last person to be with the mystic on the night of his death. (Neville's wife was hospitalized at the time.)

Neville's daughter Vicky summoned Carter to the teacher's home to consult with the coroner the morning of October 1 when his body was found. In the coroner's presence, Carter witnessed a massive amount of blood around Neville's corpse and a contorted expression on his face, as though he had choked and bled out.*

According to his death certificate, Neville died of a rupture of the esophageal varices—i.e., swollen or enlarged veins—leading from the throat to stomach with subsequent hemorrhaging, hence the profusion of blood and appearance of choking. The cause was liver damage or cirrhosis. That condition generally results from long-term alcohol abuse.

"The coroner kept asking me what happened," Carter recalled, "he said, 'Was Mr. Goddard a heavy drinker?' and his daughter said, 'Well he used to be, but not lately.'" At a dinner party the night before, Carter recalled, Neville did not even finish a full martini, nor did the men have anything further to drink when he dropped Neville off at home.

Yet Neville often spoke of enjoying alcohol, including a bottle of wine each day with lunch. In a lecture delivered on an unknown day in 1972, he remarked, "I had my full bottle of wine today with some cheese for my lunch, and thoroughly enjoyed a bit of wine and, oh, a section of Edam."

I do not view the teacher, or any artist, in a lesser light for his probable cause of death, and I realize, too, that there exist symbolical or extra-physical interpretations of Neville's passing, some referenced by Carter, which I honor in the outlook of every mature seeker.** Indeed, Neville referred to his own demise occurring, as it did, in

---

* See *Neville Goddard: The Frank Carter Lectures* from Audio Enlightenment, 2018.

** I explore this material further in *Neville Goddard's Final Lectures* (G&D Media, 2022).

his sixties, in a lecture delivered November 21, 1969: "In my own case this little garment seemed to begin in 1905, but it was always so. It was always growing into manhood and departing in its sixties. Always appearing, occupied by God, moving towards a certain point and then disappearing."

Since many readers and listeners describe their experience of discovering Neville's work in catalytic terms, I want to share my own story.

I am often drawn to a teaching based on my perception of its purveyor's character and gravitas. Something about Neville's persona gripped me even before I heard his clipped Anglican accent or glimpsed his Romanesque image. Neville, to me, conveyed personal seriousness intermingled with the most radical proposition I had ever heard: everything is ultimately rooted in *you*, as you are rooted in the infinite.

I initially wrote about Neville in early 2005 in an article for *Science of Mind* magazine. My article "Searching for Neville Goddard" was the first journalistic portrait of the mystic since occult philosopher Israel Regardie profiled him in his 1946 book, *The Romance of Metaphysics*. A colleague teased me at the time: "You only like Neville because he's so obscure and esoteric." Not exactly—but he was then a figure of opaqueness to most New Thoughters.

Just hearing Neville's name filled me with intrigue. In summer 2003, I was interviewing major-league pitcher Barry Zito, who was then playing for the Oakland A's. Barry's tough-talking but idealistic father, Joe, had tutored his son in Neville's work. The Cy Young Award-winner used Neville's method of mental creativity in his training regimen. Pitching for the San Francisco Giants, Barry became the hero of the 2012 World Series.

Neville's teaching that all of reality is self-created—that your mind is God the Creator—then formed a key part of the athlete's system of self-development, which he inherited from both his father, Joe, and mother, Roberta, who led their own metaphysical congregation in San Diego, Teaching of the Inner Christ Church.

Midway through our conversation, Barry paused and said, "You must really be into Neville." I had no idea what he meant. The athlete was incredulous. Immediately following our talk, I sought out Neville's 1966 book *Resurrection*, his last. Upon reading it, I was enthralled— and hooked ever after.

Neville's books were then available only in nondescript editions with plain beige covers. They were issued from a single publisher in Los Angeles, DeVorss & Co. (*At Your Command* was not among them—it recirculated only after Neville's resurgence.) The covers were uniform in design, featuring title, author, and the intriguing insignia of an eye impressed on a heart impressed on a tree. Neville told a Los Angeles audience in 1948: "It is an eye imposed upon a heart which, in turn is imposed upon a tree laden with fruit, meaning that what you are conscious of, and accept as true, you are going to realize. As a man thinketh in his heart, so he is."

The austere editions, more suited to Cato the Elder than a dramatic mystic, inadvertently heightened the mystery around the man. The volumes also opened a generation of readers—me included—to Neville's ideas when virtually no other entry point existed.

A final word about Barry Zito. After my article appeared, his father Joe instilled me with confidence in my writing, still a new endeavor. At my desk at a publishing company one morning, I heard that Joe Zito was on the phone. Knowing Joe's glass-eating reputation, I lifted the receiver nervously. In drill-sergeant tones, the voice on the other end announced: *"Mitch, you stick with this thing."* He meant writing. I followed Joe's exhortation. In a little over three years, I had my first book contract with Random House.

If I had to reduce Neville's method to its barest simplicity I would say that the teacher's approach to life, perhaps imported from his thespian days, is to *always be on stage*. *Feel and occupy* the life you wish to experience; immerse yourself within that life in your mental-emotive self or psyche. Do so through emotive visualization, employed particularly in states of meditation or comfortable drowsiness when the rational defenses of the intellect slacken.

Author and magician Alan Moore has spoken eloquently of the connection between fiction, language, and magic.* Moore has mentioned—and I can affirm—that anyone who's been writing for a while has a file of extraordinary coincidences in which *experience follows story*. Concepts of "make believe" are powerful in ways one may not suspect.

If I have any critique of Neville's *techniques*, it is that I am unsure he realized how difficult it is for an individual to enter and sustain a feeling state contrary to dire circumstances or emotional duress.

Thought alone cannot produce emotion—emotion overpowers thought. Were thought or intention able to control passion, much less physicality, we would have no addictions, untoward outbursts, or depleting attachments. As a trained performer, Neville found it *natural* to summon different emotional states, similar to an accomplished Method Actor. Those abilities are unavailable to most people.

Resolution to this dilemma is private for every seeker. One workaround, which the teacher often referenced and which I suggested earlier, involves using hypnagogia (not his term)—the state of cognizant pre-sleep or drowsy relaxation—to facilitate the feeling process. Hypnagogia naturally occurs twice daily: just as you are drifting to

---

* "Language, Writing and Magic," talk delivered September 6, 2016, YouTube.

and rousing from sleep. It is a period of hallucinatory sentience during which you are nonetheless capable of controlling attention. What's more, your rational barriers are lowered. This may be considered primetime to visualize a desired end. (Hypnagogia is also a period of heightened extrasensory perception (ESP) activity, as recorded in academic psychical research.) This is similar to the methods of French mind theorist Émile Coué (1857–1926), previously met in chapter VIII, whose phraseology shows up in Neville's work.

Hypnagogia is not necessarily limited to sleeping and waking hours. In Neville's telling, he entered this state daily at 3 p.m. following lunch—aided by a full bottle of wine. Neville required no abstemiousness in his system. Whether excessive consumption of alcohol also proved the teacher's undoing is a valid and somber question.

Another way of using Neville's system is to adopt an inner state of theatrical or childlike play. Not childish, child*like:* a state of internal wonder and pretending. Children excel at this. We grow embarrassed by this quality as we age but Neville spoke ingenuously of walking the wintry streets of Manhattan imagining that he was in the treelined, tropical lanes of his native Barbados, boarding a ship to some desired destination, or in a location where he wished to be.

Neville cautioned against rationalizing exactly *how* your wishes will arrive. Again from *At Your Command*:

Your desires contain within themselves the plan of self-expression. So leave all judgments out of the picture and rise in consciousness to the level of your desire and make yourself one with it by claiming it to be so now.

Unfoldment, he wrote, occurs in "ways beyond knowing"—harmonious, natural, and appropriate. In that vein, desires are neither to be feared nor conditioned:

The measurements of right and wrong belong to man alone. To life there is nothing right or wrong . . . Stop asking yourself whether you are worthy or unworthy to receive that which you desire. You, as man, did not create the desire. Your desires are ever fashioned within you because of what you now claim yourself to be.

When a man is hungry (without thinking), he automatically desires food. When imprisoned, he automatically desires freedom and so forth. Your desires contain within themselves the plan of self-expression . . .

The reason most of us fail to realize our desires is because we are constantly conditioning them. Do not condition your desire. Just accept it as it comes to you. Give thanks for it to the point that you are grateful for having already received it—then go about your way in peace . . . But, to be worried or concerned about the HOW of your desire maturing is to hold these fertile seeds in a mental grasp, and, therefore, never to have dropped them in the soil of confidence.

This relates again to an observation by twentieth-century spiritual teacher Jiddu Krishnamurti, which is that when we ask *how* we really don't want something. *How* is avoidance. When the realness of desire exists, without conflict or contradiction, the means appear—albeit sometimes after an interval—as naturally as shooting open an umbrella in the rain. The hungry person desires food—not *thoughts* of food. This must be kept in mind when assuming your feeling state. And finally:

Recognition is the power that conjures in the world. Every state that you have ever recognized, you have embodied. That which you are recognizing as true of yourself today is that which you are experiencing.

Neville's voice, even in his nascent work, summons us, finally, beyond all method, system, or liturgy. Above all, the teacher emphasized the literalness of a truth whispered in nearly every spiritual, therapeutic, and ethical philosophy: *you are as your mind is.*

I had intended to end this chapter on those words. But I am moved to a different conclusion, or at least an after-note, due to a letter I received as I was wrapping this piece of writing. Such communications often arrive propitiously. It came from a reader and seeker, Irfan Tarin, on whose words I close with his permission:

> I am from Afghanistan but living in Toronto since three years. I traveled to west in search to find answers for my questions. I have accidentally got to know about the "Infinite Potential" book of Neville Goddard . . . I don't know how to say, I am so happy after reading this book, and feel a great relief and expansion since I started reading this. Specially the mystical experiences. And the real meaning of scriptures and verses which are same both in Bible and Quran. Like God made man in his own image or all the stories of prophets and messengers and all the book. Which nobody told us the real meaning.

We in the West tend to take the search for granted. The opportunity is all but handed us at birth. Human nature often devalues what is freely given. Consider Irfan's words a gift—a reminder of your freedom to search. Use it.

Chapter XIV

Claude M. Bristol and the Metaphysics of Necessity

The American metaphysical scene has produced no other figure quite like Claude M. Bristol (1890–1951). He did not write as a spiritual visionary or scientist but rather as a journalist and businessman who related to the needs of everyday people—and who discovered a personal metaphysics that he believed could be broadly applied.

Bristol gave full voice to his ideas in his 1948 mind-power classic, *The Magic of Believing*, a book that has never been out of print. Bristol's guide to the actualizing powers of thought won legions of readers, including celebrities from Liberace to Arnold Schwarzenegger. As a writer and seeker on the contemporary metaphysical scene, I encounter a surprising range of people who swear by Bristol's insights.

The Magic of Believing is as much memoir as metaphysical guidebook and it must be understood in connection with the man himself. Bristol's life was at once testament to his ideas—and to their limits.

Bristol was born in Portland, Oregon, on March 8, 1890. He spent most of his career as a journalist, businessman, and lawyer. The author was widely known throughout the West as a crack newspaper and magazine writer. He first learned his craft as a police reporter in Portland. Few forms of training do more to sharpen and prepare you for work as a writer, journalist, or researcher than police reporting.

I also began my career as a police reporter in Northeastern Pennsylvania, so I can identify with Bristol's path. In that atmosphere, you function under tight deadlines in stressful and rarely friendly conditions. You learn to gather facts quickly and produce resolutely clear copy. Or you sink. That's where Bristol's chops as a writer came from.

He was sufficiently recognized as a journalist so that Palmer Hoyt (1897–1979), the widely respected editor-in-chief of *The Denver Post*, wrote the introduction to the first edition of *The Magic of Believing*, an unusual foray for a newspaper man into metaphysics. In what might be considered slightly backhanded praise, Hoyt opened, "Generally speaking, people are more interested in themselves and their success than anything else. For this reason Claude M. Bristol's book, *The Magic of Believing*, ought to enjoy widest readership."

While still a young man, Bristol experienced a downturn in life, which got him on the scent trail of practical metaphysics. In early 1918, he entered military service in World War I. It was the final year of that catastrophic conflict. At twenty-eight, Bristol was on the older side among so-called Doughboys. At the time, American forces were fully engaged and Bristol found himself stationed in France. He went on to write for the Army newspaper *Stars and Stripes*. But early in his mobilization he was a standard grunt hauling around ammunition and supplies in dangerous battlefield conditions. Because of an error in his transfer papers, Bristol was receiving no pay. For weeks he was unable to purchase a stick of gum, cigarette, or candy bar. He experienced an acute sense of longing every time he saw another soldier strike a match or throw away a gum wrapper.

The Army supplied his meals. He had a place to sleep on the ground. But for a long stretch he was penniless. Bristol vowed he would never again find himself in that predicament—that when he returned to the U.S., he would spend the rest of his life in prosperity.

This experience ignited in Bristol the one factor I consider crucial to every program of self-development whether metaphysical, therapeutic, or both. It is having *a passionate, definite, and unshakable aim.* Bristol wished for money, which he writes about plainly in *The Magic of Believing.* Critics could scoff at his aims, but those familiar with affluence and on distant terms with lack rarely understand the aspirations of working and middle-class people, not as idealized but as on-the-ground realities. Indeed, the driving engine of most personal progress is *urgency to repair something.*

"There is a relationship between pain and excellence," a brilliant filmmaker and my partner Jacqueline Castel told me. I honor that. This principle reverberates through Bristol's story. He suffered want— and that drove him toward desire. That desire, in turn, drove him toward his conception of practical metaphysics. When Bristol arrived home, he found various positions in journalism, finance, and eventually law. He came to divide his career across each.

Whatever he was doing, Bristol would sit at his desk and on a pad or pieces of scrap paper, whatever was at hand, he would doodle dollar signs, all day long. He did this when he was on the telephone, in meetings, or contemplating ideas. He was absolutely ignited by this want, this need for money. It never left him. Some might consider it gauche, but his wish mushroomed into a career that was not only multi-faceted but also very remunerative. It included a successful writing career.

I do not mean to leave the impression that Bristol was a one-dimensional self-seeker. "Having served as a soldier in World War I, mostly in France and Germany," he wrote in *The Magic of Believing*, "and having been an active official for many years in ex-service men's organizations as well as a member of a state commission to aid in the rehabilitation of ex-service men and women, I realized that it would be no easy task for many individuals to make outstanding places for themselves in a practical world from which they had long been separated."

Indeed, when Bristol arrived home from war, he encountered a nation in transition. The American economy was growing and the mass of young veterans, many of whom came from agrarian backgrounds and had never worked in manufacturing or large offices, were unsure how to enter the new economy. For his part, Bristol believed that the threshold of prosperity begins in the mind, an idea he determined to spread, first through lectures and later his writing.

Bristol wrote only two books. The first appeared in 1932. It was a self-published, pamphlet-sized work called *T.N.T.: It Rocks the Earth*. *T.N.T.* was a digest of some of his early mind-power philosophy—the idea that what you believe, what you feel, what you think, and your mental pictures concretize in the world around you. The short book was sufficiently successful, as was Bristol as a lecturer and financier, so that the author was able to retire at age forty-two from his Portland investment banking firm. He writes about rescuing the firm using methods from his book. As a writer, "He has met with more than ordinary success," reported *The Sunday Oregonian* on January 1, 1933. "Because of demands made upon him he has decided to devote himself to this work in the future."

It wasn't until 1948, however, that Bristol published *The Magic of Believing*. (It also appeared under the alternate title *Believe and Grow Rich*.) He was then fifty-eight years old and died soon after at age sixty-one of kidney failure on December 14, 1951.* Bristol left most of his estate to the Shriner's Hospital for Crippled Children in Portland.**

The end could only have been profoundly difficult. After nearly twenty years of marriage, Bristol's wife, Edith, a publishing executive, divorced him the prior year.*** The childless couple had a painful and public separation. In "Claude Bristol, 'Magic' Author, Sued by Spouse," the *Oregon Daily Journal* reported on September 22, 1950, that Edith "charged the prominent Portland author with cruel and inhumane treatment, claiming he used abusive language, was jealous of her and her friends and has an overbearing disposition."

A December 16 obituary by the Associated Press noted only that the author passed in a Portland hospital "after a long illness," remarking dryly, "'Magic of Believing' is a non-fiction book that says generally that a person can change the events of his everyday life by holding what Mr. Bristol termed the proper thoughts."

I spent a large part of my career in spiritual publishing. At one point, it occurred to me that a majority of the successful books I published— works that not only found their way upon launch but also seemed bound for posterity—were written by people in middle age or beyond. Bristol fit that pattern. Personally, I did not publish my first book, *Occult America,* until I was forty-three. Hence, I encourage people not to feel daunted by conventional timelines. We experience physical limitations, as Bristol markedly did. We experience limitations in geography, income, and background. But I like to remind readers

* "Bristol Services," *Oregon Daily Journal*, December 18, 1951.

** "Author Leaves Hospital Fund," *Oregon Daily Journal*, December 19, 1951.

*** "Long Illness Takes Author," *Portland Oregonian*, December 16, 1951.

that the man who produced one of the most enduring and widely read books of practical metaphysics of the twentieth century did not publish it until he was fifty-eight and in declining health.

That's among the reasons Bristol's book spoke to its audience—it grew from lived experience. As seen in his life, such experience can also be marked by pain and failure. We must view inspirational writers and speakers as three-dimensional beings, not stick figures. Neither life's joys nor tragedies are exclusive of each other. I often note, whatever the ultimate nature of reality, we do not experience life from the mechanics of one mental super law—we dwell under a complexity of laws and forces, some of which can prove overwhelmingly countervailing. Yet I likewise believe that we must honor any author for his or her best work. *The Magic of Believing* was Bristol's. As will be explored, I think his metaphysics have a place in the lives of striving people.

I noted that Bristol had good writerly training.* Many people say they want to write and wonder how to get started. (Wanting to get published is different from wanting to write—don't confuse the two.) I always say begin, like Bristol, with the basics of journalism. Learn how to write a lead paragraph. Learn the five W's: who, what, when, where, and why. Learn the basics of old-time wire-service writing. Do this and you will have a foundation that rarely fails you. This was Bristol's approach in all things, from journalism to metaphysics.

Whatever the pain of his personal life, Bristol's *Magic of Believing*, published by Prentice Hall in May 1948, proved an immediate suc-

---

* Not so good that the former newspaper man didn't sometimes mishandle facts. In a humorous barb, the *Oregon Daily Journal* reported on May 1, 1944, that when Bristol became campaign manager to Republican Joe Dunne in his Portland mayoral race: "In his announcement Bristol reviewed his accomplishments in the newspaper field, as an author, a member of the American Legion and a business executive, touched upon the legislative and public record of former [State] Senator Dunne but overlooked telling where the campaign headquarters are to be established." Dunne lost the Republican primary to incumbent Earl Riley.

cess. It went through four printings in its first year of publication and entered thirteen more printings in the following three years. By the author's death, an impressive 150,000 copies were in print.

Some celebrities of the era vowed that Bristol's book launched them on their path. Comedian Phyllis Diller (1917–2012) was a vocal fan of *The Magic of Believing*. The brashly funny performer said she suffered from crushing shyness until she discovered Bristol's guide. She recommended it throughout her life and often spoke of it in interviews.

Pianist Liberace (1919–1987) was a particular admirer of *The Magic of Believing*. In fact, in his memoir the performer recalled initially exposing his friend Diller to the book.* Liberace's biographer, Darden Asbury Pyron, said the entertainer considered it a "semi-sacred text," further noting: "he seems to have discovered the book at a critical juncture—the mid-fifties—when he was losing his grip on his career and even on his life."**

What Liberace found sufficiently impressed him so that in 1955 there appeared a "Special Liberace Edition" of *The Magic of Believing*, which featured his short introduction, image on the cover, and "seventeen photos of the maestro and his family." The following year, the flamboyant entertainer recorded a song in tribute called "The Magic of Believing," apparently in a promotional agreement.

"My attitude," Liberace said of his career, "is that nothing is impossible, it just takes a little longer."

In 2010, blogger Mike Cane ventured an interesting observation:

Now this *has* to make you wonder, especially if you grew up in the early 1960s and were exposed to Liberace and Phyllis Diller in their TV heyday. I don't think there were two more "out there" perform-

---

* *Liberace: An Autobiography* (Putnam, 1973).

** *Liberace: An American Boy* (The University of Chicago Press, 2000).

ers at the time than them. Liberace was flamboyantly effeminate during a time of widespread fear of homosexuality. Phyllis Diller never had a face for TV and had a voice that could scratch records. Yet both of them got *where they both wanted to be,* and they credited Bristol's book for that.*

Bristol's two books sat in Marilyn Monroe's library. Arnold Schwarzenegger has spoken glowingly of *The Magic of Believing.* George Noory, the host of Coast to Coast AM, credits the book with setting his career in motion. I have personally received dozens of emails from people ranging from artists to salesmen who have called *The Magic of Believing* a turning point in their lives. Such testimony might be easily discounted but it gives a sense of the depth of dedication that Bristol's work commands.

In that vein, I want to offer a true story that personally reached me. I provide this account not with an implication that something similar is going to happen to the book's readers but rather with the simple, basic promise that every word I am about to relate is true as I heard it.

One evening several years ago, I went on social media and posted a picture of my 1948 vintage edition of *The Magic of Believing,* which is signed by Bristol. Along with the image, I issued a challenge: "Let's try to approach this book with what in Zen Buddhism is called 'beginner's mind'."

I continued: "Let's imagine that it's 1948 and *The Magic of Believing* has just rolled off the presses. We are all holding first editions in our hands. Let's stay up into the night together and read this book."

---

* "Mike Cane's xBlog," December 17, 2010.

I believe that a pooling of inner resources naturally arises from group activities, such as when marathon runners up each other's pace. On the intellectual-emotive scale, unified group activities tend to heighten morale and focus. So, I issued this challenge and wrote, "Sit in a chair with me up late into the night and let's approach these ideas as though for the very first time."

When I posted this challenge, it caught the eye of a friend living in New England. He was recovering from a severe and longstanding illness. While recuperating, my friend had fallen into a desperate financial crisis. He had been unable to work. He was down to $102 in the bank. He had no health insurance, no source of income, and no immediate prospects.

He told himself, "I have nothing to lose. I may as well take up this challenge." He happened to own an audio edition of *The Magic of Believing*, which I had narrated. He played this audio edition over and over. It became his constant companion for about a week. He sometimes listened for hours at a stretch. A few days into this, he received a call from a former boss. While they were catching up, his ex-boss said, "By the way, you really ought to look at your old 401k." My friend had maintained such an account but not rolled it over when he left his job.

He sighed and replied, "Oh that—what's the big deal?" He thought there was just a few dollars in it. His ex-boss told him, "No, really, I'm being serious with you. You've got to check your 401k." The former employer said that more than $50,000 was sitting dormant in the account. My friend had no idea he had accumulated so much money. He was recovering from a debilitating illness, so his eye wasn't on finances as it would have been at another time in life. This call arrived a few days into his marathon listen of *The Magic of Believing*. Was it coincidence? Perhaps. Was he wishfully projecting a pattern onto something? Could be. Was it a miracle? Well, the news reached him in a fashion that emotionally felt miraculous.

Again, I am not suggesting that *The Magic of Believing* is going to produce some marvel in your life. But let me offer a possibility—and it is something that Bristol certainly believed himself.

I take seriously the contention that there are extra-physical dimensions to thought. There exists too much evidence to write off that prospect.* In fact, we possess so much replicated evidence of there being some extra-physical, non-local capacity to the mind—much of it derived from laboratory experiments across fields including medicine, physics, and academic psychical research—that materialist philosophy simply doesn't cover all the bases of life. The idea that matter alone creates itself and that your mind is just a byproduct of the physical organ of your brain no longer works in the twenty-first century.

Academic psychical researchers venture that when your mind is profoundly and deeply focused on something, you may be directing some kind of communication to other people capable of helping you or meeting you halfway. Bristol goes further with that question. He reasons that the mind possesses vibrational or frequency-like signals that can result not only in telepathy but in psychokinesis.

I consider Bristol's language metaphorical since we're always dealing in imagery when attempting to understand or apply something that we as a human community haven't fully grasped. But I must also add that Bristol's supposition is not as far out as it may sound.

Twentieth-century parapsychologist J.B. Rhine (1895–1980), whose research Bristol often notes, conducted ESP experiments for years at Duke University. Under rigorously controlled laboratory conditions, Rhine found that certain subjects proved capable of transmitting infor-

---

* E.g., see my "Parapsychology: Evidence & Resources for the 'Elusive Science'," Medium, March 24, 2023.

mation in an anomalous manner unaffected by time, space, or mass, extending to the psychokinetic ability of affecting throws of dice.*

Twenty-first-century psychical researchers at Princeton University found that certain subjects were able to affect the pattern of numbers appearing on a device called a random number generator, which emits infinite combinations of random numerals. Through intention, subjects created instances of symmetry where none should have appeared. The researchers' ongoing Global Consciousness Project has documented that during periods of worldwide emotional intensity, such as the terrorist attacks of 9/11, random number generators placed in select locations around the world demonstrate inexplicable patterns, or interruptions in randomness.**

Following a decade of study, Cornell University research psychologist Daryl J. Bem published a 2011 paper reporting the results of his series of experiments into precognition. In brief, Bem found that test subjects who memorized a word list scored higher in recall by repeating their study of the list following the test. Bem's data, like Rhine's, has since proved confirmatory in replicated experiments and meta-analysis.***

Although I am describing these experiments in necessarily abbreviated form, they have been subject to greater scrutiny than most trials to test the effectiveness of popular pharmaceuticals. I direct interested readers to a comprehensive analysis of psychical research and its replications that appeared in the flagship journal of the American Psychological Association: "The Experimental Evidence for Parapsy-

---

* I consider Rhine's record, and the replication of his work, in my article "The Enduring Legacy of Parapsychologist J.B. Rhine," Medium, October 10, 2022. Also see my book *Daydream Believer* (2022).

** For a summary of the Global Consciousness Project, see: "Terrorist Disaster, September 11, 2001;" "Formal Results: Testing the GCP Hypothesis;" and "Global Consciousness Project Brief Overview" at noosphere.princeton.edu.

*** "Feeling the Future: Experimental Evidence for Anomalous Retroactive Influences on Cognition and Affect" by Daryl J. Bem, *Journal of Personality and Social Psychology*, 2011, Vol. 100, No3. For further consideration of Bem's work and its replication, see my article "Is Precognition Real?", Medium, February 21, 2023.

chological Phenomena: A Review" by Etzel Cardeña, *American Psychologist* (2018, Vol. 73). I also provide a user-friendly summary in my previously noted piece, "Parapsychology: Evidence & Resources for the 'Elusive Science'" at Medium.

For these reasons, I honor Bristol's instinct that emotively charged and focused thought may be communicated, at least intermittently, in some extra-physical manner. Perhaps this occurred for my friend when his ex-boss reached out to him at the most desperate moment of his life to share news of an investment account with $50,000.

Skeptics insist that our brains are designed to impose patterns on things. That is true. But skeptics rarely apply this logic to themselves. Their immediate impulse is to rationalize anomalies according to diagnostic or logical categories they find familiar. But events like the one I just described are difficult to quantify.

This is due to the complexity of emotions involved. Seen from one perspective, a remarkable web of events exists at the back of virtually *everything* that happens to you, whether seemingly exceptional or mundane. But factors of emotional impact, timing, and profundity of need are highly individualized, making anomalous experiences difficult to quantify, reify, or measure. Not everything in life can be broken down on an actuarial table.

Recall Bristol's dollar doodling. I've often noted the importance of understanding what you truly want in life—of having a definite, absolute aim. I suggest that people write out their aim, not on a handheld device, tablet, or laptop; but in a tactile way with a pen or pencil and paper.

I believe that when you write down a wish, the very act of rendering it in a physical manner is a first step, however nascent, toward some means of actualization. Think of it: when you produce something on paper, you not only have a vow and contract, you not only have a clarified and committed purpose, but your act has, in however infinitesimal a way, altered reality or your experience of it. The writing on that paper has created something that was not previously present. This is the basis of sigil-making in chaos magic, which, like chaos theory, holds that observed events pivot on seemingly tiny or unseen complexities. Always regard first steps, however small, seriously.

Bristol spent his workdays constantly reinforcing what he wanted. Simple enough. But we are not always capable of acknowledging what we want. When you consider your aim be sure that you are being inwardly honest and not curbed by some sense of embarrassment, shame, or internalized peer pressure.

We all want to look good in the eyes of others. We want to be appreciated and admired. Yet we often harbor handed-down or customary ideas of how to achieve that. In many cases, these ideas are no more than decisions made by someone else, often in the distant past.

One of the mental traps that limits creativity and sense of self is the habit of *rote thought*, even in our most private ponderings. The things we tell ourselves over the course of life—*I want to be of service; I want a relationship; I want to be a leader in my field*—become so familiar that we eventually fail to question or verify them. Are our resolutions sincere—or habitual?

Never obfuscate what you want. That doesn't mean a desire is always wise or actionable. But it must at least be acknowledged. Truth liberates.

Bristol, in his way, made large questions about the psyche appear simple—because he believed that meaningful personal experiments *are* possible, and could demonstrate, or at least suggest, the efficacy of positive-mind mechanics in daily life, including in matters of career, creativity, and relationships.

His simplicity proved infectious. In addition to the accolades I've mentioned, *The Magic of Believing* was such a post-war favorite that Prentice Hall issued an illustrated *Magic of Believing for Young People* in 1957. The young readers' edition failed to catch on, however. At more than 200 pages, it was almost the length of the original and no simpler. But it is the kind of publishing effort I admire. Despite the enduring popularity of New Thought or mind-metaphysics literature, few editions are geared toward adolescents who might benefit from the types of self-query and experimentation that the best of such books encourage. In 1954, the publisher also issued a posthumously expanded version of *T.N.T.*, which proved more lasting.

Although Bristol's language is sometimes dated and his tone credulous, *The Magic of Believing* remains a surprising and radical journey into the possibilities of determined thought. We are still at the early stages of grappling with some of his topics, gaining a glimpse of anomalous mental capacities in a new generation of experiments in the placebo response, neuroplasticity, precognition, and perceptual theory.

Hence, as I did that day on social media, I suggest approaching *The Magic of Believing* in a spirit of enthusiasm and personal adventure. It's an old favorite that provides an unembarrassed invitation to intimately probe questions of mental-emotive causality—and the book may ignite in you a renewed sense of personal possibility.

Are we too cynical today to try?

Chapter XV

The Revelation of Joseph Murphy

etaphysical writer and minister Joseph Murphy (1898–1981) encouraged his readers and listeners to live by an entirely different scale of values.

Most of us born in the West grew up with the notion—almost wholly untested—that mood and outlook result from personal circumstance. Emotions are symptoms. Murphy's work, particularly his widely impactful 1963 bestseller, *The Power of Your Subconscious Mind*, upends that view of life.

Across thousands of lectures and dozens of books and pamphlets, Murphy described and documented a radically different and more self-determinative way of living. Mood, thought, and mental image, he taught, are *causes* rather than symptoms. Murphy considered this true in the most literal and universal sense.

More so, the metaphysician reasoned, the individual is an expression and channel of the deific creative powers referenced in Scripture. Hence, you are, at this moment and all moments, constructing your world through your emotive mental images.

Beginning with his first book *This Is It* in 1945, the Irish minister combined principles of psychology, self-suggestion, and a cosmological theology, which he had been developing and testing for many years.

It is notable that Murphy did not step out as a writer until age forty-seven. (As noted, I experienced a similar trajectory in my own writing career.) The seeker-mystic first sought to validate his ideas in the laboratory of personal experience. There are, of course, manifold perils of personal bias toward a favored thesis.* But to restrict self-knowledge to credentialed study is to deny the impulse itself.

Once Murphy found his footing as a writer and speaker, his output was prodigious. His original books (not counting myriad anthologies and reissues) surpass forty.

Equally remarkable—and a lesson in itself—is that Murphy did not produce the work that made him famous, *The Power of Your Subconscious Mind*, until age sixty-five. His career is a reminder not to view traditional milestones of age as nonnegotiable.

Since Murphy's death in 1981, the size of his readership—measured by reprints, multiple editions, digital and audio volumes, translations, and anthologies—has dramatically grown.

Part of the reason for Murphy's posterity is that he adventurously and, for many seekers, convincingly married twentieth-century psychology with the New Metaphysics, specifically New Thought, Science of Mind, Unity, Christian Science, and Divine Science.

---

* For a useful digest, see "What Is Cognitive Bias?" by Kassiani Nikolopoulou, Scribbr.com, November 11, 2022. revised October 9, 2023.

In so doing, the author gave generations of readers a dramatic new sense of self-potential. Interestingly, Murphy himself "requested that no funeral be held and that no obituary be written," according to scholar of religion J. Gordon Melton in *Religious Leaders of America* (The Gale Group, 1999).

Murphy accepted the traditional premise that we possess two minds: the rational, analytic mind called the conscious; and the inner, emotional mind called the subconscious, or what may be termed the psyche.

The subconscious is generally agreed to be the driving engine of experience—it is the hidden influence that shapes and reinforces your attitudes, affinities, perceptions, self-image, and relational patterns. But Murphy went further. He reasoned that the subconscious is *programed* by the conscious to function as a tool of causation: what we view and accept as valid or perceptually justified—whether sound or desirable—is acted upon and out-pictured by your subconscious in a complexity of ways.

Hence, Murphy reasoned that the *mission* of your conscious mind, aside from navigating circumstance, is to protect your subconscious from receiving impressions that misdirect its life-shaping energies. You must consciously filter out or temper suggestions that you do not want your psyche to uncritically accept and act on.

The stakes of this transaction are daunting. The subconscious, Murphy reasoned, mediates between individual experience and the existence of an Infinite Mind, which courses through each of us like inlets of a vast ocean. Seen differently, the subconscious or psyche is the medium through which Infinite Mind, or what is called God in Scripture and *Nous* in Hermeticism, creates and actualizes.

This view is largely at home in New Thought. It differs somewhat from Christian Science insofar as Christian Science theology sees the human mind not as a mediator between the individual and the Higher but as an illusion—sometimes called "mortal" or "material" mind, which must be allowed to dissolve like a mirage so that the one Higher Mind can shine through.

In effect, however, Murphy's philosophy agrees with Christian Science and the related metaphysical schools: materialism is ultimately a delusion and the one true reality is the fullness and unsurpassed peace of the Higher Mind. In this sense, Murphy endeavored to harmonize the New Metaphysics, biblical revelation, religious symbolism, and modern psychology.

Whether by intent or happenstance, in no book did Murphy succeed more fully than *The Power of Your Subconscious Mind*, which combined self-suggestion, historical and anecdotal portraits, psychological insights, and the cosmic theology Murphy had been developing and testing since he began his career as a metaphysical philosopher almost twenty years earlier.

Murphy produced many potent essays, sermons, and books, but this one was his culminating and most powerful statement. It is one of the two or three modern landmarks of creative-mind philosophy, perched in timing and influence between Norman Vincent Peale's 1952 *The Power of Positive Thinking* and Rhonda Byrne's 2006 *The Secret*.

Unlike those books, however, which might be found in homes with few other works of popular metaphysics, *The Power of Your Subconscious Mind*, as with Murphy's other writings, brought him a following among readers who, like the minister himself, were not casual toe-dippers but lifelong seekers.

Murphy was born on May 20, 1898, to a devout Catholic family on the Southern Coast of Ireland in Ballydehob, County Cork. He was the fourth of five children, three girls and two boys.

Murphy's father worked as headmaster of a local boys high school. His parents urged him to join the priesthood. But the young seminarian found religious doctrine and catechism too limiting. Eager to gaze more deeply into the internal mechanics of life, he left his Jesuit seminary to dedicate his energies to chemistry, which he studied in Dublin both before and following his religious training.

In the early 1920s, married yet still searching for his place in the world of career and commerce, Murphy relocated to America to seek employment as a chemist and druggist. After running a pharmacy counter at New York's Algonquin Hotel, Murphy renewed his study of mystical and metaphysical ideas.

He read works of Taoism, Confucianism, Transcendentalism, Buddhism, Scripture—and, most fatefully, New Thought. The seeker grew enamored of the New Metaphysics sweeping the Western world. The causative power of thought, Murphy came to believe, revealed the authentic meaning of the world's religions, the deeper mechanics of psychology, and the eternal laws of life.

In reaching his matured spiritual outlook, Murphy told an interviewer, as seen in chapter XIII, that he studied in the 1930s with the teacher who tutored his contemporary New Yorker and friend, mystic Neville Goddard.

Following the period of tutelage he described to Neville's Abdullah, Murphy in the late-1930s began his climb as a minister and writer, soon lecturing over radio and speaking on both coasts. He wrote prolifically on the autosuggestive and causative faculties of thought—and finally, at sixty-five, reached a worldwide audience in 1963 with *The Power of Your Subconscious Mind*, which went on to sell millions of copies and has remained one of the most enduring books on mind-power metaphysics.

The Power of Your Subconscious Mind boasts an unusual range of admirers, including actors Victoria Principal and David Hasselhoff.* (Murphy's 1953 book, *The Miracles of Your Mind*, sat in Marilyn Monroe's library.**) Parents have told me that they raise their children on the methods and ideas explored in *The Power of Your Subconscious Mind*. I've heard from committed spiritual seekers who report that this popular how-to has proven one of the deepest influences in their search. The success and longevity of Murphy's landmark rests, in part, on how it affirms and organizes some of our deepest instincts about the radical possibilities of thought and marries a range of psychological and spiritual suppositions. Among Murphy's key ideas:

1. Every religious, psychological, and ethical philosophy agrees: *What you think dramatically affects your quality of life.*
2. Your subconscious mind harbors insightful and creative power— if properly harnessed, this suggestive power can solve problems and shape circumstances in ways that you never considered possible.
3. The power of your mind is *indifferent*: Your subconscious picks up on and carries out what you dwell upon, for good or ill.
4. You can tap the power of your subconscious by setting aside time just before going to sleep at night to reflect on a cherished aim or the solution to a problem. Drift off with assurance that your subconscious is working on it.

---

* *Don't Hassel the Hoff: The Autobiography* by David Hasselhoff (Thomas Dunne Books, 2007).

** See: https://themarilynmonroecollection.com/marilyn-monroe-owned-book-the-miracles-of-your-mind/

5. Form vivid, believable, emotionally charged mental pictures—*and stick with them*. Consistency is key in training your subconscious.

6. Never *force* a mental image. Forced effort brings failure. Be relaxed, calm, and confident when impressing your subconscious. If you find this difficult, step away and return to it when you're in a calm and confident state.

7. Once you have acted to impress your subconscious, do not dwell on the ways and means of accomplishment—these will reach your conscious mind in the form of hunches, happy accidents, and breakthrough ideas.

8. Neither disdain nor worship money. Understand money as a natural, healthful part of life. Your subconscious will act gainfully on that belief.

9. Specialize in work you love and strive to know as much as possible about it. *Passion and focus* act powerfully upon your subconscious.

10. Your subconscious is not to be trifled with. Scrutinize your desires regularly to ensure that they are ethically sound and for the presumed benefit of all concerned.

In sum, Murphy taught that if you want to make one definite and gainful investment in your future, learn how to cultivate an affirming, meditative, and flexible pattern of thought, informed by the principle that *thoughts are destiny*.

I admire Murphy's scruples, life journey, and efforts. But I do not mean to leave the impression of total comfort with his ideas.

I believe that Murphy, like most of his New Thought contemporaries, failed to come to terms with global or individual suffering, much less develop a persuasive or mature spiritual response to calamity, other than to reassert the therapeutic primacy of the psyche, or what might be deemed the "try again" response.

Indeed, when confronted with questions of evil and chronic suffering, New Thought writers, Murphy included, tended to slip into circular reasoning or contradiction, unable to fully account for tragedy and limitation in their model of a self-created world.

Murphy fitfully sought to contend with this problem in his 1954 book, *The Meaning of Reincarnation*. In it, he blamed the thought patterns of parents for an offspring's illness or disability. Murphy later moved away from that indefensible proposition to suggest that the pooled thoughts of *all* humanity, extending to antiquity, could be the responsible factor in incomprehensible suffering.

The minister further attempted to confront the question of tragedy in his 1971 book, *Psychic Perception*, where he described the individual as subject to thoughts of a "world mind" or "race mind," which contained the substance of every thought—good or ill, nourishing or withering—that every individual had ever conceived. Hence, as he saw it, an infant born ill could be a victim of this "world mind."

Yet to assume, as Murphy wrote, that *every* thought has a timeless ripple effect—so that a person could be impacted by something randomly conceived centuries or millennia earlier—places us at the mercy of a near-infinitude of influences and outcomes. This amounts to tacit acknowledgment of randomness or accident—*the very things Murphy argued do not exist.*

Today, some New Thought writers and seekers attempt to ascribe natural disasters, wars, pandemics, and famines to mass or personal karma. I do not believe that the law of karma or some ersatz version of it—the concept itself is forebodingly vast and varied within traditional Vedic moorings—is intended to flatten complexity. Karma is not putty to plug ontological gaps.

Indeed, on the spiritual path, we measure verities through intimate experience. If a person hasn't been through global calamities that is reason enough not to attempt judgment. Judging the suffering of another is tantamount to throwing a stone rather than gleaning a truth.

I believe that in our known sphere we experience many laws and forces; the law of mind, I warrant, is ever operative but is impacted by other experiences in our physical framework, just as gravity is impacted by mass. I wish it was a subject area where Murphy had gone further.

To his credit, I believe that certain of his insights coalesce with traditional Vedic ideas about reincarnation, especially when he describes all of humanity emerging from and returning to original thought substance. In this regard, Murphy's outlook on reincarnation runs closely to that of occult explorer Madame H.P. Blavatsky (1831–1891).

How then to regard Murphy? One of the maladies of modern intellectual culture is, I believe, prevalence of an "all or nothing" attitude, in which we are expected to either wholly accept or reject every aspect of a writer's outlook. That would leave the search impoverished and monochromatic (which, for many people, it is).

The thrill of reading Murphy is that, questions and dissents aside—and such things ought to populate every mature seeker's experience—he exudes the *practical joy* of possibilities of expansive thought, of perceptual basis of experience (in which I firmly believe), and of protean aspects of idealistic philosophy.

On these topics, the alternative spiritual culture has produced few better writers—and perhaps no greater or more impactful work than *The Power of Your Subconscious Mind*.

Chapter XVI

America's Positive Thinker: Norman Vincent Peale

t was the ultimate insult. In the early 1960s, the editors of the radical literary quarterly *Dissent* hosted a small conference in New York City with bestselling therapist Erich Fromm to discuss the Frankfurt School philosopher's new manifesto of "ethical Socialism." At one point, socialist icon and presidential candidate Norman Thomas, "sharp-witted in his age," recalled editor Irving Howe, exclaimed to the author, "Erich, it's a nice piece of writing and I don't disagree with a word, but you know, to me it reads like a sermon by Norman Vincent Peale!"*

Red with anger, the analyst stalked out.

Thomas's barbed appraisal reflected a widely held attitude among intelligentsia—enduring to this day—that the Reverend Norman Vincent Peale (1898–1993), author of the 1952 landmark *The Power of Positive Thinking*, was an apostle of fluff. Comparisons to Peale were a scarlet letter of unseriousness.

---

* *A Margin of Hope: An Intellectual Autobiography* by Irving Howe (Harcourt, Brace, 1982).

Yet the Dutch Reformed minister and mega-selling author, whose book is now more than seventy years old, has outlasted in readership nearly all of his contemporaries who promulgated a message of therapeutic practicality, including Fromm and once-popular religious writers Rabbi Joshua Loth Liebman and Bishop Fulton J. Sheen.

Indeed, Peale's postwar volume, on its publication spending a then-unprecedented ninety-eight weeks at number one on the *New York Times* bestseller list, still hits top positions on the *Publishers Weekly* list of religion bestsellers. Recent to this writing, publisher Simon & Schuster rereleased several of Peale's titles.

Yet the man who lodged the term "positive thinking" into the American psyche was pained by his lack of acceptance among lettered peers. In actuality, Peale was a widely read attendee of Boston University's School of Theology who headed one of America's oldest pulpits at Marble Collegiate Church on New York's Fifth Avenue from which he collaborated with Freudian analyst Smiley Blanton in opening the innovative Religio-Psychiatric Clinic in 1937.

Agonizing over whether his bestselling message of winning personableness had detracted from his theological gravitas, Peale wrote that his father, also a minister, set him straight:

> Norman, I have read and studied all your books and sermons and it is clearly evident that you have gradually evolved a new religious system of thought and teaching. And it's O.K., too, very O.K., because its center and circumference and essence is Jesus Christ. There is no doubt about its solid Biblical orientation. Yes, you have evolved a new Christian emphasis out of a composite of Science of Mind, metaphysics, Christian Science, medical and psychological practice, Baptist evangelism, Methodist witnessing and solid Dutch Reformed Calvinism.*

---

* *The Tough-Minded Optimist* by Norman Vincent Peale (Simon & Schuster, 1961).

But Peale, it seemed, was his own worst enemy. Contrary to his ebullient public persona, Peale never stood aloof from partisan politics. Indeed, he had a history of coarse political statements. In 1934, he warned congregants that "a sinister shadow is being thrown upon our liberties," a thinly veiled reference to the New Deal.* In 1952, he supported an archconservative movement to draft General Douglas MacArthur to run for president. In 1956, Peale used his pulpit to criticize Democratic presidential candidate Adlai Stevenson for being divorced, leading to Stevenson's famous quip, "I find Saint Paul appealing and Saint Peale appalling."

But it was in the fall of 1960 that Peale ignited a true storm of controversy. During the Nixon-Kennedy campaign—Nixon was a congregant and confidant—Peale publicly aligned with a group of conservative Protestant ministers who opposed the candidacy of John F. Kennedy on grounds that Kennedy, a Roman Catholic, would ultimately prove loyal to the pope. The benignly named Citizens for Religious Freedom announced: "It is inconceivable that a Roman Catholic president would not be under extreme pressure by the hierarchy of his church to accede to its policies . . ."** Conspiracists feared that the young senator was, in effect, a Vatican "Manchurian Candidate."

A flood of negative coverage led to calls for Peale's resignation from his pulpit, and several newspapers dropped his syndicated column. Peale succeeded in convincing his parishioners that he had simply wandered, Forrest Gump–style, into a situation of which he had no foreknowledge. Speaking from his Marble Collegiate pulpit, Peale said of his decision to join the group: "I never been too bright, any-

---

* *God's Salesman: Norman Vincent Peale and the Power of Positive Thinking* by Carol V.R. George (Oxford University Press, 1993).

** "Protestant Groups' Statements," *New York Times*, September 8, 1960.

how."* The line elicited sympathetic laughter from the pews. Within Marble Collegiate, the rift was healed.

But a darker Peale reemerged in private. In a 1960 letter to a female supporter, Peale wrote: "I don't care a bit who of the candidates is chosen except that he be an American who takes orders from no one but the American people."** He went on to ask her how a "dedicated Protestant as yourself could so enthusiastically favor an Irish Catholic for President of our country which was founded by Calvinistic Christians?" Upon Kennedy's victory, Peale despondently wrote friends: "Protestant America got its death blow on November 8th."

To Peale's critics, the minister's attack-and-deny tactics on Kennedy were no surprise. Detractors saw him as a smiley-faced cipher—a propagator of happiness with no ethical core. Indeed, it must be acknowledged that Peale's philosophy of positivity and self-worth was incapable of meeting life in all of its difficulties and tragedies. His outlook did not include a theology of suffering. Peale seemed incapable of persuading readers, as his avowed literary heroes Ralph Waldo Emerson and William James once did, that the individual facing illness, tragedy, and death could find dignity and purpose only by seeing himself as part of the cycles of creation, in which loss plays an inevitable part.

It must also be said, however, that if those intellectuals who rolled their eyes at Peale's gospel of affirmation had taken the care to read his books, they would have discovered serviceable ideas. Peale's outlook could ford a river—his advice could prevent a marriage from crumbling when an unspeakable criticism, of the kind that can never be rescinded, was uttered in the heat of argument. Peale's integration of psychology into church life dramatically lessened the post-war stigma of seeing a therapist. Indeed, Peale was the best-known clergyman to

---

* "Minister Backed by Congregation" by Homer Bigart, *New York Times*, September 19, 1960.

** For Peale's letters here and immediately following see George (1993).

embrace psychotherapy—the literature from his Religio-Psychiatric Clinic described the "sacredness of human personality." Peale encouraged the faith traditions to stretch and grow in order to stay relevant. In 1936, four years after taking his pulpit at Marble Collegiate, he privately wrote a congregant in a letter shared with me: "As time passes men's ideas change; their knowledge is enlarged; and before long a creed leaves much to be said and says some things that are no longer tenable."

Peale possessed spiritual depth—but "the world did not see that depth," his successor the Reverend Arthur Caliandro (1933–2013) recalled to me when I was writing *One Simple Idea*. Still, supporters and critics alike harbored questions about Peale's theology and his innermost judgment. The minister was most at home among business elites and corporate climbers. Caliandro remembered an elderly Peale's attraction to Donald Trump upon first seeing the real-estate magnate on television. Peale was always "very impressed with successful people" and self-promoters, Caliandro recalled. "That was a weakness."

Indeed, among the movers and shakers who filled Peale's pews were the family of an adolescent Trump. The influence stuck. "I still remember [Peale's] sermons," candidate Trump told the Iowa Family Leadership Summit in 2015. "You could listen to him all day long. And when you left the church, you were disappointed it was over. He was the greatest guy."* *The Power of Positive Thinking* is among the few books to which the ex-president alludes.

Did Peale create a philosophy that elevates self-belief above ethics, as alarmingly seen in Trump's fantasies of stolen elections? Is that, finally, the key to his book's endurance?

The chief criticism of Peale's work arose from his principle that self-assurance brings accomplishment. Critiquing the modern urge

---

* "How Norman Vincent Peale Taught Donald Trump to Worship Himself" by Gwenda Blair, Politico Magazine, October 6, 2015.

to self-belief, philosopher George Santayana (1863–1952) noted, "Assurance is contemptible and fatal unless it is self-knowledge."* The philosopher highlighted a contradiction in Peale's approach—which is that blindly self-confident people, rather than accurately assessing their strengths and achieving their ends, are often dangerously delusive.

Yet the part of the equation that Santayana and other critics missed is that Peale didn't promulgate a conceited idealism to the exclusion of self-questioning, a lesson Trump typically blew past. In a facet of the minister's positive-thinking approach, only by a coordinated effort of thought could an individual begin to grasp or question what he actually wants from life and who he really is. The Protestant minister's outlook proved electrifying and freeing to millions of readers raised on religion as a punitive institution. Peale's core message, recalled Caliandro, was, "Not only can you be forgiven, but you could achieve, you could accomplish."

Today, Peale's message has inspired a wide range of therapeutic evangelical voices, including Joel Osteen, one of the few evangelical leaders who acknowledges him as an influence and has appeared on the cover of the ongoing monthly Peale founded, *Guideposts*.** Other evangelists publicly keep their distance, leery of Peale's integration of mystical themes with Bible-based Christianity. In *The Power of Positive Thinking*, Peale adopted some of the affirmative-mind movement's key concepts, including "Law of Attraction," "in tune with the infinite," and the efficacy of magnetic "prayer power."

In the end, *The Power of Positive Thinking* endures because it extols the possibilities of the individual in a manner that sits comfortably with both the church-going public and alternative or New Age seekers. Whatever one makes of Peale's message, or its fallout, the minister

---

* *Character and Opinion in the United States: With Reminiscences of William James and Josiah Royce* by George Santayana, vol. 11 of *The Works of George Santayana* (Scribner's, 1920).

** E.g., see *Guideposts*, April 2012.

is among the few figures who bridged that divide and other cultural redlines. Indeed, today in the hallways of Harlem's A. Philip Randolph Campus High School, a student-painted mural, adjacent to projects on mass incarceration, quotes Peale: "Change your thoughts and you change your world."

Chapter XVII

The Strangest Secret of Earl Nightingale

The emergence of business motivation as an electronic medium—first on vinyl albums, cassette tapes, and DVDs and later through podcasts, audiobooks, and apps—grew from the aching search of a child of the Great Depression.

He was a Marine who survived the attack on Pearl Harbor, a successful broadcaster and salesman, and, above all, a relentlessly curious man who hungered to know what set apart successful people.

His deep, sonorous voice became familiar to millions after he recorded "the secret" to success on a pioneering vinyl record in 1956. His name was Earl Nightingale (1921–1989).

Nightingale was born in 1921 in Long Beach, California. By the time Earl was twelve, in 1933, his father had abandoned the family. Earl, his mother, and two brothers lived destitute in a "tent city" near the Long Beach waterfront, home to people displaced in the Depression.

Earl's mother supported the family by working as a seamstress in a WPA factory. The adolescent Earl despaired not only of the family's poverty but also of the people he came in touch with. Everyone around him seemed backbiting, sullen, and directionless.

"I started looking for security when I was twelve," Nightingale recalled.* What he specifically meant was that he wanted to determine why some people were poor while others thrived. He yearned to join the latter group.

As a twelve-year-old, Earl ignored broader socio-economic factors. This reflected a blindness to the outer mechanics of life, political and otherwise, which endured across his adulthood. Nonetheless, the wish to succeed, however narrowly framed—and perhaps because of it—drove him to read voraciously in search of "the answer." He haunted the Long Beach Public Library, poring over every available work of religion, psychology, and philosophy.

At seventeen, Earl was no closer to solving his riddle. Thirsting for independence and needing three meals a day, he joined the U.S. Marine Corps on the eve of World War II. In December 1941, Earl became one of twelve survivors out of a company of a hundred Marines aboard the U.S.S. *Arizona* during the attack on Pearl Harbor.

He made it through the war, emerging not only with his physical wellbeing but also with the full maturation of a personal gift. He possessed a remarkable speaking voice—rich, deep, sonorous. His intonation was flawless. When stationed after the war as an instructor at Camp Lejeune in North Carolina, Nightingale moonlighted as an announcer with a local radio station. From there he found radio jobs in Phoenix and then at a CBS affiliate in Chicago.

---

* "Success at 35: Retirement at $30,000 a Year" by Frank Hughes, *Chicago Daily Tribune*, March 29, 1956.

At CBS in 1950, the twenty-nine-year-old became the voice of the aviator-cowboy adventurer Sky King on a radio serial of the same name. Nightingale excelled in the rock-'em-sock-'em role for six years. But a more fateful development occurred soon after landing the part. The Depression-era boy discovered his secret to success.

After reading hundreds of works of psychology, religion, mysticism, and ethics, Nightingale experienced a personal revelation. It arrived while poring through Napoleon Hill's *Think and Grow Rich*, which became his lifelong source of inspiration.

Nightingale realized that in the writings of every era, from the Taoist philosophy of Lao Tzu to the Stoic meditations of Roman emperor Marcus Aurelius to the Transcendentalist essays of Ralph Waldo Emerson, the same truth appeared, again and again. He had been reading it for years but simply not seeing it. It came down to six words: *We become what we think about.*

That was it. *We become what we think about.* It was the "answer" for which the Marine vet and radioman was searching.

While remaining the voice of Sky King, Nightingale left the CBS station for a new broadcasting gig, which allowed him to write his own spots. (The only criticism to which Nightingale ever seemed sensitive was whether he wrote his own material—he was adamant that he did.) At Chicago's WGN, Nightingale not only wrote and hosted his own hour-and-a-half talk show—where the everyman philosopher offered homespun wisdom, inspirational stories, and slice-of-life anecdotes—but he also worked out a deal to profit from products he pitched on air.

Nightingale promoted *Think and Grow Rich* through a local bookstore and received a cut of every copy sold. He followed suit with other products, literally from soup to soap. He soon began pitching retirement-insurance policies sold by the Franklin Life Insurance Company. This enterprise was less successful. Nightingale's pitches moved few policies. Then he seized upon a different idea: rather than selling policies, he would recruit salesmen for the company.*

"If you, my listener, are a salesperson or a wife of a salesperson and your husband is making less than twenty thousand a year, I came across an idea that is fantastic," Nightingale intoned.**

He asked people to mail in cards with their address and invited respondents to recruitment meetings for Franklin Life. Nightingale brought top salesmen into Franklin's fold that way. This was no oily pyramid scheme: some of them remained with the firm for decades, a Franklin executive recalled. Nightingale was a pitch artist—but he sold a fair deal.***

The announcer discovered he was better at recruiting and revving up salesmen than selling goods or policies himself. From that point forward, Nightingale's number-one product became motivating other

---

* Nightingale's business activities at WGN and his recruitment of insurance salesmen are recounted by Francis J. Budinger, the former president of Franklin Life Insurance Company, in "Francis J. Budinger Memoir" (1980), an oral-history interview conducted by Josephine Saner, Special Collections department, Norris L. Brookens Library, University of Illinois at Springfield.

** Nightingale's pitch is recalled from memory by Budinger. Nightingale also described some of these activities in his book *Earl Nightingale's Greatest Discovery* (Dodd, Mead & Company, 1987).

*** Additional sources include Nightingale's 1957 original professional recording of *The Strangest Secret* (Earl Nightingale Recordings); an updated version of *The Strangest Secret*, published in book form by Nightingale-Conant in 1998; Nightingale's 1960 abridgment and recording of *Think and Grow Rich* (Success Motivation Institute); *Learning to Fly as a Nightingale: A Motivational Love Story* by Diana Nightingale (Keys Company, 1997); "Radio, TV Broadcaster Earl Nightingale, 68," *Chicago Tribune*, March 29, 1989; "Earl Nightingale, the Millionaire Who Retired, Was Not and Did Not," by Clarence Petersen, *Chicago Tribune*, February 8, 1970; "Bob Proctor from 'The Secret' Shares His Insights on Learning, Creating Prosperity and the Law of Attraction" by Allison Kugel, PR.com, April 2, 2007; and "Lloyd Conant of Motivational-Record Firm," *Chicago Tribune*, April 4, 1986.

people. Journalists and academics who turn up their noses at business motivation and hard-driving sales jobs—which underwrite countless tuition checks—rarely understand the market-to-mouth world in which Earl functioned.

In the mid-1950s, Nightingale purchased his own franchise office of Franklin Life, an idea probably put to him by a new friend, W. Clement Stone, a highly successful Chicago insurance man and conservative donor who had cowritten books with Napoleon Hill and founded the Napoleon Hill Foundation. In addition to friendships with presidents Richard Nixon and Gerald Ford, Stone was also a benefactor of scientist J.B. Rhine's parapsychology labs in Durham, NC.

Nightingale got into a routine of delivering inspiring talks to his salesmen. One day in 1956, before taking an extended vacation from the office, Nightingale privately recorded a motivational message for the men to hear in his absence. His thirty-minute message told the story of his discovery of the six-word formula: *We become what we think about.* He called his presentation "The Strangest Secret."

In clear, simple terms Nightingale described how this formula was the fulcrum on which all practical philosophies rested. It was a "secret," he explained, only insofar as we overlook it, just as we undervalue or ignore those things we are freely given: love, health, sensations, and, above all, the uses of our minds.

"The human mind *isn't used*," he said, "merely because we take it for granted."

The vinyl phonograph record electrified everyone who heard it. It got passed around, shared, and borrowed. Nightingale returned home surprised by the demand for it. No commercial advice record had ever before been produced. The pitchman saw the possibilities.

Calling on friends in the music business, Nightingale recorded a studio version of "The Strangest Secret," and Columbia Records agreed to distribute the album. *The Strangest Secret* became the first spoken-word album to receive a Gold Record, for sales in excess of one million copies.

With orders booming, Nightingale partnered in 1959 with another Chicagoan, direct-mail advertiser Lloyd Conant. Together they formed Nightingale-Conant, which became the nation's first recording company focused on motivational fare. The company offered Nightingale's recordings, first on vinyl and later on cassettes. In decades ahead its catalogue expanded to include self-help icons such as Anthony Robbins, Robert Kiyosaki, and Deepak Chopra.

Nightingale had minted an industry. And in his search for truth about human nature, he stumbled upon a new kind of product: *selling people on the promise within themselves.* He made himself the field's first marketer and promoter. Like the radioman that he was, Nightingale performed and produced the early merchandise, first in the form of *The Strangest Secret* and later in his widely syndicated radio program, *Our Changing World*, which he wrote and narrated beginning in 1959.

Nightingale was evangelizer, philosopher, and pitchman rolled into one. In partnership with mail-order expert Conant, he also became manufacturer, fulfillment manager, and catalogue retailer. Nightingale's business model was simple: Do it all. And do it yourself.

Nightingale's commercial outlook was more than the result of Depression-era determination and personal guile. Critics of Nightingale and other motivational pitchmen often make the mistake of contrasting selling with believing, as though one naturally precludes the other. Nightingale was, above all, a believer. To listeners eager for his message, Nightingale's voice and viewpoint were sincere, deeply affecting, and practical. He encouraged honing individual ability. He read voraciously and urged listeners to do the same. He inveighed against conformity, blather, and hive-think.

By the time Nightingale received his Gold Record in 1971, he left no question about the potential of motivational media. When he died of heart failure in 1989, soon after his sixty-eighth birthday, Nightingale had lived just long enough to see the motivational genre grow into a profitable business of publishers, organizations, and individuals.

Within a decade of Nightingale's passing, the medium of records and cassette tapes that he knew gave way to CDs, DVDs, and, finally, digital downloads.

Today, whenever a psychology, self-help, or marketing message is heard or viewed through podcasts, apps, or audiobooks, an echo sounds from 1956 when Earl Nightingale recorded his "Strangest Secret."

Chapter XVIII

Secular New Thought: Maxwell Maltz and Psycho-Cybernetics

O ne of the most exciting and popular New Thought programs of the 1960s and beyond was ardently secular in nature. It grew from the work of a clinician who had the simple realization that *self-image is destiny*—and self-image is alterable. It was called Psycho-Cybernetics.

This trenchantly non-spiritual program of self-development and reconditioning was devised by a renowned reconstructive surgeon, Maxwell Maltz (1899–1975), in 1960, and won the allegiance of a wide-range of professional athletes, as well as cultural figures including actress Jane Fonda, First Lady Nancy Reagan, and surrealist artist Salvador Dali. Dali and the surgeon forged a close friendship and even vacationed together. In 1966, the surrealist master created a painting "Darkness and Light" inspired by Psycho-Cybernetics, which he gave Maltz as a gift. It later appeared on the cover of an updated edition.*

---

* As an editor at Penguin Random House, I had the opportunity to review personal correspondence between the author and artist, which sat in the files of Maltz's publisher Prentice Hill, which PRH had acquired.

In short, Maltz believed that self-image, more than any single factor, determines the vector of one's life—and *self-image is malleable to individual will.*

His epiphanic moment arrived this way: As a pioneering cosmetic surgeon, Maltz was among the first generation to perfect reconstructive surgical techniques. Educated at Columbia, Maltz began treating patients in the 1920s; they included victims of burns and accidents, and others who suffered deformities or birth defects (real and exaggerated), which impaired their daily functioning. After years of medical practice, Maltz made a startling observation: most of his patients *did* experience a marked improvement in self-image following successful surgeries—yet a small but persistent number *did not,* and the clinician wondered at this. Why, he asked, was the low self-image of some patients apparently resistant to an improvement in appearance? And what is this thing that we call "self-image?" Where is it from?

Maltz grew convinced that your self-image is, to a large extent, the result of self-perceptions and unconscious messages that you internalize and constantly, often unknowingly, repeat to yourself starting from your earliest age. Such a pattern can be crippling or uplifting—and it *can* be changed.

This insight formed the basis of Maltz's 1960 bestseller, a book that retains loyal readership today. In *Psycho-Cybernetics,* Maltz argued that your mind functions according to the self-regulating system of cybernetics, a term popularized in 1948 by mathematician Norbert Wiener. Cybernetics describes the mechanism behind a heat-seeking missile, which, once programmed, carries out its directive with flawless self-correction. In a similar sense, you too function, Maltz wrote, as a sophisticated, circuit-loop mechanism—yet unlike engineered apparatuses, or even computers, you operate on *self-suggestion.*

Maltz's program for reconditioning is not for the weak-willed. It is rigorous. In brief, it requires:

1. At least a half-hour a day of deep relaxation meditation.
2. Another half-hour of self-guided visualization-based meditation, in which you picture yourself and your life exactly as you want it to be, within the categories of reason. (Canniness and emotional functionality are prerequisites to the program.)
3. A steady, supplemental practice of affirmations, visualizing, and journaling.

Lest this sound too easy, consider: Everything in our lives—especially in the age of hand-held devices unknown in Maltz's time—conspires to rob us of periods of authentic meditation, meaningful self-reflection (versus morbid self-interest), and inner quietude. Have you ever tried to meditate for two thirty-minute periods a day? It's more difficult than it sounds, especially if you already have a regular meditative practice to which the Psycho-Cybernetics exercises are added or accommodated.

So, *does it work*? My personal experience is: yes—but with two major caveats:

1. The program requires, as alluded, a great deal of self-discipline and inner effort. There is a secret key to every self-help program. It is absolute, ravenous hunger for self-change. Absent that, self-help is a hobby. With the right degree of hunger, any legitimate program—from the twelve-steps to talk therapy—can make a difference. But never underestimate the depth of passion that must be present to sustain and drive your efforts. As C.S. Lewis put it in *Mere Christianity* in 1952: "All depends on really wanting."

2. Maltz died in 1975, before the neurologic and biologic antecedents of our psychology were well understood. I think he underestimated the influence, and mysteries, of temperamental and
   characterological traits. For example, every sensitive parent
   notices that his or her children enter the world—from earliest
   infancy—with pronounced personality markings, which follow
   them all their lives. My two sons, in their teens as of this writing, displayed temperamental traits from literally the moment
   they emerged from the womb. I recognize these characteristics
   in them today. The nature-versus-nurture debate is like a circle with no demarcation where one influence ends and another
   begins. I believe that Maltz, partly due to his generation, overes-
   timated conditioning and failed to consider the impact of intrinsic personality, and how biochemistry tends one person toward
   exuberance and another toward depression.

What's more, I am certain that Maltz, as a cosmetic surgeon,
would have acknowledged that overall appearance, too, places considerable weight on the lever of self-perception.

Nonetheless, all but the most sectarian determinists would agree
that conditioning is a seismic force. Indeed, the fact of intrinsic personality traits makes conditioning all the more critical insofar as your
conditioned self informs how you navigate those aspects of character
that seem implacable.

Books sometimes take a turn in the road before finding their audience.
Psycho-Cybernetics was issued by Prentice Hall in 1960, and reprinted
that year by enterprising publisher Melvin Powers (1922–2013) at his
Wilshire Book Company in Los Angeles, where it found its major
success. Powers, who also republished the popular *Three Magic Words*

by U.S. Andersen, had an eagle eye for mind-power classics that had been neglected or overlooked in earlier editions. U.S. Andersen was the pen name of Uell Stanley Andersen (1917–1986), a retired pro-football player, novelist, and metaphysical writer. Andersen's *Three Magic Words* first appeared in 1954 under the title *The Key to Power and Personal Peace,* as published by Hermitage House (a New York press that had incidentally issued L. Ron Hubbard's first edition of *Dianetics* four years prior). Andersen's book was republished in 1956 under its current title by Thomas Nelson & Sons, and later by Powers' Wilshire Book Company. In its retitled version, *Three Magic Words* gained wide popularity. (Let it never be said that titles don't matter.)

Psycho-Cybernetics effectively set the template for all secular forms of popular self-help and motivational philosophy. If you attend a business-oriented or life-coaching self-help program—one with a non-spiritual tone—chances are you are imbibing material from Maltz.

I have a special love for Maltz's book and program because it conveys a sense of epic hope about the potential of the individual to redirect his life, without requiring any belief system at the door. *Psycho-Cybernetics* envisions the individual as capable of conquering greater heights than, say, Cognitive Behavioral Therapy (CBT), which can seem to just rearrange the lawn furniture of the mind.

The book's only requirement is a zeal to experiment. Different people will, of course, have different results from, and responses to, Maltz's approach. But consider: what more noble undertaking is there than to strive to improve your nature, and strengthen your sense of self-direction? All of it attempted without a sectarian bent or a necessary leap of religious faith.

Seen in this light, Maltz's program was among the most popular expressions of humanist philosophy of the twentieth century.

Chapter XIX

The Journey of Oral Roberts

Televangelist Oral Roberts is often remembered as the founding father of the "prosperity gospel," the doctrine that prayers and affirmations can deliver wealth. He is also remembered as a religious pitchman and gung-ho fundamentalist, tainted with greed and ignorance. But his full story is both more complicated and positive than that—and to understand American religion, it must be properly framed.

At the dawn of the modern media age, Roberts expanded the evangelical message from saving souls to helping seekers find happiness in the here and now. In a revolutionary departure, the minister encouraged people who grew up in punitive brands of faith, where disobedience led to hellfire, to instead see God as a powerful—and practical—force for good in their earthly lives.

Roberts's transformation from small-town pastor to media eminence began in 1947, when he was a twenty-nine-year-old minister in Enid,

Oklahoma. The young Pentecostal was torn between a "feeling of destiny" and the grim outer reality of living near the poverty line, a situation faced by many Southern preachers in the first half of the century. (Source notes appear at the end of the chapter.)

During a period of personal depression, Roberts spent days and nights poring over Scripture—which he randomly opened one morning to 3 John 2: "Beloved, I wish above all things that thou mayest prosper and be in health, even as thy soul prospereth." For the young Roberts, the verse cast Christianity in a fresh light, challenging the emphasis on guilt and repentance in which he and many of his ministerial contemporaries had been raised. "We have been wrong," he told his wife. "I haven't been preaching that God is good."

Roberts's new message of "positive faith," in which religion could help with personal needs—from addictions to job searches—took him to a larger congregation in Tulsa and eventually around the world and on television. In 1963, he founded Oral Roberts University. He eschewed the sin-and-salvation sermonizing of Billy Graham, whose decades-long dominance of American evangelism was rivaled only by Roberts's. "I don't believe in the judgmental gospel that Billy preaches," Roberts said in 1972. "I ran away from it as a boy. Billy meets the needs of a lot of people . . . I reach other needs."

Roberts also gained fame—and notoriety—for his healing crusades. In his heyday as a religious healer, from the late 1940s through the early 1960s, thousands would wait on long lines at tent revivals to be prayed over by the minister. At the same time, Roberts discouraged the movement's worst excesses, urging followers never to resist medical care and to follow up with doctors. He readily acknowledged the psychological dimension of his healing campaigns, too. Even critical journalists never detected fraud.

Indeed, Roberts's notions about a collaborative relationship among religion, psychology, and medicine foreshadowed the rise of a later generation of mind-body health advocates, such as Norman Cousins and Andrew Weil. Speaking of his revivals in 1958 with a United Press International (UPI) reporter, Roberts said: "I hope God lets me live another thirty years, for I think by then we'll see an unbelievably close alliance between science and the kind of healing I encourage."

One prominent evangelical supporter noted Roberts's capacity to view religion "wholistically," using a variant of *holistic*—a term rarely heard in evangelical circles. "Gradually the Spirit began to show me," Roberts recalled in *The Holy Spirit in the Now* in 1974, "that in the Bible healing is for the whole man. It's for the body, it's for the soul, it's for the mind, for finances. It's for any problem that needs to be healed."

In the 1970s and '80s, as the Roberts ministry shifted its emphasis from healing to prosperity, critics began to focus on whether his chief loyalty had turned from God to mammon. Roberts certainly enjoyed good restaurants and golf courses, and he had a large family home in Tulsa and a getaway house in Southern California. But even during Roberts's peak, his lifestyle, while very comfortable, was not extravagant. He opted to live out his final years in a fairly ordinary Orange County condo.

Contrary to media depictions of Roberts as a predatory firebrand, for much of his career the minister emphasized joyful prayer and forgiveness. Among followers who had been raised in a stern form of worship, Roberts's message of "eternal optimism," rather than sounding myopic, could deliver the same kind of liberating shock that many Americans of an earlier generation had experienced when first discovering the positivity-oriented spirituality of many of the New Thought figures explored in this book.*

---

* Preceding Roberts in emphasizing a positive gospel was the Christian evangelical Word of Faith movement, which got its inception in the theology of E.W. Kenyon (1867-1948), a Massachusetts-born minister and writer who began his career in the late-nineteenth century. Kenyon honed his style at the Emerson School of Oratory in Boston in 1892. The two-year Emerson School featured an immersive program of literature, writing, and oration. It was not connected to Ralph Waldo Emerson, but was founded by a Unitarian-Universalist minister, C.W. Emerson. The school was steeped in New Thought. One of Kenyon's instructors during his 1892–1893 academic term (the only one he attended)

That put Roberts among the earliest evangelical leaders—and by far the most influential—to preach a "positive and joyous mental attitude," which fundamentalists viewed as suspiciously ecumenical. The same fundamentalist ire today surrounds media minister Joel Osteen: While non-evangelical critics are likely to dismiss Osteen as a smiley-faced cypher, they do not grasp the relative openness of evangelical pulpits such as Osteen's, which avoid political pronouncements and espouse religious inclusivity.

I should note that Roberts was not the first religious figure to harness mass-media for a message of causative, positive faith. That distinction must go to New Thought pioneers Charles and Myrtle Fillmore who in 1889 founded the vibrant and ongoing Unity movement.

Born in 1854 on an Indian reservation near St. Cloud, Minnesota, Charles and his wife and intellectual partner Myrtle grew inspired by the teachings of Emma Curtis Hopkins and other New Thought luminaries—both spouses reported faith-based healings. Eager to share their discoveries, the Fillmores formed Kansas City prayer and discussion groups. Drawing upon Charles's printing background and his well-timed real estate purchases in the growing city, they launched the magazine *Modern Thought* in April 1889. It was dedicated to metaphysical healing, New Thought, and Christian Science, and also to occult philosophies and methods, such as Mesmerism, Spiritualism, Theosophy, clairvoyance, astrology, and palmistry—topics that Charles later sharply rejected.

---

was Ralph Waldo Trine, author of *In Tune With the Infinite*. Kenyon's fellow students included motivational hero Elbert Hubbard and his wife, Alice, a New Thoughter and suffragist. Hubbard later returned as a faculty member. Another graduate with high pedigree in New Thought was philosopher and Phineas Quimby-chronicler Horatio Dresser. Still another instructor during Kenyon's academic year was Leland Powers, a Christian Scientist who went on to found the School of the Spoken Word, an oratory college that Science of Mind founder Ernest Holmes attended in 1908.

Modern Thought marked the beginnings of the Unity School of Practical Christianity. In years ahead, Charles insisted that the school was explicitly Christian—based in *"Pure Mind Healing* only," and not the occult subjects that had once moved him.

Magazines, pamphlets, correspondence courses, and mail-order prayer services quickly followed. In a crucial move in 1890, the Fillmores formed the Society of Silent Unity, a distance-prayer service whose workers prayed for anyone who wrote in. Silent Unity quickly became the signature Fillmore operation. In 1907, Charles added telephone technology to Silent Unity, staffing the phone lines with trained, round-the-clock prayer attendants. Unity was probably the first ministry to use the phones in this way. The service continues today.

The Fillmores' ministry also made early use of radio, targeted mailings, correspondence courses, pamphlets, and well-produced magazines aimed at the large demographic range of Unity's congregants. This included the children's monthly *Wee Wisdom*, which launched the literary career of bestselling novelist Sidney Sheldon when it published the ten-year-old's first poem in 1927. Although theologically rejected and even scorned by most evangelical pulpits, the New Thought-based church pioneered a media model that was readily adopted by them.*

Given Oral Roberts's own theological eclecticism and emphasis on buoyant faith, it is not surprising that the language of positive thinking also permeated his books, sermons, broadcasts, and articles. One of his closest friends and confidants, North Carolina businessman S. Lee Braxton, was deeply attached to positive-thinking literature, which he began pressing upon Roberts as the minister was making his name in the late

---

* Twentieth-century New Thought innovator Frank B. Robinson (1886–1948), who ran a mail-order religion called Psychiana from his hometown of Moscow, Idaho, also deserves credit for harnessing early media strategies. Robinson is extensively profiled in my *Occult America* (2009).

1940s. Braxton identified Dale Carnegie's *How to Win Friends and Influence People* as "the book that really put me in business." Speaking at Braxton's funeral in 1982, Roberts noted that every year since 1949 he had reread one of the motivational books that Braxton had given him, *How I Raised Myself from Failure to Success in Selling* by Frank Bettger.

Typical passages from Roberts's writings came straight from the positive-thinking playbook: "Whatever you can conceive, and believe, you can do;"* "Like Begets Like;" "Expect a Miracle;" "Change your outlook on life;" "God is your source;" "Give that it may be given to you;" and "I am in tune with God"—this last echoing Ralph Waldo Trine's *In Tune With the Infinite*. Reader testimonials in Roberts's *Abundant Life* magazine featured headlines such as "A Raise, Plus a Bonus;" "New Job as General Manager;" "A Bonus Surprise from Day to Day;" and "Sales Have Tripled."

Traditionalists often choked on Roberts's innovations. In 1969, he came under fire for his weekly television program, *Something Good Is Going to Happen to You*. In a bid for younger viewers, Roberts included as regulars the World Action Singers, a mini-skirted song-and-dance troupe noted—without pleasure—by *Christianity Today* for their "animated singing and slithering." Hate mail started. To his mind, many of the critics resembled comedian Dana Carvey's hectoring Church Lady from *Saturday Night Live*. Roberts's biographer David Edwin Harrell, Jr., recalled the minister's reply to one angry letter writer:

> Where are the young people? They are not in your church, you are
> not reaching them . . . What's wrong with their bodies? Their bodies

---

* Compare this to Napoleon Hill's statement "What the mind of man can conceive and believe, the mind of man can achieve . . ." from *Success Through a Positive Mental Attitude* by Hill and W. Clement Stone (Prentice Hall, 1960, 1977).

are clean. These young people don't go out and drink and use drugs and commit adultery. These are clean young people. I like to see them move their bodies. Young people are in movement in this country and if you want to reach one of them you'd better move a little bit.

Not everyone was displeased with the new directions. In 1972, Roberts received an admiring, handwritten note signed by "John Lennon," who told him: "A lot of people I know loved your show."

Roberts's attempts to update his ministry were more than just cosmetic. Wayne A. Robinson, who edited Roberts's publications in the late 1960s and early '70s and later wrote critically of him, noted the minister's interest in modernist theology—a development that sometimes put him at odds with his own board of regents at Oral Roberts University. "He was especially impressed with the existentialists," Robinson wrote in 1976 in *Oral: The Warm, Intimate, Unauthorized Portrait of a Man of God*, "and his sermons began to speak to the importance of *this* moment—the *Now*, the irrelevance of *doctrine* to man when he is in *need* and in *pain*, and the importance of relating one's belief to one's own experience and existence."

To be finally understood, Roberts must be seen as a figure at the heart of the classic American mission to remake religion as *practical*. Roberts combined two key but diffuse aspects of American faith: 1) the quest for personal salvation—which characterizes most evangelistic and mainline congregations—and 2) the brand of therapeutic, self-help spirituality that is often associated with the culture of New Age and New Thought.

Roberts joined these approaches into a distinctive theology, which sets him apart from most of today's prosperity gospelers. He provided millions of supporters with a Christianity that sought to address the problems of everyday life—from money to marital woes—in equal part to the search for salvation. Roberts's departures later became a mainstay of media ministering, making the Oklahoma evangelist one of the most impactful and innovative religious leaders of recent times.

Notes on Sources

In documenting the career of Oral Roberts, enough cannot be said to the credit of journalist David Edwin Harrell, Jr., author of *Oral Roberts: An American Life* (Harper & Row, 1985) and *All Things Are Possible: The Healing and Charismatic Revivals in Modern America* (Indiana University Press, 1975). Harrell's biography of Roberts, in particular, is a model of critical sympathy in mining the life story of the controversial (and often misunderstood) evangelical leader. Except where otherwise noted, quotes from Roberts are from Harrell's volumes. Roberts's comments on the "close alliance" between science and religious healing appeared in "'Faith-Healing' Tactics Decried by Roberts" by Albin Krebs, *The News-Times* (NC), February 14, 1958. For Roberts's Orange County retirement, see the Oklahoma Historical Society's Voices of Oklahoma project at: voicesofoklahoma.com/ interviews/roberts-oral/oral, in which interviewer John Erling notes: "His condominium was filled with very average furnishings . . ."

On the career of the Fillmores, I have benefited from *Charles Fillmore* by Hugh D'Andrade (Harper & Row, 1974); James W. Teener's doctoral dissertation, *Unity School of Christianity* (University of Chicago Divinity School, 1939); *The Unity Movement* by Neal Vahle (Templeton Foundation Press, 2002); and *The Household of Faith* by James Dillet Freeman (Unity School of Christianity, 1951). Sidney Sheldon's recollections are from an undated interview with his publisher HarperCollins.

For a sampling of the positive-thinking phraseology in Roberts's work, see his books *If You Need Healing—Do These Things!* (Healing Waters Revival Ministry, 1947); *Miracle of Seed Faith* (Oral Roberts, 1970); *The Miracle Book* (Pinoak Publications, 1972); *A Daily Guide to Miracles* (Pinoak Publications, 1975); and *Don't Give Up!* (Oral Roberts Evangelistic Assn., 1980). Also see Roberts's remarks to author

Will Oursler in *The Healing Power of Faith: Exploring the World of Spiritual Healing* (Hawthorn Books, 1957).

The provenance of the "John Lennon" letter is sometimes questioned. Its history and content are thoughtfully considered in "The Gospel of John Lennon" by Lindsey Neal, ThisLandPress.com, March 7, 2011.

Chapter XX

The Meticulous Seeker: Ainslee Meares

honor the perspective of journalist Norman Cousins (1915–1990) who wrote in his classic *Anatomy of an Illness* in 1979: "Not every illness can be overcome. But many people allow illness to disfigure their lives more than it should. They cave in needlessly. They ignore and weaken whatever powers they have for standing erect."

As a critical but "believing historian" of alternative spirituality, I urge exquisite care and caution in approaching questions of anomalous healing. There is no room for shorthand, generalities, or false hope.

That said, I do *not* discount the possibility of extraordinary—even miraculous—episodes of recovery pertaining to the psyche, which I define as a compact of thought and emotion. Such episodes are very rare but no less authentic as documented in mainstream medical literature.

If the psyche possesses causative or extra-physical capacities, i.e., if it goes beyond cognition and motor commands, which at various points in this book I argue it does, that prospect opens onto vistas that the human search, while millennia old, has only begun to detect.

In that vein, since the mid-1960s, a handful of physicians and clinicians have been making an effort to document one of the most astounding yet verifiable facts in the field of cancer research: spontaneous remissions of terminal cases.* In researching this question at the New York Academy of Medicine library, I found that about twenty such cases appear in world medical literature each year.** Many cases, clinicians agree, are probably unreported.

Based on estimated spontaneous regression rates worldwide—about one out of every 100,000 cases of cancer***—it can be extrapolated from the number of new cancer cases reported annually in the United States that about fifteen episodes of spontaneous regression occur here each year.

There is no medical consensus around the causes of spontaneous remissions. Clinicians hypothesize that in rare cases patients may have been misdiagnosed, or patients may have been suffering from a severely impaired immune system, which, for reasons unknown, was restored to normal or exceptional functioning, perhaps due to the healing of an undetected virus or infection. Clinicians also acknowledge the possibility of mental therapeutics.

"Of all possible mechanisms cited for regression," wrote G.B. Challis and H.J. Stam in the journal *Acta Oncologica* in 1990, "the psychological is the only category which is not clearly biological."

In surveying the extant literature, these researchers found that "only three authors are primarily responsible for reports of regressions by psychological means in the scientific literature"—and only one, Australian psychiatrist and researcher Ainslie Meares, "pro-

---

* See *Spontaneous Regression of Cancer* by T.C. Everson and W.H. Cole (W.B. Saunders, 1966).

** "The Spontaneous Regression of Cancer: A Review of Cases from 1900 to 1987" by G.B. Challis and H.J. Stam, *Acta Oncologica* 29, Fasc. (1990).

*** Challis and Stam (1990).

vided sufficient information to be able to include the cases in our tables."*

Ainslie Meares (1910–1986) presented a special case in point. In the 1970s and '80s, Meares oversaw and published research on the practice of intensive meditation by terminally diagnosed cancer patients for whom traditional treatments, such as chemotherapy, had been discontinued; in other cases, he employed intensive meditation (sometimes three hours a day) with patients who had "advanced cancer" but were still undergoing treatment. He documented notable therapeutic episodes in both groups.

In a 1980 report on seventy-three patients who had advanced cancer, Meares found that intensive meditation helped relive pain, depression, and anxiety, and contributed to a more peaceful and dignified death when cases proved terminal.** In addition, Meares wrote of cancer patients who undergo intensive meditation: "There is reason to expect a ten percent chance of quite remarkable slowing of the rate of growth of the tumour, and a ten percent chance of less marked but still significant slowing. The results indicate that patients with advanced cancer have a ten percent chance of regression of the growth."

Meares also documented a small, but not isolated, number of cases where terminally diagnosed patients spontaneously regressed while following a protocol of intensive meditation. In an article in *Australian Family Physician* in March 1981, he described the case of a fifty-four-year-old married woman with two grown children who had recovered

---

* Citations to Meares' key journal articles appear in the bibliography following this chapter.

** "What Can the Cancer Patient Expect from Intensive Meditation?", *Australian Family Physician*, Vol. 9, May 1980.

from breast cancer following meditation.* When a mastectomy failed to check her cancer growth, the patient had refused chemotherapy and embarked on a program of anabolic steroid use and natural supplements (which Meares neither studied nor endorsed).

She began to show healing after seeing Meares for meditation sessions each weekday for one month, using a technique of sitting still and experiencing her "essential being," as he described it, without concentration of any kind. (In general, Meares restricted his research to subjects who had seen him for at least twenty meditation sessions of one hour or more daily. Although he does not specify the length of time this fifty-four-year-old woman sat daily, some of his patients meditated up to three hours a day.) He wrote of her remission:

> A single case, considered by itself, may not be very convincing. But if we consider the particular case in conjunction with other patients who have responded in similar fashion, the relationship of treatment and outcome becomes more clearly established. In other words, the present case is not an isolated incident. It is one of a series of cases of regression of cancer following intensive meditation in some of which the regression has been more complete than in others.

I was informally describing all this one evening in 2016 to a research pathologist at Harvard Medical School who specializes in breast cancer. I broached the topic with him of these rare but documented cases of spontaneous remission. Some cases, as noted, are evidently autoimmune related; but we also talked about the correlations with intensive

---

* "Regression of recurrence of carcinoma of the breast at mastectomy site associated with intensive meditation," *Australian Family Physician*, Vol. 10, March 1981.

meditation. The researcher's response: "I have to be objective. But I have noticed that patients who display a positive attitude toward their treatment tend to do better. My colleagues have noticed this, too. We don't know why that is."

It is difficult to write about this kind of subject, even inconclusively, because it tends to polarize.

Readers with New Age sympathies are apt to seize upon such discussions as validation that mind-body medicine, perhaps coupled with some kind of detox program, represents the royal road to health. Meares said no such thing, and he was scrupulous, as any responsible researcher would be, never to plant false hopes.

Yet there is an equal and opposite extreme, in which a physician, or more often a polemical skeptic, approaches such a discussion with no sense of proportion, perceiving *any* such talk as atavism or wishful thinking. (Indeed, after I had noted the Harvard researcher's remarks on social media, another research physician I know objected that we were entertaining rash conclusions; he missed our expressed intent to avoid either conclusions or leading questions but rather to frame a discussion.)

What's more, it is important to note that no researcher denies the biological factors cited earlier—nor the psychological factors in the Meares cases.

I give the final word to Meares because his tone and carefulness exhibit what is needed today in our spiritual culture and beyond. He wrote this in "Cancer, Psychosomatic Illness, and Hysteria" in *The Lancet* of November 7, 1981:

In medicine we no longer expect to find a single cause for a disease; rather we expect to find a multiplicity of factors, organic and psychological. It is not suggested that psychological reactions, either psychosomatic or hysterical, are a direct cause of cancer. But it seems likely that reactions resembling those of psychosomatic illness and conversion hysteria operate as causes of cancer, more so in some cases than in others, and that they operate in conjunction with the known chemical, viral, and radiational causes of the disease.

This, to me, is the kind of voice our society should cultivate generally—in politics, spirituality, and medicine. It is the voice that sustains an informed question, which is the vantage point from which all new understanding is ventured.

Bibliography

To facilitate further inquiry, I include citations to Ainslee Meares' key journal articles on this topic.

"Atavistic Regression as a Factor in the Remission of Cancer," *The Medical Journal of Australia,*" July 23, 1977.

"Regression of Osteogenic Sarcoma Metastases Associated with Intensive Meditation," *The Medical Journal of Australia*, October 21, 1978.

"Meditation: a psychological approach to cancer treatment," *The Practitioner,* January 1979, Vol. 222.

"Regression of Cancer of the Rectum After Intensive Meditation," *The Medical Journal of Australia*, November 17, 1979.

"Remission of Massive Metastasis From Undifferentiated Carcinoma of the Lung Associated with Intensive Meditation," *Journal of the American Society of Psychosomatic Dentistry and Medicine*, Vol. 27, No2, 1980.

"What can the cancer patient expect from intensive meditation?", *Australian Family Physician*, Vol. 9, May 1980.

"Regression of recurrence of carcinoma of the breast at mastectomy site associated with intensive meditation," *Australian Family Physician*, Vol. 10, March 1981.

"Cancer, Psychosomatic Illness, and Hysteria," *The Lancet*, November 7, 1981.

Chapter XXI

The Reluctant Icon: Vernon Howard

By the late-twentieth century, prosperity ministries and extreme motivational seminars created a chasm between the ideals and reality of popularized metaphysics and positive-thinking spirituality.

Yet one of the most distinctive and skilled spiritual thinkers of the era deftly avoided this pitfall. He was a man who began his career in the tradition of the success gospel but eventually distanced himself from it. Leaving behind his old life, and with it the ethical and material dilemmas of spirituality-for-sale, he defined a wholly fresh concept of mind-power.

His name was Vernon Howard (1918–1992). While this mystical writer and philosopher lacked fame, following, or renown, he possessed an extraordinary, and probably singular, gift for distilling the complexities of the world's religious and ethical philosophies into aphoristic and ardently practical principles.

Indeed, Howard, a California transplant born in Haverhill, Massachusetts, was probably the most remarkable and independent voice to emerge from America's culture of practical spirituality; though as his outlook matured, it became impossible to pin any label on him.

In the first leg of Howard's writing career, from the late 1940s to the early 1960s, he produced books that could have come from the conventional New Thought catalogue. They bore such titles as *Success Through the Magic of Personal Power; Time Power for Personal Success; Your Magic Power to Persuade and Command People*; and *Word Power: Talk Your Way to Life Leadership*.

Howard's folksy oeuvre extended to works of popular reference, trivia, and children's nonfiction, such as *Lively Bible Quizzes* and *101 Funny Things to Make and Do*. To the outside observer, the Los Angeles–based author was just one more scribe-for-hire, of the type found in any large city.

But in the mid-1960s, Howard's outlook underwent a remarkable maturation. His personal genesis began with a wish to escape from the cycles of euphoria and depression that characterize the life of any ambitious writer. He told the *Los Angeles Times* in 1978 (with full source notes at the end of the chapter):

> I started realizing the uselessness of the extraneous. People could tell me I was a good writer and I realized all it did was make me hungry for more applause. And when that didn't come, I'd get hurt. I decided I had to find something without applause so I could live independently, without the approval of other people.

Howard found his own solution to this predicament. He left his career as a commissioned author of success literature (as well as his marriage) and resettled in the relative boondocks of Boulder City,

Nevada. "Not exactly a community noted for breeding literary mystics," observed the *Las Vegas Review-Journal* in a 1979 profile.

Journalists sometimes poked fun at Howard's newfound hermitage. The *Review-Journal* headline announced, "Not all mystical sages are big stars." *Human Behavior* magazine that year ran a piece, "Searching for the mystic path with Boulder City's cosmic master."

But from his desert idyl, in the late 1960s until his death in 1992, Howard developed into a wholly distinct spiritual thinker. He produced a remarkable range of pamphlets, parables, articles, books, and lectures in which he expounded with total clarity and directness on the need to abandon the fleeting rewards of outer life in exchange for authentic and self-directed inner existence.

In a sense, Howard's teachings boil down to the parable of Jacob and Esau. Esau sells out his birthright for a bowl of pottage—not realizing that he has sacrificed his life for a fleeting reward, which quickly gives way to pain and resentment.

Howard urged readers to see how we do this at *every instant* of life. He encouraged listeners to exchange the baubles of worldly achievement—and the depression or anxiety that summarily follows—for rewards of real truth: a contented, flowing inner state—a feeling of *natural rightness,* innate to all people once obfuscations are removed.

Howard's psychology centered on two key ideas, which ran throughout his work. They can be summarized this way:

1. **Humanity lives from a false nature.** What we call personal will is no more than a fearful, self-promoting, *false "I."* This counterfeit self chases after worldly approval and security, reacting with aggression one moment and servility the next. The false "I" craves self-importance

and status, which, in turn, bind the individual to pursuit of money, careerism, and peer accolades. To be truly happy, this false self must be shaken off, like a hypnotic spell. In its place, the individual discovers his or her True Nature, which emanates from a Higher Will, or what is sometimes called God.

2. **Human behavior is characterized by hostility, corruption, and weakness.** Friends, neighbors, lovers, coworkers, and family members often manipulate or exploit us, wreaking agony in our lives. "It's not negative to see how negative people really are," Howard wrote. "It is a high form of intelligent self-protection to see thru the human masquerade." On this, he was uncompromising. When someone makes a habit of diminishing you, Howard taught, you must resolve inwardly—and, as soon as you're physically able, outwardly—to remove yourself from that person, without constraint by convention, apologetics, or hesitation. Once we see through human destructiveness, we attract relationships of a higher nature.

Howard's bluntness could arrive like a refreshing drink of water—typified by an undated interview with student and writer Guy Findley:

G: What is real power?

VH: The absence of your false power. Now, you see when I tell you that you're going to be puzzled by it. Get rid of your nonsensical power and then you'll know what's on the other side of it. But people won't do that. They want to argue and they want to say, "Oh, I know what power is." You don't know what power is. What you know is weakness. Because as long as you have human power, you have weakness only.

And further:

Have you ever noticed a small child, how easily he's distracted? He has a little toy he plays with. You put a piece of candy in front of him and he forgets the toy. You hand him something else, a little colored ball, and he sets the candy down. Human beings are like that. They start off with a purpose of some kind and then you put a little piece of candy in front of him—you put marriage in front of him, or a romance—or you put a promotion at work in front of them—Eh! "Who needs God? I got a promotion. I'm an assistant manager!" See? So the world is so filled with false delights that people would rather have in place of persisting. Now, one way to overcome that latching onto distractions is to see that every time you get that promotion down at work or every time someone compliments you, that nothing has changed.

Howard eventually attracted a circle of about fifty students in the Boulder City area. "We send our message out but we have no concern for the results," he told a reporter. "What does the size of our audience have to do with the truth?" One evening he announced to a roomful of listeners: "We're here every Thursday night. If you don't like what you hear, don't come back." He only occasionally ventured out of his Southern Nevada town to deliver talks in and around Los Angeles.

Howard did, however, reach a larger audience through video-taped lectures, which students broadcast through the early medium of public-access cable television, along with a prodigious output of books and tapes. "He says he lives comfortably just on royalties," the *Los Angeles Times* reported in 1988.

Many of Howard's video presentations are today preserved online. You can begin them, as with his books, from any point. In a mark of Howard's virtuosity, the entirety of his message appears in all of its parts. He spoke extemporaneously, without notes, rarely betraying a hesitation, stumble, or missed beat.

In his talks, Howard appeared exactly as he did in daily life: casually dressed in a polo shirt or short-sleeved button-down, physically robust though slightly paunchy. Seated at a spare table, he looked like any ordinary, late-middle-aged man—not quite professorial (his edges were too rough) but more like an avuncular phys-ed teacher. But Howard's voice and gaze were those of a distinctly poised and purposeful individual: a simple man with a profound message—namely, that inner freedom awaits you the moment you turn to it, provided you learn to mistrust the vaunted "goodies" of outer life and those who proffer them.

In a carryover from his years as a success writer, Howard gave his books sensationalistic titles, such as *The Mystic Path to Cosmic Power* (his most popular and, some say, best book); *Esoteric Mind Power; Secrets for Higher Success;* and *The Power of Your Supermind.* His ever-practical pamphlets—with titles such as *Your Power to Say No* and *50 Ways to Escape Cruel People*—were advertised in popular psychology magazines and grocery tabloid the *Weekly World News.*

A typical ad for one of his pamphlets read: "Worried? *50 WAYS TO GET HELP FROM GOD."* The ads were in no way cynical. Tucked amid competing advertisements for weight-loss programs and wrinkle creams, Howard's ads reflected the dictum to *go out to the highways and hedges and bring them in.* The former success writer knew how to reach people in need.

I have, from time to time, wondered whether his overwrought titles restricted rather than expanded his appeal. In some regards, Howard seemed to use this approach not to broaden but limit his audience—deliberately rejecting approbation from lettered culture. Nothing does more to dilute the search than peusdo-seriousness, intellectual jockeying, and ambition *within* the search. Howard would have none of it.

As noted, Howard's writing could be picked up almost at random—any chapter, any page, any pamphlet or book—and the reader could fully enter his philosophy. There existed no prerequisites, no partially thought-through ideas. Howard's gift was fully and continually illustrating and restating core truths in dramatically fresh ways, a talent evinced by Ralph Waldo Emerson (1803–1882), Neville Goddard (1905–1972), and few other modern writers. Although Howard could not be classified, his psychological insights coalesced with ideas found in the work of spiritual teacher Jiddu Krishnamurti (1895–1986) and, at times, the vitally important twentieth-century spiritual philosopher G. I. Gurdjieff (1866–1949). A confluence with classical Buddhism and Christianity was also evident.

But Howard's language and methods reveal a down-to-earth, hands-on immediacy that perhaps no other contemporary spiritual figure demonstrated. He insisted that any program of self-development had to palpably improve the hours of ordinary life. On this, he was uncompromising.

He was likewise resolute on questions of human cruelty—a crisis he believed most therapists and spiritual thinkers underestimated or failed to grasp. The teacher entreated listeners to separate from cruel people, without justifications or concern for social approval.

Cruelty, he taught, often takes the form of subtle putdowns, chronic provocations, or cutting asides, for which the bully always claims plausible denial. The payoff for the predator is a perverse thrill or "false feeling of life." Hence, Howard counseled separation—*not* confrontation or "communication" (the midwife of self-defeat), which only grants the aggressor the friction he savors. Moreover, the predatory persona is often the first and loudest to cry *injustice!* In a statement certain to engender pushback, Howard said: "Show me the victim and I'll show you the bully."

One evening he erupted at students:

> All I'm really trying to say is: why don't you just LEAVE PEOPLE ALONE! They've got problems of their own. They don't need your jokes or your smart remarks.

Because I used to play Howard's lectures at home or in the car, my then-young sons would chide me, "Vernon Howard is mean!"—a note one of them snuck into my journals. I explained that Vernon was simply trying to shake us awake. To which I would now add that his plainly worded aphorisms—which he encouraged listeners to live with for six months—conceal unexpected lifelines. (This chapter closes with a small sampling.)

Howard's approach meshes with William James's philosophy of pragmatism. The only viable measure of a private belief system, James wrote, is its *effect on conduct. If a thing works,* it doesn't matter what detractors say. And *if it doesn't,* then the philosophy has no claim on sensitive people—it may belong in books of social history and museum cases but not in the folds of daily life.

Empiricism, in James's view, requires measuring an idea without reference to how it compares with widely held reasoning but by what an individual can perceive of its nature, consistency, and, above all, impact. Pragmatism requires evaluating an ethical or religious idea by *experience of use,* including within oneself.

Many philosophies avert questions of *result* by rearranging or disavowing the concept. Howard took the opposite tack: "Will you trust a religion or philosophy that does not produce a truly poised and decent human being?"

That question is, I believe, one to which every spiritual teacher must submit—as Vernon Howard eagerly did.

Aphorisms from Vernon Howard

We attract negative people and events because we wrongly and unconsciously value them.

You'll never be taken in by a false prophet when you are no longer a false follower.

A successful day for many people is one in which no one discovered what he is really thinking.

A chief feature of false life is that it cannot stand alone, but frantically demands allies to support its false positions.

A weak person's duty is to try to shove his responsibilities onto you, and your duty is to refuse them.

It is unnecessary to obey any arising reaction which tells us to act against our true interest.

It is not risky at all to risk the dislike of someone in favor of being and acting what is true.

Your past can be changed in an astonishing way by seeing it with these higher truths.

We must never forget that wrongs about life and boredom always go together.

A man is punished only by the level he occupies, as when deceit deceives the deceitful.

Wherever you are, perhaps with friends or at a party, ask yourself, "Do I really want to be here?"

Never do anything that causes distress in a hostile person. By doing this you deny him his painful thrill, and since he is no longer rewarded he will leave you alone.

You can recognize only your own level.

Every one of your human relationships must be on your terms or not at all.

Fear is the product of truth refused.

If you do not use your business for ego-expansion, it will never be a problem to you.

A man's psychic level instantly signals itself to others.

Quietly ignore a cruel man.

Notes on Sources

Vernon Howard's statement "I started realizing the uselessness" is from "He's on the Highway to Higher Truths" by Anne LaRiviere, *Los Angeles Times*, January 1978. The observation about Boulder City is from "Not All Mystical Sages Are Big Stars" by Ed Vogel, *Las Vegas Review-Journal*, July 21, 1979, which is also the source for Howard's quote "we send our message out." Howard's statement "it's not negative" is from his pamphlet *Be Safe in a Dangerous World* (New Life Foundation, 1981). Additional helpful articles include "Searching for the Mystic Path with Boulder City's Cosmic Master" by Eleanor Links Hoover, *Human Behavior* magazine, March 1979; "New Age Prophet Offers Mystic Road Map to Inner Bliss" by Steve Chawkins, *Los Angeles Times,* May 5, 1988; and "New Life Foundation Founder Howard Dies of Natural Causes" by Carri Geer, *Las Vegas Review-Journal,* September 3, 1992. Howard's statement "will you trust a religion" is from *1500 Ways to Escape the Human Jungle* (New Life Foundation, 1978). Howard's books, pamphlets, audios, and DVDs are published by the New Life Foundation (anewlife.org), which issues a regular newsletter.

Epilogue

Optimism of the Will:
A Response to Christopher Lasch

close this book with a different kind of Happy Warrior. Historian and philosopher Christopher Lasch (1932–1994) was among the most tren- chant and informed critics of alternative spirituality, New Age, and New Thought, as he was of many facets of what he considered America's cultural decline. I deeply miss Lasch's presence on the American scene, even as I dissent from facets of his outlook, particularly his critique of new religious forms. Since we have heard from some of New Thought's brightest lights, I believe we should also consider the perspective of one of its most compelling and sincere critics. In this epilogue, adapted from Daydream Believer, *I endeavor to fairly represent Lasch's criticism—and my reckoning with it.*

In spring of 2018, I participated in a live, online chat with listeners of the late-night radio talk show Coast to Coast AM. At the top of the chat, I received a thoughtful and detailed question from a participant named Matt C. He asked me to respond to the critique that social thinker Christopher Lasch had made of New Age and alternative spirituality, which Lasch saw as mired in narcissism.

Before his untimely death from cancer at age sixty-one, Lasch wrote penetratingly of the increasing segmentation of American society; the distance of social, economic, and cultural elites from the needs of the overall public; and the increasingly maladapted forms by which we seek personal gratification.

As Matt C. described it, Lasch regarded "New Age, Gnostic, and Occult movements as essentially resulting from primary narcissism," in which starry-eyed followers seek to elude death and personal limitation by erasing boundaries and melting into a numinous whole with the universe. (Philosopher Ken Wilber offered a similar critique of New Agers who misperceive unaccountability and reversion to childishness as reflections of authenticity or "growth.") The other form of narcissism that defines New Age and alternative spiritual movements, in the listener's summation, is "destructive secondary narcissism, which we associate with egomania and an attempt to restore a sense of lost omnipotence." This occurs when the go-getter personality perceives himself as the center of the universe, possessed of boundless power and entitlement.

In a 1990 afterword to his 1979 classic *The Culture of Narcissism*, Lasch further wrote that New Age revives ancient forms of Gnostic spirituality, stipulating that both modes of practice, with greater sympathy to the poetic pathos of Gnosticism, rely upon infantile fantasies. "The New Age movement," Lasch wrote, "has revived Gnostic theology in a form considerably adulterated by other influences and mixed up with imagery derived from science fiction—flying saucers, extraterrestrial intervention in human history, escape from the earth to a new home in space . . . The New Age movement is to Gnosticism what fundamentalism is to Christianity."

I responded that while I have tremendous respect for Lasch, I believed that he and many academic critics "lacked familiarity with

New Age material and its distant antecedents." As I saw it, Lasch "was uncharacteristically under-prepared to critique this aspect of our culture. What Lasch failed to grasp is that New Age, rather than being steeped in narcissism, is actually a re-sounding of ancient Gnostic themes. It is a varied search for understanding." (Lasch and I both compared New Age with Gnosticism—but with different estimates of the latter's value.*) I defended New Age "simply as a radically ecumenical culture of therapeutic spirituality. It shares the attitude of radical search with ancient Gnosticism." I stand by those remarks. But, looking back, I do not feel that my reply adequately encompassed the depth of Lasch's critique.

If the mind-power thesis as I have presented it is roughly correct, then the issues framed by the Coast listener place the practitioner in front of a daunting question: *What is mind power for?* Is it just a metaphysical ego trip? Or a mode of escapism?

To address this argument, let us assume, as I do, that the mind's causative properties are, too some degree, authentic—something Lasch would have disputed; he probably would have viewed such an outlook as a delusive diversion in the direction of either primary narcissism (i.e., melting into the numinous) or secondary narcissism (i.e., egomania). But I abide by the viewpoint—and claim it as my privilege: we all live by assumptions, whether spiritual, materialistic, or some variety. Traditionally, our only empiricism on the path is conduct and experience. I cannot prove or disprove the functionality of my or another's private philosophy beyond the measure of behavior and credible testimony. I augment that approach with corresponding insights from the sciences, as I bring to bear elsewhere.**

---

* See my "The New Age and Gnosticism: Terms of Commonality," *Gnosis: Journal of Gnostic Studies*, Volume 4: Issue 2, 2019, also reprinted in *Uncertain Places*.

** E.g., see my articles "The Enduring Legacy of Parapsychologist J.B. Rhine," Medium, October 10, 2022, and "Is Precognition Real?", Boing Boing, August 17, 2022, as well as my chapter "The Parapsychology Revolution" from *Daydream Believer*.

If the individual is indicted by a drive to rejoin an idealized numinous state and thus escape the frictions, uncertainties, and imminent end of life—which he or she may seek by erasure of boundaries and assumption of "oneness" with a deity or supernatural forces—or another individual seeks security by an equally childish quest for self-inflation and rejection of obstacles to wish fulfillment and gratification, then such a person must stand in judgment before the question of the purpose and significance of *metaphysics of any kind*—and particularly the type to which I prescribe, which emphasize attainment. In that vein, Lasch would detect in me, and in my prescription, the malady of secondary narcissism: inflation of self.

I referred to attainment. Someone once told me that he did not know what I meant by attainment. At this, I can only smile. If a smoke detector went off at 4 a.m. and someone yelled: "*we have to get out of here!*" no one would ask, "what do you mean?" *We know.* The form that attainment takes is immediately and privately felt by, and distinctive to, every individual. But is the wish to create, produce, earn, generate, or live in a certain way—in short, *is ambition*, even of an ethically developed variety—a *worthy end* of the spiritual search?

I have wrestled with this question for many years. I have come to a perspective on it. At this stage of my search, I have ceased to distinguish between what are considered eternal and temporal values. I believe that any such division is artificial and gets inured in us by the force of familiarity.

Much of Eastern and Western religious thought tells us that we live in a hierarchical cosmos, and things that are essential, eternal, sacred, and everlasting belong to the "greater you," to a higher degree of existence toward which you progress as you shed worldly attachments and illusions, sometimes broadly called *maya* or *samsara*, and come to realize that attachments foster suffering. I believe that this idea, so foundational and familiar, does not suit the life and search of the contemporary seeker. I think it warrants reexamination.

In my observation, we have fallen into a rote and recitative division in which we think in terms of attachment and nonattachment, identification and nonidentification, personality and essence, ego and true self, temporal and eternal. I do not know how you would determine the lines of demarcation among those posited opposites.

A friend used to joke that if you demonstrate some behavior and like it, you say it must come from essence; if you demonstrate something and dislike it, it must come from personality. How would we distinguish where personality ends or blends into essence or where a more temporal desire gives way to a more eternal desire? And how would I evaluate what is urgent in another's life?

At this point in my search, I have come to believe that *the essential purpose of life is self-expression.* Self-expression can take any number of forms that are intimate and necessary to the individual. This is not the same as consumption. Consumption of a gross variety aims to salve a lack of self-expression.

I am opposed to nothing other than barriers being thrown up between the seeker and his or her sense of self-expression. The only thing that I stand against, the only moral code I employ on the path, is that I would never intentionally do anything to block or deter another person from striving for the same human potential that I wish for myself.

Even in our age of decentered and discursive information, we imbibe too many homiletic ideas about what constitutes the search, what reflects progress on the path, and how one would evaluate that progress. As alluded, I believe that the evaluation of the success—a term of which we should be unafraid—of a philosophy, therapy, religious or spiritual viewpoint is *the conduct and experience of the seeker.* This includes the capacity to enter into and sustain satisfying relationships, find one's way in the material world in some manner that is reasonably self-sustaining, and, above all, foster capacity and outlets for self-expression.

In Scripture, we read that the creator fashioned the individual in its own image. In the late-ancient Hermetic manuscript called *The Emerald Tablet*, a similar note appears in the principle: "as above, so below." If we take either of these notions seriously, if these ideas actually mean something to us—and they are at the heart of the Abrahamic and Hermetic religious systems—they must mean that you the individual are capable of creating within your own sphere, as you were created.

Created from what? Hermeticism teaches that all of existence emanates from an infinite presence from which nothing can be added or subtracted; this original substance has no proportion; it cannot be measured, limited, or contained within concepts of time, space, or dimension. The one thing that we consensually understand as fitting that definition is mind.

The Hermeticists used the Greek term *Nous* to describe an Overmind or life essence that they saw as the source of all creation. These Greek-Egyptian thinkers believed that each individual emanates through concentric spheres of creation from this essence or higher mind.*

As a being born of mind, the individual is naturally endowed with corresponding creative abilities within the physical framework in which he or she dwells. But this schema also holds that we are *limited* by the laws and forces of our cosmic framework. "Ye are gods," the Psalmist says, "but ye shall die as princes."

Observation dictates that we live under immensely diffuse laws and forces—of which I believe the law mental causation is one. From what I have written up to this point, it could be inferred that thought

---

* According to Hermetic literature, the supreme mind or *Nous*, uses as its vehicle a threefold process consisting of: 1) subordinate mind (*demiurgos-nous*); 2) word (*logos*); and 3) spirit (*anthropos*).

is the ultimate arbiter of experience. So much within our world, emergent from both the sciences and religious tradition, suggests this. In referencing *a law of mental causation*, I must add that a law is, by definition, ever operative. This does not mean, however, that it is *experienced uniformly*. H2O is always water, but water can, of course, be vapor, liquid, or solid depending upon temperature. Gravity is constant—it is mass attracted to itself—but you experience gravity differently on the moon than on earth or Jupiter or in the vacuum of space, where gravity seems absent but is still felt because objects are drawn in contact. The law of mental causation may work similarly: it is constant but myriad forces mitigate your experience, sometimes deterring its apparent function. Hence, and contrary to Lasch's suggestion, we do not categorically flee from limits when experimenting with the mind-power thesis.

At the same time, we do witness extraordinary congruencies between events and thought or spiritual appeal. Is there even a difference between thought and spiritual appeal? The sensitized mind may be what we colloquially call spirit. We know from academic ESP studies that the mind evinces extra-physical qualities.* Extra-physicality is my basic definition of spirituality. As such, mind and spirit may occupy the same scale. Let me share a personal experience, which touches on that prospect.

Several years ago, I was part of a very demanding esoteric order. Many people in the group were intellectually refined and the rigor of the search was deeply felt. Physical demands were placed on us. Seekers could be pushed to their limits. I can assure you that nothing does more, or works more quickly, to skewer fantasies about yourself than being awakened at an inconvenient hour in an unfamiliar or physically uncomfortable place to perform some difficult task—you discover your

---

* E.g., a meta-analysis of psychical research data appeared in the flagship journal of the American Psychological Association: "The Experimental Evidence for Parapsychological Phenomena: A Review" by Etzel Cardeña, *American Psychologist*, 2018, Vol. 73, No. 5.

limits quickly. People who are accustomed to succeeding in familiar or comfortable settings, who are considered "wise owls" in their domestic realms, or who see themselves as spiritually advanced, get leveled on a very different scale.

One winter, we were planning a camping trip near the New York-Pennsylvania border. If you have ever gone winter camping in the northeastern United States, you know it can be tough going. I once prevailed upon a friend to join me on a recreational winter camping trip and he adamantly refused. Why? I asked. "Because the best you can possibly hope for is to have a terrible time," he said. My friend was, of course, right; we spent the excursion basically trying to stay alive. But this group trip was planned with a sense of purpose. We were gathering in the woods to join together in the search.

My teacher gave me a particular task in preparation. He mixed in a little humor with it, but it was nonetheless a veritable and meaning-ful effort. He said that the women in the group were going to sleep in tents in the freezing nights. The men were staying in a cold-water cabin—basically a large, uninsulated shack, which was little better. My teacher said that if the female campers had to get up at night to relieve themselves, in order that they would not have to venture into the icy woods, I was to go out and buy buckets for their tents to serve as chamber pots. But these buckets, he said with a glint in his eye, had to be of a particular type. They had to be pink and heart shaped. If, after really trying, I could find no pink, heart-shaped buckets, it would be acceptable for me to buy red, heart-shaped ones. And if I really found myself out of options, I could finally buy red buckets of a standard shape.

This was before digital commerce exploded, so the search for an unusual item required phone calls and foot visits. I lived on the east-side of Manhattan and I embarked on a search across New York's boroughs for pink, heart-shaped buckets. I did not want to disappoint my teacher and I felt that the task was important on several levels. I put everything into it. I called and visited bed-bath stores, hardware stores, home-good stores, and contractor stores, crossing myriad places off my growing list. I got nowhere. I could not find pink, heart-shaped buckets. So, I decided to switch to Plan B and look for red buckets, first heart shaped and, if that proved futile, of a standard shape. That did not seem too difficult.

But, oddly enough, here I was in New York City—one of the commercial hubs of the world—and I could not find red buckets of either type. Again, I called and visited hardware stores, paint stores, you name it. Nothing. Early one evening, out on a household errand, I told myself, "Well, it's time to call my teacher and admit that I failed. I've searched everywhere for pink, heart-shaped buckets. I searched for red, heart-shaped buckets, and then just regular red, circular buckets—but came up empty." Something told me to wait a bit longer. Do not call him yet.

As this was running through my head, I was standing outside of a little around-the-corner neighborhood grocery store, someplace you run to pick up eggs or milk. I entered the store and headed toward the back to the cold-foods section. When I reached the rear of the store, right there stood a gleaming, brand-new pile of *pink, heart-shaped buckets*. In near-disbelief, I grabbed a stock boy and asked, "What color are those buckets?" He said, "Pink." I asked, "And they're heart-shaped?" Regarding me somewhat strangely he agreed and volunteered, "They just came in today."

I was astonished not only because the odds and circumstances of finding my hallowed item right then and there seemed infinitesimal—this is so even if you use the "law of large numbers," which dictates that across a large population weird things must happen to *someone*—but there was an additional factor. It is critical to note that even when dealing with actuarial tables, large numbers, and statistical probabilities, there is one thing that statistics cannot really get at: the emotional stakes and personal meaning of an experience. The individual is invested with a certain *something* in relation to the thing encountered—whether a yearned-for relationship, job offering, home listing, crisis averted, stranger who helps, friend who has been long out-of-touch, and so on. The emotional stakes and private meaning of a situation can heighten its rarity and pertinence beyond any measure of chance. That is what I experienced in this situation. It exemplified for me an ineffable truth: there is something lawful about mental exertion.

Some social scientists (and, more often, science journalists and bloggers) label virtually any personal effort to observe connections between self and the world by the brutally compact term—at once naive and cynical—*confirmation bias*. This is a clinical term for prejudice. We all suffer from it. But to over-apply such judgment to the individual search requires limiting questions of emotional and ethical existence to the structures of credentialed study. The overuse of such concepts also means subtly (and futilely) attempting to upend the ageless imperative to *know oneself* in favor of professionally determined protocols of perception. It means indirectly claiming that self-inquiry is illusory outside licensed probity. From Lao Tzu to Proust to Plath, all is, strictly speaking, mere anecdote, of no greater application to the truth of the human situation than the elections of a subject responding to forced-choice survey questions in a lab or marketing study.

To focus on just one aspect of the mind-causation thesis, it seems to me that the trigger of conveyance behind thought and circumstance is the uniqueness, dedication, and totality of an individual's focus, mental and otherwise. Why should this be? In Hermetic philosophy, all actions, cycles, and events represent a kind of rhythmical swing. This reflects the principle "as above, so below," which I see as a natural over-law. A pendulous, rhythmical swing *necessitates a mirroring swing*.

Switching for a moment to standard mechanics, Isaac Newton made the observation, which has been validated in both macro and particle physics, that objects separated over vast distances exert precise mirroring effects over one another, for which we are unable to fully account. String theory is among the theses developed to explain this mirror effect. Within the schema of string theory, all of reality, from the particulate to the universal, is joined by networks of interwoven strings, providing unseen and extra-dimensional antecedents for observed events, including those we call chance.

In terms of human endeavor—and I speak somewhat metaphorically, but what else is metaphor than a concept of actuality?—when we dedicate ourselves to an ideal, and we bring totality of effort—mental, emotional, and physical—to concentrate on that point, we set in motion a rhythmical swing. There must be a corresponding motion. That motion moves along the arc of your focus, provided there is no overwhelming counter movement based on another event, action, or physical barrier within your framework.

Psychologically, I am describing mechanics captured in G.I. Gurdjieff's statement from *Meetings with Remarkable Men* as "the law-conformable result of a man's unflinching perseverance in bringing all his manifestations into accordance with the principles he has consciously set himself in life for the attainment of a definite aim."

Is this more than supposition? Is it just a pretty way of describing persistence? To consider that, follow me briefly down a different path. It strikes me that our senses are nothing more than organic instruments of measurement. If we want to get down to definitions that even a philosophical materialist could love, what else are sight, smell, touch, taste, and so on, than instruments of measurement, which transfer data to your central nervous system or psyche?

Researchers in particle physics have amassed indelible evidence over the course of more than ninety years that a subatomic particle exists in what is called a "wave state" or a state of superposition: the particle appears in an infinite number of places simultaneously and is not localized, or actual, until a sentient observer decides to take a measurement, or a technical device, such as a photometer, periodically takes one.

There exists debate over whether a device represents a method of measurement distinct from an observer, as well as whether the "collapse" from wave to particle results from an observer's individual psyche or "transpersonal mind behaving according to natural laws," as observed by Bernardo Kastrup, Henry P. Stapp, and Menas C. Kafatos in a May 29, 2018, *Scientific American* article, "Coming to Grips with the Implications of Quantum Mechanics." This *transpersonal mind*, the writers continue, "comprises but far transcends any individual psyche," a description similar to the Hermetic concept of *Nous*. The authors compellingly argue that even if a device is used for measurement—and thus localization—perception and intent, either of the individual, the meta-mind, or both, remains the determining force.

No one challenges quantum mechanics data. It is uncontroversial. Only its implications are. I invite intrepid readers to look up the aforementioned *Scientific American* article: they will find, I aver, that my descriptions of quantum theory are, if anything, conservative. We are, in fact, witnessing a kind of reality selection in the quantum lab, not strictly pertaining to particle behavior but to the nature of observation and creation—or, again, selection—from among infinite, coexisting realities. A decision to measure or not measure sets in motion innumerable possibilities. This is the "many worlds" interpretation of quantum physics. A law, as noted, must be constant. Not necessarily transferable to every situation and not liberated from mitigating or surrounding circumstances, but not isolated in data or effects.

The logical conclusion to which quantum mechanics has brought us in the early twenty-first century is that consciousness, or the psyche, cannot be extracted from physics and material existence. All is entangled or *whole*. Hence, if our senses function as devices of measurement, it nudges us in the direction of self-selection. I sometimes encounter critics lampooning or disparaging the New Age perspective on quantum physics—and it must be acknowledged that excesses and cherry-picking *do* exist. But when those observers who are actually in the know venture their own description, it often sounds a lot like the New Age interpretation. Some brave critics, such as Brian Millar writing in 2015 in *Parapsychology: A Handbook for the 21st Century*, concede, "There is . . . some truth in the New Age canard." Indeed, one hears a lot less complaining from the mainstream today than say, fifteen or twenty years ago, about mystical interpretations of quantum theory. This is not because we as a human community have grown tired of complaining (our ever-renewable resource). It is because, similar to the UFO thesis (and I hope soon the ESP thesis), the center has moved closer to the metaphysical interpretation.

Indeed, the implications of quantum data are increasingly important because we are encountering *parallel insights* in other sciences. This turns us to the field of neuroplasticity. Researchers in neuroplasticity use brain scans to demonstrate that thought—a familiar word of which we do not possess a clear definition, even as we advance toward concepts of artificial intelligence—actually alters the neural pathways through which electrical impulses travel in the brain. This results in changes of targeted behaviors, including in areas of addiction and obsessive-compulsive disorder (OCD).

One of the field's pioneers, UCLA research psychiatrist Jeffrey M. Schwartz wrote, "I propose that the time has come for science to confront serious implications of the fact that directed, willed mental activity can clearly and systematically alter brain function; that the exertion of willful effort generates a *physical force* that has the power to change how the brain works and even its physical structure."

Schwartz linked his UCLA findings to developments in quantum physics. "The implications of direct neuroplasticity combined with quantum physics," he observed in his 2002 book *The Mind and the*

Brain, "cast new light on the question of humanity's place, and role, in nature." The co-emergence of the two fields, Schwartz argued, "suggests that the natural world evolves through an interplay between two causal processes."

If thought can alter neural pathways, and affect corresponding behaviors, then brain biology must be understood as the *product of thought* as much as the other way around. This process, Schwartz wrote, "allows human thoughts to make a difference in the evolution of physical events."

Hence, I am engaging in more than metaphor when I speak of rhythmic correspondences, sensory measurements, and mental selectivity. All of this suggests that we are, in some very real respects, *protean beings*—participants in self-creation—and to a far greater degree than has been commonly understood or acknowledged.

With that contention made, let me return to the practical mechanics of mind causation. I believe that nothing on the path does more to stifle your sense of morale, purpose, possibility, and selfhood than being told what you are *supposed* to find or how you are supposed to live or what your spiritual values are supposed to be or what the search is supposed to be about. Self-determination is vital to everything I have been describing. Including if it contradicts my proclivities.

In my observation, the ability to direct your mental-emotive energies requires a measure of assurance and hopeful expectancy. This is commonly observed in placebo studies. The belief that something *can happen*—and that your mind plays an extra-cognitive role in this—is critical.

Another elusive concept, *faith*, is an umbrella term for these catalytic factors. We often define faith or hope as a belief that all will turn out right in the end. In actuality, I do not possess that outlook or temperament. If anything, I have struggled my entire life with anxiety. This is probably why I dedicated myself to the field of positive-mind metaphysics. I have never really suffered from depression but anxiety can get its claws in me at 4 a.m. when I ought to be sleeping but my mind and emotions are racing. Years ago, I delivered a talk at a wealthy retirement community in New York's Hudson Valley. After I finished, an audience member approached me and asked, "How do you sleep at night?" At first, I thought I had offended her. I then realized what she meant. "Your brain," she continued, "it's always going." She was right. "Oh yeah, that's true," I said. "I actually don't sleep very much." So, that's my struggle. Then where does a sense of hopeful expectancy come from? How does faith or great expectation enter the picture?

In my observation, faith is bound up with, and in some ways equivalent to, persistence. *Meaningful persistence* is faith. That is the experience described in the story of the pink, heart-shaped buckets. My effort did not involve optimism. Unless you call it *optimism of the will* to use the term attributed to revolutionary political theorist Antonio Gramsci.* Through passion of dedication, my full psyche was in play. The psyche is a compact of *thought and emotion.*

It is important to note that thoughts, emotions, and physicality run on separate tracks. They are distinct forces. If thoughts ruled us, no one would have a problem with anger, addiction, overeating, and so on. Your thoughts would suffice to curb the unwanted consumption or outburst. Emotion and physicality are often stronger than thought. Hence, we can seldom talk ourselves out of a mood or craving. We can use our minds (which run on a continuum with spirituality) to help circumvent

* Gramsci adopted the phrase "pessimism of the intellect, optimism of the will" from French political writer Romain Rolland. Gramsci reflected poignantly on the concept in a letter written from prison in December 1929: "[A] man ought to be so deeply convinced that the source of his own moral forces is in himself... that he never despairs and never falls into those vulgar, banal moods, pessimism and optimism. My own state of mind synthesizes these two feelings and transcends them: *my mind is pessimistic, but my will is optimistic* [emphasis added]. Since I never build up illusions, I am seldom disappointed. I've always been armed with unlimited patience—not a passive, inert kind, but a patience allied with perseverance." Quoted from "On Revolutionary Optimism of the Intellect" by Leo Panitch, *Socialist Register*, Vol. 53, 2017.

mood or craving; but those things are enormously powerful and they sometimes must receive their due. They run on their own tracks and are owed something. Moods and cravings are not just to be corralled and reorganized; they may have a valid claim on us. I point this out simply to highlight that thought is not the only mediator of power.

As an amalgam of thought and emotion, the unified psyche is powerful: it is the totality of your psychology. This compact forms only when you progress in the direction of a passionately felt need. That is why I consider desires sacred; they are key to human growth and striving. A desire does not necessarily liberate you from things that are *owed to others*. But a desire points you in the direction of authenticity. As such, a desire should be carefully understood and, whenever principle permits, heeded. Do not allow a noninvasive desire to get taken from you. Desire must not be taken away because *persistence in its direction summons the forces called faith, expectation, belief in self, and investment in the greater possibility of the individual*.

That which you experience with your whole psyche, and move toward in every effortful way, sets in motion the pendulum effect I described. Barring some countervailing force, this motion, like a bow pulled and released, lawfully swings in the direction of what is focused on. Again, these are not random metaphors. I am describing concepts that appear in Hermeticism and that find shared insights in the scientific fields I have referenced and will further. These concepts are also warrantied by seekers across centuries. I have provided you with a testimony of my own.

I have not forgotten about my self-selected interlocutor, philosopher Christopher Lasch. If causative mental agencies are more than escapist fantasy, or an expression of secondary narcissism as Lasch suggested, how does that prospect relate to the broader challenge the philosopher issued? In the afterword of *The Culture of Narcissism*, Lasch sharpened his critique of religious or social models that extol gratification—and pointed to his vision of a sounder, stabler approach to life. He observed compellingly:

> The best hope of emotional maturity, then, appears to lie in a recognition of our need for and dependence on people who nevertheless remain separate from ourselves and refuse to submit to our whims. It lies in a recognition of others not as projections of our own desires but as independent beings with desires of their own. More broadly, it lies in acceptance of our limits. The world does not exist merely to satisfy our own desires; it is a world in which we can find pleasure and meaning, once we understand that others too have a right to these goods. Psychoanalysis confirms the ancient religious insight that the only way to achieve happiness is to accept limitations in a spirit of gratitude and contrition instead of attempting to annul those limitations or bitterly resenting them.

My wish is not to foster an imagined escape from life's obligations or a justification to bend others to our desires. Indeed, the chief sign of weakness masquerading as agency is when someone continually burdens others to repair his moods, support his psyche, or dispense rewards. Nor am I positing a system without limits or barriers. Unwillingness to bow to or acknowledge frustrations can become a form of theater in which the indestructible being conceals his or her own lack of self-belief.

In the *Corpus Hermeticum*—the primary body of Greek Hermetic texts translated during the Renaissance—humanity, for all its potential greatness, is conscripted to dwell within a framework where physical laws must be suffered. The individual is at once a being of boundless potential and natural limits—a paradox that creates the tension of existence.

"The master of eternity," reads the dialogue called *Asclepius*, "is the first god, the world"—or great nature—"is second, mankind is the third."* In the Hermetic framing, man, a being ever in the state of advancing or becoming, is considered superior to the gods, whose existence is fixed; but man in his present mode of living nonetheless remains subservient to coarser aspects of nature.

Book I of the *Corpus Hermeticum* teaches: "mankind is affected by mortality because he is subject to fate"—fate is a term for nature's governance—"thus, although man is above the cosmic framework, he became a slave within it." In Hermetic teaching man's mystic prowess is bound by organic tethers.

I believe in experiential philosophies that elevate and encourage our expansion toward self-expression and heightened existence—without denying existential trauma. Such outlooks bring purpose, intention, striving, focus, and *beingness* to our existence. The philosophy of mind causation, on the terms explored here, not only abets authentic selfhood but forms its foundation.

As I see it, nothing in this approach abrogates or fundamentally conflicts with Lasch's analysis, other than his blanket disparagement of New Age. More importantly, the mind causation thesis contributes a defensibly greater possibility to the human situation than what appears in Lasch's or many other secular psycho-social outlooks. As seeking people, we must avoid delusional excesses, which occur on *either extreme*—mystical or materialist—of how one views the psyche.

Within New Age culture, as Lasch justly critiques, we are often conditioned to think in elusive or inflated concepts of self-development and its horizons. People of a spiritual orientation might use terms like *realized, enlightened,* or *illumined.* I find such language excessive. People of a psychological bent might use terms like *well-adjusted, actu-*

---

* I am quoting from Brian P. Copenhaver's seminal translation, *Hermetica* (Cambridge University Press, 1992).

alized, or *fulfilled.* Those concepts are more graspable; but, like the vocabulary of cognitive-behavioral therapy, psychological terminology can proscribe the individual to a life of diagnostic contentment rather than support a more expansive sense of attainment. I reaffirm my contention that *the true aim of life is self-expression.* And we possess tools—including mind causation—in that effort. Such prospects are not to everyone's spiritual and ethical tastes but nor do they require a break with philosophical sobriety.

It may be asked whether personal guardrails are necessary to prevent the effort I describe from resulting in exploitation of others or despotic "reality distortion." In that vein, I am inspired by a principle from Ralph Waldo Emerson's journals of January 15, 1827:

> The nature of God may be different from what he is represented. I never beheld him. I do not know that he exists. This good which invites me now is visible & specific. I will at least embrace it this time by way of experiment, & if it is wrong certainly God can in some manner signify his will in future. Moreover I will guard against evil consequences resulting to others by the vigilance with which I conceal it.

You alone are responsible for your experiments: not every impulse requires acting on or revealing; certain wishes must be abided in quiet; certain are to be considered from the scale of reciprocity and debts owed. Here I am reminded of a statement by philosopher and critic of science Paul Feyerabend: "I am for anarchism in *thinking,* in one's *private life,* BUT NOT in *public life.*"* I have no right to demand that another person or institution mirror my self-conception. But I commit an equal violation if I do not know myself and exercise the full faculties of my psyche.

---

* *Against Method,* fourth edition, by Paul Feyerabend (Verso,1975, 1988, 1993, 2010).

I have insisted that self-expression is critical to a satisfying—if not unerringly successful—existence. I believe that paucity of self-expression results in anxiety, depression, ennui, addiction, and is often diagnosed and coded in the therapist's office without this factor—the power and agency intrinsic to self-expression—named or acknowledged. In that sense, I am more a child of the sixties and seventies, perhaps, than Lasch would approve. He writes, "The best defenses against the terrors of existence are the homely comforts of love, work, and family life, which connect us to a world that is independent of our wishes yet responsive to our needs."

The philosopher's biographer Eric Miller calls Lasch's writing his "most fundamental vocational impulse" and "enduring passion," describing the prodigy authoring his "first complete book" by age eleven.* So I ask: would Lasch, denied the writer's pen, the teacher's lectern, the public's ear, have found sufficient defense in those "homely comforts?"

One area where the philosopher and I soundly agree is when he writes: "We demand too much of life, too little of ourselves." Our values are similar. Our metaphysics are not. I hope that I have responded to Lasch's estimable critique of New Age and modern metaphysics while providing a useful and persuasive counter approach to life.

In the end, what matters is not vehicle—but conduct and arrival. This is the aim of the Happy Warrior.

---

* *Hope In a Scattering Time: A Life of Christopher Lasch* by Eric Miller (Eerdmans, 2010).

Appendix

Character of the Happy Warrior

BY WILLIAM WORDSWORTH, 1806

Who is the happy Warrior? Who is he
That every man in arms should wish to be?
—It is the generous Spirit, who, when brought
Among the tasks of real life, hath wrought
Upon the plan that pleased his boyish thought:
Whose high endeavours are an inward light
That makes the path before him always bright;
Who, with a natural instinct to discern
What knowledge can perform, is diligent to learn;
Abides by this resolve, and stops not there,
But makes his moral being his prime care;
Who, doomed to go in company with Pain,
And Fear, and Bloodshed, miserable train!
Turns his necessity to glorious gain;
In face of these doth exercise a power
Which is our human nature's highest dower:

Controls them and subdues, transmutes, bereaves
Of their bad influence, and their good receives:
By objects, which might force the soul to abate
Her feeling, rendered more compassionate;
Is placable—because occasions rise
So often that demand such sacrifice;
More skilful in self-knowledge, even more pure,
As tempted more; more able to endure,
As more exposed to suffering and distress;
Thence, also, more alive to tenderness.
—'Tis he whose law is reason; who depends
Upon that law as on the best of friends;
Whence, in a state where men are tempted still
To evil for a guard against worse ill,
And what in quality or act is best
Doth seldom on a right foundation rest,
He labours good on good to fix, and owes
To virtue every triumph that he knows:
—Who, if he rise to station of command,
Rises by open means; and there will stand
On honourable terms, or else retire,
And in himself possess his own desire;
Who comprehends his trust, and to the same
Keeps faithful with a singleness of aim;
And therefore does not stoop, nor lie in wait
For wealth, or honours, or for worldly state;
Whom they must follow; on whose head must fall,
Like showers of manna, if they come at all:
Whose powers shed round him in the common strife,
Or mild concerns of ordinary life,
A constant influence, a peculiar grace;
But who, if he be called upon to face

Some awful moment to which Heaven has joined
Great issues, good or bad for human kind,
Is happy as a Lover; and attired
With sudden brightness, like a Man inspired;
And, through the heat of conflict, keeps the law
In calmness made, and sees what he foresaw;
Or if an unexpected call succeed,
Come when it will, is equal to the need:
—He who, though thus endued as with a sense
And faculty for storm and turbulence,
Is yet a Soul whose master-bias leans
To homefelt pleasures and to gentle scenes;
Sweet images! which, wheresoe'er he be,
Are at his heart; and such fidelity
It is his darling passion to approve;
More brave for this, that he hath much to love:—
'Tis, finally, the Man, who, lifted high,
Conspicuous object in a Nation's eye,
Or left unthought-of in obscurity,—
Who, with a toward or untoward lot,
Prosperous or adverse, to his wish or not—
Plays, in the many games of life, that one
Where what he most doth value must be won:
Whom neither shape or danger can dismay,
Nor thought of tender happiness betray;
Who, not content that former worth stand fast,
Looks forward, persevering to the last,
From well to better, daily self-surpast:
Who, whether praise of him must walk the earth
For ever, and to noble deeds give birth,
Or he must fall, to sleep without his fame,
And leave a dead unprofitable name—

Finds comfort in himself and in his cause;
And, while the mortal mist is gathering, draws
His breath in confidence of Heaven's applause:
This is the happy Warrior; this is he
That every man in arms should wish to be.

Index

About the Author

Mitch Horowitz a historian of alternative spirituality and one of today's most literate voices of esoterica, mysticism, and the occult. Mitch is the PEN Award-winning author of books including *Occult America, One Simple Idea, The Miracle Club, Daydream Believer, Uncertain Places, Practical Magick,* and *Modern Occultism. The Washington Post* says Mitch "treats esoteric ideas and movements with an even-handed intellectual studiousness that is too often lost in today's raised-voice discussions." *Filmmaker Magazine* calls him "a genius at distilling down eso-

Photo by Josh Romero

teric concepts." A former vice president at Penguin Random House, Mitch has written on alternative spirituality for *The New York Times*, *The Wall Street Journal*, *The Washington Post*, *Time*, *Politico*, and a wide range of 'zines and scholarly journals. Mitch's writing has called attention to the worldwide problem of violence against accused witches, helping draw notice to the human rights element of the issue. Mitch's books have been translated into French, Arabic, Chinese, Italian, Spanish, Korean, and Portuguese. His work is censored in China.

Printed in the USA
CPSIA information can be obtained
at www.ICGtesting.com
JSHW011708190224
57671JS00016B/344